Shifting Ground

Shifting Ground

Spanish Civil War Exile Literature

Michael Ugarte

Duke University Press   Durham and London 1989

Library of Congress Cataloging-in-Publication Data
appear on the last printed page of this book.

Parts of the material on Max Aub and Luis
Cernuda have appeared in the journals *Hispania*,
MLN, and *Monographic Review*. I would like to
thank the editors of these journals for their permis-
sion to reprint this material.

In memory of my father, Francisco Ugarte, one more in the long line of Spanish émigrés from fascist Spain.

Contents

IV   The Poetics of Exile: Luis Cernuda

V   Self-Exile: Juan Goytisolo

Preface

This project began, I think, in the summer of 1964 when my father prescribed a series of readings for me on the history and civilization of modern Spain. Surprisingly, I found that some of these readings were not simply instruments my father used to torture his students, but that there was actually something in them for me, and that they could serve to answer (at least partially) any teenager's most crucial (albeit ingenuous) questions: who am I, where did I come from, and what in the name of God brought me to this dull little town where the most pressing social problem is the need for a new traffic light? As my father talked to me about the Spanish Civil War, and about the people, like himself, who left as a result of the conflict for both political and economic reasons, he could not keep himself from interjecting a story or two. Many of these stories, embellished with minute details along with frequent affirmations that they were the absolute truth ("me acuerdo perfectamente"—I remember it perfectly), dealt with himself, his trials, as well as his triumphs and joys.

Years later, as a graduate student, and then as a full-fledged teacher of Hispanic literature and civilization, I continued to be obsessed by the issues addressed by my father, not the least of which was the difficulty of leaving one's homeland. Through my discoveries of exile novels, poetry, and essays, particularly the ones dealing with the Spanish Civil War, I have found that my father's stories are no exceptions to the wide range of literary patterns that exile seems to set into motion, the most common being autobiographical conveyance. Although I do not propose to write anything approaching a theory of exile literature, I do argue that the experience of exile gives rise to certain literary tendencies and questions which are inherent in any attempt to duplicate a real experience in writing. Also, my claim is that Spanish exile literature has much in common with other literatures of banishment, in spite of the fact that each case of exile has its own historical and geographical specificity.

Any writer, particularly the academic one, must draw the limits of his or her subject, and this was perhaps the most difficult task in the otherwise pleasantly cathartic experience of putting together this book. The problem was (is) that exile by its very nature, as I cry out on several occasions, seems to erase its own limits as it develops. I chose to solve the problem not by making the subject more manageable, that is, by narrowing the scope of my discussion, but through what I hope has been a more interesting (although unwieldy) approach: I have used those very self-effacing limits as my point of departure. Exile has to do with the borderlines and dividers that an individual is forced (or desires) to traverse. In literary terms it has to do with crossings of languages, of settings, of times. Thus, like the exile, I have taken the risk of crossing into certain unfamiliar territories and can only hope that the reader will find the journey worthwhile.

There are many people and organizations that played a role in the completion of this work, and I would like to express my gratitude to them.

Principally, it was the John Simon Guggenheim Memorial Foundation that is responsible for having given me the opportunity not only to complete this study but to do so in a place that is something of a lost home to me: Madrid. For good reasons Guggenheim has supported some of the very writers who are the subjects of this book, and because of this I am humbled (if not embarrassed) that I am included among them. I would also like to thank the staff at the Fundación Pablo

Iglesias who were so kind and helpful to me in finding the material I was looking for. In addition, the University of Missouri-Columbia Research Council has given me some financial support.

Through their encouragement and support, there are a number of very important individuals in my life who helped me see this project through. More than anyone, my companion through it all has been Maurita McCarthy Ugarte whose observations and suggestions have been invaluable. Her sensitivity to literary matters as well as political ones is felt in much of the book, especially the part on Nabokov. Also influential have been Jackson and Karen Lears who generously and lovingly provided the intellectual stimulation and intimacy that one so desperately needs to keep working on a project like this one. To all the Learses (Jackson, Karen, Rachael, and Adin) I am genuinely grateful. A very special thanks is also due to my children, Francisco and Molly, for they have always been an inspiration to me in matters intellectual.

There is also a group of Hispanists on this side of the Atlantic whose influence is present in this work not only through my personal contact with them but through their own contributions to Hispanic studies. I would particularly like to thank Professor Edward Baker who introduced me to the novels of Max Aub years ago when I was studying at the University of Washington; John Kronik who has helped me in ways that even he does not realize; my colleague Dan Gulstad at the University of Missouri who gave the professional encouragement I needed; and Gustavo Pérez Firmat for a very perceptive and helpful reading of the manuscript.

On the other side of the Atlantic, thanks are due to certain Spanish intellectuals who gave me their time and suggestions as well as some intellectually invigorating conversation: Manuel Andújar, Carlos Guerméndez, José Luis Abellán, and Javier Alfaya.

My uncle, Don Artemio Precioso, is yet another person who played a part in this book by filling me in on details in the lives of many Spanish exiles, including my own grandfather, Artemio Precioso, a writer who was forced out of Spain during the dictatorship of Primo de

Rivera. My uncle's political commitment to solving ecological problems after his own period of banishment from Spain was a great inspiration to me, a sign that there is political life after exile.

A special note of gratitude is also due to Linda Dowell for kind (too kind) preparation of the manuscript, especially since I am still in awe of and utterly intimidated by the computer. But even here there might be hope.

I

The Unknown Quantity of Exile

Introduction

An unnamed king in Vladimir Nabokov's novel, *Pnin*, remarks at one point that he prefers the "unknown quantity of exile" to abdication (p. 71). If one were to dwell on the phrase, one might designate exile as the unknown quantity of X: it is an unidentified person, one who has been something but is no longer, a hypothetical being or thing, something which has no tangible existence, a quantity whose specific value is unascertainable, unreachable through mathematical calculation or linguistic definition. It is the signature of one whose identity has been stripped, whose very existence is, for one political reason or another, no longer verifiable with a name.

It is the unknown quality of exile, in addition to its quantity, which will be the focus of these pages. I do not wish to offer a theory of exile literature, for by its very nature exile resists theory and systematization. It lies in the realms of politics and history as well as literature, or, as we shall see, it dwells uncomfortably between them. Its dimensions are both diachronic and synchronic, it is a collective experience and a deeply personal one, there are recognizable patterns (both behavioral and literary), but no individual case follows a prescription. The deviations from preconceived patterns create new ones, and as the literary critic, historian, or social scientist attempts to unravel the subject of exile, the more it seems to defy the order and logic of academic discourse.

Paul Tabori, an official with the United Nations, wrote *Anatomy of*

Exile, which is one of the few attempts to deal exhaustively with the subject. Tabori found at the outset of his project that he had entered a monstrous territory, the limits of which kept disappearing as he drew them. The author of this strange history of exile from the apes to the war in Vietnam is, by his own admission, no literary critic, even though a good percentage of the exiles he deals with are writers. But the process through which he pieced together his anatomical puzzle is revealing. He sent a copy of a letter to more than five hundred people considered by themselves or by others to be in exile and asked them to relate through correspondence their experiences and sentiments not only on their particular condition but on exile in general. The response was as overwhelming as the subject of his research. By the termination of his study, which turned into a series of cursory renditions of hundreds of lives, he was still receiving letters, memoirs, books, and diaries, all accounting for an experience of some sort of displacement. Santos Sanz Villanueva, in his study of the Spanish novel written in exile after the Civil War, points out that there were few Republican refugees who did not suffer the ordeal of exile, pencil and paper in hand, ready to record every anecdote, every encounter (Abellán, IV, 182).[1] Max Aub, himself one of the most important intellectuals included in the ranks of the Spanish refugees, writes that much if not all of his vast literary corpus was completed with the intention of bearing witness ("dar cuenta de la hora," *Hablo como hombre*, p. 40). Exile, for Aub and many others, is a catalyst for writing. Banished from familiar environments and haphazardly thrown into new and usually more difficult situations, the victims share an uncontrollable need to write, to recall, to testify. It happened to Ovid and to Dante as well as to countless other writers whose texts have gone unnoticed. But the very absence of a listener, a hardship suffered by both Ovid and Dante in their day, seems to kindle the exile's fiery need to speak, to make use of a disappearing language. The endangered language of exile with all its political, historical, and even psychological underpinnings and consequences as it manifests itself in the aftermath of civil war in Spain is the subject of these chapters. It is indeed a reckless subject whose resistance to categories is not unlike the exile of flesh and bone who rebels not only against a given order but against that order's characterization of him.

But if order and system are not part of my anatomy (or counter-anatomy) of literary exile, what recourses are left? Mercifully, the question is not rhetorical, for unlike certain noble attempts to destroy the boundaries between academic and literary discourses and thus bridge the gap between criticism and literature (as in the work of Roland Barthes, Octavio Paz, Phillipe Sollers, Severo Sarduy) my study humbly remains the work of a literary critic (a Hispanist to boot). In spite of formalism's limitations, especially its facile dismissal of philosophical and historical (or "extrinsic") dimensions of literature, I willingly recognize my need to resort to the tools of the formalist's trade. Thus instead of a system or theory of exile literature, I offer something perhaps not as ambitious yet more worthy of a subject as untamable as exile: a series of readings, speculations, and reflections at times theoretical, at others practical. My wish is to contribute to an understanding of Spanish exile literature's particular importance for our century and for literature itself through a close inspection of particular cases, mainly those produced in the wake of the Spanish Civil War which is a case in itself. I use the word "case" much in the same sense as would a psychologist who writes a "case study" of an individual who partakes of certain symptoms of a malady but not of others, an individual whose "case" tells us, in the long run, as much or more about himself or herself as about the community of those who share the affliction.[2] Although certain designs of exilic language recur, as I hope these pages will show, I never pretend that anyone who goes into exile will by definition and by natural consequence evince these patterns in speech or in writing. Exile is both a phenomenon and a person, and the tension between these two categories is the tension of this book.[3]

Much has been written on the literature of banishment, but nothing that calls itself a theory of exilic language. The closest thing is perhaps the work of George Steiner, but even his analysis presents itself more as a series of reflections than as a system. In *Extraterritorial* and *After Babel* Steiner underscores the importance of linguistic crossings throughout the literature of the twentieth century in the wake of what he calls "the failure of humane literacy in the face of barbarism." Such a failure coincides, happily for Steiner, with "the language revolution," the notion that the "coding and transmission of ordered information is crucial for the definition of man" (*Extraterritorial*, p. vii), and this idea, he argues, might serve as a response to the twentieth century's crisis of morals. While the subsequent pages may not be what Steiner wishes when he calls for more in-depth study of linguistic crossings, and while I am certainly not as intent as he on relocating the "semantic center," I situate my discussion precisely within the frame of that so-called language revolution in an attempt to discover how the experience of Spanish Civil War exile is coded and transmitted in certain textual reproductions of that experience.

The "language revolution" from the Russian Formalists and the Prague Circle, through Anglo-American New Criticism, to the structuralists and poststructuralists has, in my view, forced literary critics of all persuasions to be more conceptually precise in their unravelings of texts. In this regard the study of exile literature leads inevitably, perhaps unfortunately, to the question of categories and the reasons for including certain authors and texts under the amorphous heading of exile literature. First, does one begin with the author or the work? Most discussions of the subject start with the writer, yet if an author qualifies for exile status, are all of his or her works worthy of consideration? If not, is the basis of judgment something as mechanical as the difference between works written before the departure and those produced after? Is there not a predisposition to exile? And if the reverse is true, that the text determines exile, as very few literary scholars have argued, what are the aesthetic criteria? Must exile be political? Is it an experience, an outlook, or a condition? Must exile literature be produced outside the author's native land and no longer considered such after the return, or, as these pages will suggest, once in exile, always in exile? And what of that native land? Can a person be in exile from his or her native environment regardless of national boundaries? Just how does one define the word "outside," and where is "outside"? I hope that my discussion of the subject will begin to answer some of these questions; yet I maintain that to provide full answers, if such is possible, is to relieve the tension of my claim: that no literature can be excluded from the ranks of exile, that, in effect, to study exile literature is to study literature itself.

What follows, then, is a discussion of Spanish Civil War exile literature within the context of literature itself. My linguistic crossings are not so much those that deal with real changes in an author's language, such as Conrad's leap from Polish to English, Nabokov's from Russian to English, or Beckett's from English to French; they have to do with the crossing and overlapping of different codes: from politics to aesthetics, from reality to fiction, from author to text, from autobiography to novel, from testimony to literature, from real experience to poetry. Exile, both the phenomenon and the person, always finds itself on the margins of something, in a liminal position between two places, times, or, for the critic, two areas of study.[4] For this reason my analyses must stray at least one step beyond formalism, for to leave reality or politics out of a discussion of exile literature is to ignore its reason for being, its catalyst. Again the tension between politics and literature is inherent in exilic writing and in the thrust of the chapters that follow.

1 Spain and Other Cases

Though it might sound paradoxical, one could argue that the political unity of Spain in 1492 was based on exile. The Moors had finally lost their only remaining *taifa* at Granada, the kingdoms of Aragon and Castile lost their national boundaries, and most important, Spanish Jews were given the choice of conversion or expulsion, both of which gave rise to a particular brand of exile. The home of the Sephardics was not only Zion, that mythical land where exile is no longer a fact of life, but Toledo, Burgos, Segovia, Cordoba, and other medieval centers of commerce, science, and theology. These people were as much members of their local communities as they were of the larger congregation of Jewry whose unity was perhaps more spiritual than social or geographic. As a result of the edict of expulsion by the Catholic kings, Spanish Jews were sent one farther step into exile, and those who opted for the local community by externally rejecting their religion were no less in exile than those who left. But to pinpoint the moment of exilic origin as Tabori attempts to do with his rendition of the first written account of exile (*Anatomy of Exile*, pp. 43–45) seems as futile as a search for the first instance of writing. The cases of ancient Israel and Spain testify to this particular myth of origins. Jews were well into exile before they reached the Iberian Peninsula, and the accounts of exile as well as evidence of its political mechanisms within the medieval code of justice date well before 1492. The Cid is not only a real case of a man banished from his native land, one whose existence can be verified with historical documentation, but an archetype: both a literary model for later writing and the rewriting of a previous model. Similarly, the exodus of the Jews is both historically verifiable and a story whose permutations seem endless. It is a case which has been studied and imitated both within and outside the bounds of the religious community, as the following familiar words of Psalm 137 attest:

> By the rivers of Babylon,
> There we sat down,
> Yes we wept
> When we remembered Zion.
> We hanged our harps upon the willows
> In the midst thereof.
> For there they carried us away captive,
> Required of us a song,
> And they that wasted us
> Required of us mirth, saying,
> Sing us one of the Songs of Zion.
> How shall we sing the Lord's song
> In a strange land?

Claudio Guillén, in "Literature of Exile and Counter-Exile," points out that the writer of an Ovidian exilic elegy did not have to be an exile in the strict sense of the word (p. 273). His examples are Plutarch and Du Bellay, and if hard pressed, one could think of Spanish figures such as Garcilaso de la Vega.[1] Guillén's observation is disturbing, for it distorts the picture of exile as a historical precondition for writing. It also has the effect of muddying an already muddy puddle by turning exile, in spite of all its political resonances, into something as seemingly inconsequential as a story. For one who has actually been the victim of political, ethnic, or racial ostracism, especially if that person is a member of a community of victims, to reduce exile to a tale or a parable seems coldly unsympathetic. Yet the historical and political fact of exile is itself a nebulous idea, and one cannot lose sight of the historiographical nature of this fact: that history comes to us by way of language. Again instead of a grandiose model, we have cases within the historical spectrum. The case of Spain follows its own model, yet unlike those who insist on molding Spanish literature and history into a self-contained unit ("Spain is different"),[2] I maintain that the very specificity of Iberian exile testifies to the difference and specificity of other national experiences.

The fact that the unity of Spain is based largely on exile is indicative of a collective consciousness. It affirms that Spaniards are not bound together as Spaniards without the mechanisms of expulsion as an essential part of the group's social and juridical practice. Exile in Spanish history is institutional. Spaniards and Latin Americans have their own word for the phenomenon: *destierro*. *Exilio*, from the Latin *exsilium*, which is the same root for the other Romance variations (French —*exile*, Italian—*esilio*, Portuguese—*exilio*), is ironically a Gallicism. *Destierro* carries certain connotations specific to Spanish sensibilities. To be "unearthed" (*desterrado*) is to have lost the essential link between land and soul. Exile is punishment by expulsion. *Destierro* is also punitive, but in addition it signifies the loss of a necessary and integral human component. Thus one who is *desterrado* is only partially human. For this reason to use exile as a form of punishment is a particularly drastic measure.

The criminological aspects of exile, along with its semantics, once again reveal that there was always a model for the process of banishment, a model which is no less apparent in Spanish literature. As if to imitate what is expected of a man stripped of his home, the Cid weeps and mournfully turns his head to catch a final glimpse of Castile as he rides away. Those initial verses of the epic poem set the tone for further adventures. But perhaps more important, they are indicative of the reciprocal nature of exile. We who are not banished from our lands participate in the Cid's grief because we are familiar with the story of a forced departure as well as with the code which makes it possible. The Cid must leave his home and family, but those who stay, like Jimena who tearfully bids her master farewell, must also bear the loss of this noble warrior. Within the comforts of our nurturing land we too become victims of a cruel sentence. Also part of the reciprocity of exile is the overt or covert presence of the accuser. The dialogue between the banished one and those who carry out the sentence is one-sided at first, but the possibilities of an infinitely more complex dialogue arise as the process unfolds.

Although it has been suggested that exile is antithetical to social intercourse of any kind, the precise opposite of the notion of group or society (Williams, "Exile," pp. 8–9), the Spanish case, in literature as well as history, suggests that it is a cornerstone to the collective consciousness of the nation. As canonically important as the *Poem of the Cid* is to the development of the peninsula's literature, it is merely one instance of the story of exile, a structure which appears and reappears at given moments, and at times haphazardly, in the history of the nation's writing. Many other works whose themes and circumstances have to do with some sort of exile have entered the files of the Spanish literary canon: Juan Valdés's *Diálogo de la lengua*, Fray Luis de León's *Los nombres de Cristo*, the works of the romantic émigrés during the reign of Ferdinand VII, Unamuno's *Agony of Christianity*, Jorge Guillén's *Cántico*, to name only a few. These texts embody the values and experiences of a nation, and as such enjoy a type of institutional power as icons of the culture. However, to place an exilic work in the canon is problematic because those very shared values come under fire. Often Spanish exilic texts are both wittingly and unwittingly anti-canonical. Their authors are in exile due to their rebellion against a particular social or political order, and by shifting the locale of writing, they question the canon's authority. To say, "I shall write elsewhere," is to take a risk: it involves a career as well as an understanding that the rules of the linguistic code are subject to different scrutinies.[3]

But although there are cases in which an exilic text appears in the canon, clearly the opposite occurs more often. Literature written in exile as well as texts which deal with the issues of exile tend to lie sleepily at a distance from any list of highly meritorious works. Marginality is far more a trademark of exilic literature than fame, authority, or importance as defined by literary histories and anthologies. The risk taken by a writer who chooses exile and the forced risk of one who has no choice usually turn out bad ones. If success involves being at the right place at the right time, a young exile writer with little or no reputation in the homeland may fail even before he or she gets off the ground. The cases which result in the acclaim of another culture or in latent recognition by the homeland seem insignificant in the face of the quantity of writers who died as pathetically as some of the characters they created. The marginality of exile is particularly apparent when one considers the condition of all the intellectuals, essayists, novelists, playwrights, and poets who left Spain when the Republic succumbed to the forces of insurgent fascism.

It is difficult to pinpoint the reasons why Spanish Civil War exile has produced relatively few world renowned literary figures, especially in comparison to cultures that have encountered similar hardships in the twentieth century, such as Germany and Russia. Perhaps it is due to the constraints of time: an exile usually must sacrifice present-day laurels to posterity. There are also ideological considerations behind the recognition of the literary accomplishments of a country such as Spain, which always seems to be on the "wrong side" in the eyes of the west. Even within the Spanish political spectrum of the thirties, neither of the two main factions appealed to the Allies, the ultimate victors. On the other hand, awareness of the work of German anti-Nazis, the growing diaspora of Jewish intellectuals, and the collective suffering of both groups gave rise to a favorable acceptance of these exiles in postwar Europe and North America. Works by writers such as Franz Werfel, Thomas Mann, Bertolt Brecht, and Nelly Sachs are seen as expressions of an atrocious universal experience. The situation of the Russian émigrés, while every bit as pathetic as Nabokov and others describe,[4] has the advantage, particularly in the United States but also in Europe, of representing the rubble created by the Bolshevik disaster of 1917, a catastrophe sparked by what conservative U.S. politicians and journalists view as the most barbaric and diabolical political regime on the face of the earth. The popularity and eventual canonization of Alexander Solzhenitsyn with the Nobel Prize attests at least as much to the ideological import of his work as it does to its literary merit. On the other hand, the awarding of the 1956 Nobel Prize to Juan Ramón Jiménez, an exile poet whose political motivations are barely detectable in his verse, shows a certain indifference to the social, political, and existential dilemmas surrounding the Civil War in favor of aesthetic considerations. That Juan Ramón Jiménez should receive such a prestigious award could cast doubt on my argument (admittedly on the defensive side); yet it is equally significant that his poems have not been widely translated. Another Spanish Nobel laureate, not in exile but always critical of the regime which killed his dear friend, Federico García Lorca, appears even less often on the sacred lists. His name, Vicente Aleixandre, is likely to be mispronounced, if remembered, by the makers of those lists.

Exile literature, at least in the twentieth century and perhaps in older literature as well, is uneasily included in the canon, and as I have been suggesting, it unwittingly questions the list's authority. The seemingly arbitrary criteria used to classify it as such mean that Spanish exile literature has the same position worldwide as the national literary canon of Spain. Why some exilic figures are included and not others is as puzzling as the inconsistencies and vagaries of human behavior itself. One is inevitably led to speculate over possible reasons for this and to attempt to come to grips with the wealth of apparently unrelated material produced by the phenomenon of exile.

A quick look at the conventionally accepted reading of twentieth-century Spanish literary history immediately reveals the powerful influence of the Civil War on texts written before, during, and after 1936. The war, along with all its causes and consequences, is indeed an unavoidable consideration, but one wonders if the intrusion of history into modern Spanish novels, poems, essays, and plays is not more complex, especially in the light of exile. The division of Spain in the early decades of the century between tradition and modernity reached its culmination when a portion of the population was forced to leave or depart of its own accord. Historians and critics have described the two Spains with a variety of familiar contrasting phrases: the victors and the vanquished, nationalists and Europhiles, centralists and believers in regional autonomy, all of which may be summed up with José Bergamín's binomial: "España peregrina y España solariega" (pilgrim Spain and ancestral Spain).[5] These modifying phrases are binomials whose antithetical conceits are as indicative of unity as they are of contrast. For some critics of twentieth-century Spanish literature, exilic Spain serves as traditional Spain's foil and thus depends on it for its existence.

Yet the characterization of Civil War Spain as a series of contrasts which ultimately reveal a harmonic whole cannot be entirely accurate, given the international chaos of the time and the flight of this chaos outside the national boundaries. Beneath the surface of Bergamín's phrase, "España peregrina," lies a deeply rooted tension between the notion of diaspora and that of pilgrimage. The former designates a journey or journeys with no direction, while the ultimate purpose of a pilgrimage is to return home wiser and spiritually richer as a result of the trip. While the most immediate image of exile may be the contrast between the old home and the new one, the permutations of that image, especially considering the hypothetical quality of the new home—in reality no home at all—seem endless: the home versus a trip, a political regime versus a person, a concrete reality versus a hypothesis, one home versus x number of new ones. Exile involves a contrast between two or more unlike qualities; thus, as unattractive as it might seem for the literary critic, exile calls for a comparison of peaches and pears. Spanish exile, in spite of the all too familiar characterization of Spain as a "land of contrasts," is no exception.

The familiar and unfamiliar names of those who left during or after the war as well as their itineraries have been the objects of much attention in the last few years both within and outside the peninsula.

One would think that all the attention (much due, of course, to the death of Franco in 1975) would result in the discovery of evidence which might serve as a basis for a new history (or counterhistory) of Spanish literature in the twentieth century. Yet the tireless compilers of the facts, Vicente Llorens, José Ramón Marra-López, José Luis Abellán, Germán Gullón, Aurora Albornoz, Manuel Andújar, Carlos Martínez, and others only seem to establish the already accepted labyrinthine nature of Spanish Civil War culture. Very few new names have been added to the national canon, if any: there has been no attempt to rewrite the history of the post-Civil War novel with a new text at the forefront to replace Cela's *La familia de Pascual Duarte*.[6] Max Aub, Arturo Barea, Ramón Sender, and Francisco Ayala remain as insignificant outside of Spain as they ever were and are now losing the headway they made in the sixties and seventies in the wake of stay-at-home writers such as Juan Benet and Gonzalo Torrente Ballester. It seems that Spanish Civil War exile authors have not had the literary criticism they deserve.

A case in point is José Luis Abellán's six-volume study of exile from Spain after 1939. It is a historical survey of the people and politics of Spanish Civil War exile mixed with literary criticism, literary history, and political analyses. The author of the initial volume, political in scope, is Vicente Llorens, one of the victims. Perhaps because of his own exilic status, his study reveals a certain desperate need to record names and make lists, as does Tabori's manual of broken lives. Llorens relates, for example, that Juan Comorera, who had been the secretary general of the Catalan Communist Party, fled first to France in 1939, then to the Soviet Union, and from there to Mexico. For a reason Llorens does not offer, Comorera decided to return to Spain in 1951, was arrested in 1958 and sent to prison in Burgos where he died the following year (Abellán, I, 109). Admittedly, the intentions of this introductory volume are more historical than literary, yet the underlying dilemma in the life of Juan Comorera and others like him is never touched upon by the subsequent essayists of this study: the fruitlessness of exile politics and the ultimate necessity of converting those politics into a story. Exile is one of the few phenomena in history in which language is seen as a more effective tool for social change than political action. Comorera's life—the stuff novels are made of—is emblematic of the pattern of exile (its "unknown quantity") as well as the richness of that experience: lives dying to be written, hoping for a reincarnation through writing. Llorens and the other critics must have asked themselves what significance these lives had in the scope of their respective studies, political and literary. Yet they resisted elaboration due no doubt to their need to include as much as possible. Perhaps it was also due to the uncontrollable plenty, even excess, of these lives and to the excesses of the phenomena these critics valiantly attempted to catalogue. One wonders how many other lives, too wild and too inconsequential to be included even in a minor list, have gone neglected due to the conventions of our discipline, so that we who contribute to the compilation of the list will never know of their existence. The best course is, as Borges said in another context, to pretend that the literary history of exile has already been written and offer a paraphrase, a commentary (*Ficciones*, p. 15).

2 Issues and Patterns of Exile Literature

Because of its political nature, positing a synchronic literary concept of exile is perhaps as "vain and laborious" (again Borges's words) as the recording of its literary history. Perhaps there will never be a comprehensive theory of exile literature, at least not a satisfactory one, precisely because of its political and historical specificity. Yet there are also literary reasons why such a theory might be considered unfeasible. The very phrase, "theory of exile literature," sounds strange, as if one could devise a theory of a particular type of literature solely according to a political circumstance. All one could hope to do is to characterize that type of literature. A committed formalist might object vehemently to the notion of a literary category based on an author's condition: Can we have a theory of texts, he or she might ask, written by people suffering from cancer?

In spite of my suggestions to the contrary, the formalist protest is a good one, for it reveals the problematic nature of the subject matter. How does one theorize on exile literature? Do we start with literature, with exile politics, with the literary history of a given country, or with the social history of that country? To theorize on literature, on the other hand, is another matter entirely, for literature arguably can have an inner specificity, something that all its concrete manifestations share, as the Russian formalists argued in the early part of this century.[1] Thus if there is anything theoretical about my reflections on exile writing, the goal is not so much to arrive at a systematic understanding of the uniqueness of exile literature but to understand how an experience of exile might be linked to the unfolding of any creative process.

Ironically, someone as attentive to historical circumstances as Fredric Jameson might also wince (along with the formalist) at the approach I have taken to the subject. For Jameson the acceptance of a synchronic concept of literature without the consideration of its diachronic development is a denial of the workings of history itself (*Prison House of Language*, pp. 6–22). Jameson's criticism of literary synchrony, and by extension the entire formalist movement, pinpoints some of the problems of dealing with exile literature. Yet even Jameson must admit that literature has a tendency to repeat itself regardless of the historical moment. Likewise, in the case of exile, a case in which literary expression is only one in a series of social and psychological consequences, a comparison of its structural development in two or more apparently unrelated instances reveals more than a few similarities. At times these parallels are striking indications of how language and literature tend to repeat themselves as they evolve. Even within the relatively narrow range of literature covering Civil War Spain, one detects certain designs which persistently recall the strategies of texts written under similar circumstances yet outside that frame of reference. Indeed, there is something peculiarly universal about exile literature.

Francisco Ayala, one of the better-known Spanish exile novelists, maintains that exile, especially in the case of Republican Spain, gives rise to barriers which prevent writers from stepping beyond the limits of their political experiences. They ironically become more nationalistic than those who cast them out and therefore less concerned with the universal. Ayala proclaims that, in the long run, all writers are in exile and thus should not be obsessed with narrow political issues. In like manner, Juan Goytisolo, a member of a younger group of exiles, has declared that no Spanish émigré writer with the exception of Luis Cernuda has been able to transcend the specific issues that brought about their exile (*El País*, November 11, 1985). Yet perhaps Ayala's and Goytisolo's own political experiences have blinded them to the possibilities of universality in the texts of their fellow displaced writers. Ayala's statement that all writers are in exile underscores a factor which Ayala himself, as well as Goytisolo, seems to ignore: that the intensely personal and specific experience of exile is paradoxically a marker of its universality.

Ovid, whose case is a model for much exile literature, was unwilling and unable to transcend his geographical and psychological distance from Rome. In spite of the fact that he wrote in the language of the Getes, those with whom he spent his life as a banished Roman, he constantly and eloquently laments the loss of his own language in his poem of exile, *Tristia*:

> Often I search for a word, for a name, I search for a location,
> But there is no one to give me the information I need.
> Often when I try to say something—I'm ashamed of it!—
> The words which I seek fail me, I have forgotten how to speak.
> (p. 87)

Exile was not only the mainstay of Ovid's existence, it was the source of his writing. Had he not committed the unknown crime which banned him forever from his homeland, the exilic elegy would have had its model in another poet. Ovid's importance as an object of literary imitation is a reminder that an individual experience can become a universal one in its very specificity.

Perhaps the most illuminating feature of exile literature is that its characteristics underscore some of the most pressing issues of literary analysis. As one begins to unravel the problems common to a variety of texts written as the result of some sort of displacement, one becomes increasingly aware of the mechanisms through which any literary text develops. The particular nature of exilic experience (displacement, the importance of correspondences and relations, comparisons, temporal and spatial disunity, self-duplication and division) leads the writer, perhaps unwittingly, into a dialogue with him or herself on the very nature of writing and on the problems that arise from an attempt to record reality. Thus my contention is not that exile literature is a unique brand of literature with a language and a set of conventions all its own. On the contrary: exile literature lays bare the workings of literature itself.

The independent nature of exilic experience, its position both in collective and specific realms of human thought and conduct, informs one of the most constant features of exile literature: the propensity for testimony, even when the writer's apparent intention is otherwise. The I of exile needs evidence for having experienced something, and it is the nebulous nature of this evidence, the fact that it is a linguistic creation, that gives exile literature its characteristic tension. The gap between the reality and the description of what happened seems to grow wider as the exile writes. The subject, often the exile himself, and at other times another I whose experiences are similar, becomes an object. Similarly, the rendition of the experience turns into the object of another description, as in the typically exilic apology for not recalling an event exactly as it took place. The existential need to recover something lost (a land, an identity, a place of origin) results from the absence of an integral part of one's being—a fact which causes the exile to perceive of him or herself as something less than human, as the Spanish word, *destierro*, suggests. Introspection is the natural consequence of the nebulous testimony as well as of exile itself.

For these reasons, the exile resorts frequently to autobiography as one of the most effective defenses against the condition. From Ovid's *Tristia* and Saint Augustine's *Confessions*, to the memoirs of Rousseau and Blanco White's *Life* in Spain and England, to the autobiographical underpinnings of Joyce's *Portrait of the Artist*, the written testimony of the life of an author has often been a direct effect of some sort of banishment or rupture. As James Olney's seminal work on autobiography has shown, to write a life is to create a new self out of a variety of former selves (*Autobiography*, p. 24). In many ways exile also creates a new self; it creates the distance one needs to objectify the self, to look back at it from a different situation, a different land. For some banished writers exile represents a form of death, a phenomenon which tends to make the former life seem complete, an integral structure: birth, life, death. That structure is not unlike a literary one, an ordered construction with a beginning, middle, and end, even if those parts or substructures are not placed in chronological order. The autobiographical I serves as the center of a story which orders and structures the real experience; it turns the real story into a fiction, even if there has been no conscious attempt to do so. The uneasy relationship between language and real life brought to bear by autobiography is also present in the replication of exilic experience with a testimony of that experience.

Dante's *Divine Comedy*, clearly a landmark of transcendental literature and universal in its very conception, can also be read as an autobiography. Dante's protagonist is both himself as well as the exilic everyman as he searches for his way home to paradise. Direct references to Florence and to the political intrigues which sparked Dante's exile abound in the work. Yet Dante clearly views his own text as the story of an I who is as distant from the author himself as a subject is from an autobiographer. Dante creates a person, as does the writer of an autobiography, but the closure of the gap between them is the intent of the writing as it is the goal of an exilic search. From this perspective the *Divine Comedy* becomes a self-referential text in which the wish to reach the heavens is realized by the writing of the text itself; to wander in exile in search of an idyllic home mirrors the activity of writing.

Linked to the exile's need for a testimony of his or her own life is an obsession which has afflicted more than a few exiles throughout the history of world literature: memory and its dialectical counterpart, oblivion. During the recording of an exilic testimony memory often squeezes out other phases and aspects of the experience and becomes the guiding theme as well as the recourse. Understandably, the urge to recall is primordial in one whose existence is tenuously dependent upon those recollections. The reading of exilic texts as recollections of objects, people, landscapes, smells, streets, thoughts, words, and all the other trademarks of the literature of nostalgia is likely the most apt approach to this type of writing, or at least it is a reading which the exilic writer seems to have in mind as he or she amasses the props of a newly staged life. The thought process which exile initiates places remembrance in a privileged position, a difficult circumstance for the exile due to its diabolical shiftiness.

Memory is a phenomenon whose characteristic relativity proscribes the apprehension of any object or situation as a self-sufficient entity, for comparison is a necessary component of that apprehension. Relations between the present and the past, between the earth on which the exile stands and the earth of a former land, including all the animate and inanimate objects which comprise those two lands, give rise to parallels and to an assessment of things in terms of corresponding phenomena elsewhere. The here of one in exile persistently recalls the space of a there, and vice versa. The result is an existence which resides somewhere between now and then, here and elsewhere. In addition to all the possible losses an exile may suffer—home, language, freedom, a way of life—the banished person lacks tangible objects which can stand without comparison and affirm the exile's existence in time. Nothing in the land of exile seems to have its own self-contained unity. Like the unfamiliar tree whose observation and apprehension from a new residence is based on the trees of a different earth, the exile's own existence is grounded (or ungrounded) on a similar relation. The exile is by definition incomplete without the memory of a former existence, the necessary yet deceptive proof of his or her being.

An unavoidable ramification of the exilic obsession with memory is the importance an exile must attach to time, not only in the understanding of the world but in the written transcription of that world. In an essay on the literary ramifications of exile, Vicente Llorens (*Literatura, historia, política*, p. 9) hints at the crucial importance of time in the life of an exile regardless of any specific historical case.

> A life of exile assumes an essentially unstable alteration of human existence which is paradoxically and tenuously balanced between two opposing points: the present and the future. Lacking one of these, the exile suffers a type of irremediable mutilation, if his situation is not even more irreparable when he is deprived of both, completely paralyzed, stripped of the remainder of a life.[2]

The condition reminds Llorens of a verse by Rafael Alberti, one of Spain's most celebrated Civil War exile poets: "pasado muerto, porvenir helado" (the past dead, the future frozen) (pp. 9–10). The relativity of time is something that exilic life unabashedly exposes. So much so, as Llorens and Alberti suggest, that paralysis and death become the mainstays of existence. The constant temporal shifts and the inability to observe one's own life in terms of a chronological whole based on the conventional triad of past, present, and future is one of the effects of the sentence of exile.

The literature of nostalgia (another common trait of exilic writing) is at first glance a welcome relief from anguish due to the loss of temporal continuity. Yet hidden behind the palliative of a nostalgic re-creation of the past lies the glaring image of the present, a picture which, like the land of exile itself, shapes that re-creation. Its "reality" is put into question by the very word, nostalgia: a deceptively positive reading of the past in terms of a present which is worse by comparison. Behind nostalgia there is an implicit recognition of its own powers of evasion and, by extension, its artificiality. The first volume of Ramón Sender's *Crónica del alba* (*Chronicle of Dawn*) is, in many ways, a model for nostalgic literature because the text seems aware of its own tensions. The boyhood delights and adventures of José Garcés, the autobiographical protagonist, lyrically and melancholically described, stand in tenuous juxtaposition to the prologue in which the reader learns that the pictures which follow are painted from the grid of a concentration camp (pp. 9–15). That the life of José Garcés is based on that of the author himself adds an even more lugubrious texture to the tender joys of a nurturing past.

In such a state of displacement, made especially difficult by psychological trauma and existential disequilibrium, the exile is often hard pressed to justify the sacrifices he or she has had to make and thereby explain the reasons for the affliction. Even when the expatriate chooses to leave, the departure is based on an act or acts which spawned the wrath of those who consider the former citizen a transgressor. The consequence, as a great deal of exile literature, regardless of its century, attests, is a type of discourse whose rhetoric manifests moral concerns.[3] Exilic speech thus reveals a morally defensive tone in the midst of a struggle between the official voice of the home and that of a distant critic whose defense often becomes a lesson in conduct. The Jews' biblical assimilation of exile is founded on an ethical imperative just as Dante's moral discourse is the intention as well as the structure of his opus. The religious intentions of these early texts distinguish them from those of a more godless era, yet one wonders if that supposedly godless age is not as dependent on moral issues as was the age of Dante, especially in the context of exile. In the twentieth century the events which sent over a million people into exile from Germany and killed over six million others are known in the vernacular of our age as the "holocaust," a word whose moral resonances give pause to its survivors in exile, both Jews and Gentiles. The work of Thomas Mann written outside of Germany during and after the war, as well as that of Brecht and the poetry of Nelly Sachs, is an example of work, completed under similar circumstances, whose moral compulsions are both a result and a cause of a departure. The Russian case is parallel, as Solzhenitsyn's *Gulag Archipelago* and Pasternak's *Doctor Zhivago* attest. Even a writer as apparently indifferent to moral issues as Nabokov seems to hide his own pressing ethical concerns with a supercilious narrative tone (as in *Pnin*), which unexpectedly leads the reader into a moral dialogue with the author. Exile, by its compromising nature and the fact that it is a political act, engenders a type of defensive moral discourse which cannot traverse certain ideological limits. The political powerlessness of exile creates a certain awareness of the inconsequential nature of moral discourse, particularly that of the banished citizen in comparison to that of the accuser.

Yet the superiority which the exile attributes to him or herself over the political and social order of a former place is as much aesthetic as it is moral. The human taste for tensions, ambiguities, and paradoxes places the exile on a much higher ground than that of the accuser, not only due to an inevitably self-conscious perspective from outside the home but also because of the wider range of possibilities which exile can afford. The expatriate is bombarded with new influences, angles which were not part of the former composition of life. He or she is also aware of a continuing conflict at home between the regime and fellow transgressors who decided to stay. The opposite, however—that the exile's allies within might know of developments and changes as a result of the departure—is less likely in light of the regime's attempt to destroy the memory of the departed citizen. But for the exile writer —usually one who desperately wishes that his voice play some role in the process of change—aesthetic superiority subverts the utility of the leave-taking. In literary terms, the moral discourse of exile is often too rich, too ambiguous, too pluralistic, and as a consequence too unclear to have an effect. In the long run an exile can merely hope that another voice, one from an exotic place whose unfamiliar turns of phrase are often the result of another language, will serve to add dissonance to the monotone of the powers at home. Moral issues, especially in the twentieth century but in others as well, are too multifaceted for a writer seriously to presume superiority; and when such subjects are the focus of an exilic discourse the language, at times unwittingly, seems to betray its own sanctimonious position.[4]

Elusiveness of moral discourse is one among many indicators of exile literature—a literature whose vacillations seem to add further confusion to an already complex network of enigmas. The uncertainty of the condition gives rise to what has been called "the experience of ambivalence," a phenomenon shared by a great many exile writers and texts (Ferguson, "The Exile's Defense," p. 277). The dichotomies which arise in exile's initial stages (homeland versus new land, past versus present) later seem to erase their own antithetical coherence as the condition (or infirmity, as some have called it) intensifies. Vacillation, disequilibrium, ambivalence become the mainstays of uprooted lives and displaced texts. In addition to the lack of firm ethical ground on which to stand, the division between the place of origin and the new locale engenders a series of imbalances which cross the parameters of many dimensions of existence whose linguistic representation is ambivalence itself. Conflicts between images — as in the stillness and finality of a destination and the constantly moving space of a trip, the moral rectitude of a regime and a dissident member, that regime's rendering of history versus that of the exile, continuing separation from home and the possibility of return and reconciliation, a self in a former environment and a new self, a human being at one with the earth and a person fragmented by an unfamiliar soil — all of these are not so much binary concepts built on an inner structural coherence as they are unequal sides of an equation which will never compute. The exilic adaptation to a new residence is the unfolding of a creative process. Ambivalence is perhaps the best word to characterize the nature of an experience as well as the tone of a text in which there is a structural merger between two unlike entities: literature and life.

Exile intensifies the tenuousness of the relationship between language and reality, for the life of exile is, in many ways, the life of fiction. Nothing is apprehended without the grid screen of memory and comparison; naming and renaming are constant activities. All the signifieds within the land of exile keep slipping away as they are subjected to a process of mediation between the new land and the old. Exile calls for the assimilation of a different way of being, a new language which is itself nebulous and seems always to turn on itself. Again what remains is the ambivalence of the wandering word without the security of a home to nourish it with a single meaning. In this scheme exile can be considered as yet another manifestation of Nietzsche's "prison house of language."

That the issues surrounding exile give rise to fundamental questions concerning literature is evident in light of the problems raised by modern literary theory in the last two or three decades. The arbitrariness of the linguistic sign leads to a dilemma of signification in which the existence of language as a reliable tool in the apprehension of reality is seriously questioned. This paradox is not unlike the exile's difficulty in perceiving reality because of the need to focus on a shifting scenery, a landscape whose distant relation to that reality questions the possibility of its apprehension. Considering the exile's particularly intense desire to re-create a former reality, whether it be for political or existential reasons, and that this exilic search is, in a sense, a linguistic one, the condition is an apt model for literary theorists.

It is no wonder that Jacques Derrida has written about exile, if only on one occasion, for exile in language is a choice topic for one who espouses radical skepticism. One can regard the Derridian notion of difference, perhaps one of the most important contributions to philosophy in the latter part of this century, as a peculiarly appropriate allegory for exile. As signs must always defer to other signs in an infinitely negative process in which meaning can never be imminently present, the exilic journey mirrors this process of deferral by the constant reliance on relations to assimilate a new reality. The apprehension of the sign, like the assimilation of an exilic experience, operates on an imbalance. The signified is never present to the signifier, or the object is never contained within the word. The sign itself has no locality; like exile it is groundless. In one of the essays from *Writing and Difference*, titled "The Question of the Book" (pp. 64–78), Derrida deals with Edmond Jabès, a Jewish poet who considers his own Jewishness a catalyst for an eternally exilic search which is his writing. Jabès links his Jewish identity to exile, and in turn, to the unfolding (the reading) of a sacred book, its laws and its prophecies. In Derrida's essay these parallels lead to a general discussion of writing as exilic wandering. He refers to the nebulous place or site of the exile as the locus of a linguistic activity which he describes as a journey to nowhere. "When a Jew or a poet proclaims the Site, he is not declaring war. For this site, this land, calling to us from beyond memory, is always elsewhere. The Site is not the empirical and National Here of a territory. It is immemorial and thus also a future. . . . The land also keeps itself beyond any proximity" (p. 66).

In the same essay the French philosopher posits the text as weed, an outlaw whose commentary (for Jabès's exegesis) is a necessity, the end result of a desire which is no result at all because it does not, cannot, end. This commentary is "the very form of exiled speech. . . . Writing is originally hermetic and secondary" (p. 67). Derrida goes on to invoke the metaphor of the desert with all its starkness and possibilities of mirages and aimless wandering—an image of his idea of absence, which is, he says, the "heart of the question" of Jabès's work: a "song of absence. . . . Absence attempts to produce itself in the book and is lost in being pronounced; it knows itself as disappearing and lost, and to this extent it remains inaccessible and impenetrable. To gain access to it is to lose it; to show it is to hide it; to acknowledge it is to lie" (p. 69). The paradoxes of exile (a sad condition whose remedy is, to continue in Derrida's ironic vein, a further contributor to the symptoms) are markers of the Derridian conception of writing in that exile exposes its own losses (absences). The activity of the poet is not unlike that of the Jew or the exile.

> *Absence* of the writer too. For to write is to draw back. Not to retire into one's tent, in order to write, but to draw back from one's writing itself. To be grounded far from one's language, to emancipate it or lose one's hold on it, to let it make its way alone and unarmed. To leave speech. To be a poet is to know how to leave speech. To let it speak alone, which it can do only in its written form. *To leave* writing is to be here only to provide its passageway, to be the diaphanous element of its going forth: everything and nothing. (p. 70)

The "crossing of exile and language" is no less prevalent in classical texts than it is in the twentieth century, as several critics have observed.

The figure of exile is as pervasive in the permutations of literary myths as the fall, and in a basic sense, it is similar. In an essay on St. Augustine, Margaret Ferguson points to a Platonic notion of exile in which the universe falls into "an abyss of unlikeness" when God releases control of it. To be always the same is a property of the divine, and exile, seen as a flight from sameness, is a fundamental problem in the human condition. Ferguson seizes this and other images of the fall into exile as a point of departure for a discussion of St. Augustine's conception of language as a faulty and deceptive vehicle to God, because "no words can adequately represent an atemporal and holistic significance." Thus St. Augustine, the critic argues, anticipates the Derridian critique of the mimetic notion of language ("Saint Augustine's Region," pp. 844–845). Similarly, Giuseppe Mazzotta's treatment of Dante, while on the surface not swayed by modern tenets of literary theory, is not indifferent to the linguistic subversions which arise when a text is read through the grid of an exilic play of differences. The following description of the *Divine Comedy*, a work in which exile, as Mazzotta contends, is Dante's "most profound metaphor" (*Dante: Poet of the Desert*, p. 145), could very easily serve as a characterization of much of modern literature.

> It is the ground of exile where questions that seemed settled once and for all are rethought in their original and problematical character: it is the imaginative area where faith is exposed to the possibility of faithlessness and errors; it figures a radical displacement where memory is shifty and any univocal meaning is elusive and itself exiled. In this condition, one must be willing to take hints, follow leads, surrender to encounters. . . . One must be a restless nomad like the poet until the end comes. (pp. 273–74)

The models of exilic language in Dante, Saint Augustine, and Jabès, especially as their texts are elaborated by modern critics and theoreticians of literature, allow us to compare other texts written from that nebulous place of exile even if the social and political circumstances are different. The notion of an exilic fall from grace, the play of differences between a Here and an Elsewhere, and the relational nature of exilic reality are no less apparent in Spanish Civil War exile literature than in Dante and his banished cohorts. As we shall see in the numerous accounts of banishment from Spain, such as Rafael Alberti's autobiography, *La arboleda perdida* (*The Lost Grove*), or Max Aub's diary of an unhappy return, *La gallina ciega* (*The Blind Chicken*), or Luis Cernuda's *La realidad y el deseo* (*Reality and Desire*), the exilic fall is the texts' very conception and leads to the same issues and patterns which Ferguson, Derrida, and Mazzotta find so compelling in exile literature.

However, a critic can never lose sight of the concrete politics which give the exilic text its specificity. Is there not a significant difference between the concept of exile in Dante, for example, and the one we know in the twentieth century? Is Dante's political dilemma, his banishment from Florence in the midst of family struggles for power, a different issue altogether from the spiritual exile of the narrator-character of the *Divine Comedy*? Or does Dante's banishment from Florence in 1302 have anything to do with those who were cast away from their Spanish homeland as a result of a civil war? In the last analysis there is a crucial difference between the everyman theory of exile and one that is grounded in historical considerations; or in another light, there is a discrepancy between poetic and narrational problems and political or real ones. For the beginning of an answer I return to the interplay between literary diachrony and synchrony as elucidated by the Russian formalists (and Jameson) as a way of explaining aesthetic convergences within a constantly changing process. Yet even this is not wholly satisfactory just as any theory will always be challenged by a specific text. And as the following Spanish and non-Spanish case studies of exile will show, each instance seems to reshape the model, comment on it, extend it. Exile is a telling reminder of the inherent gap between a literary theory and a specific text; for, as I have stated, the very word "exile" is both a phenomenon and a human being of flesh and bone.

3 Three Paragons of Exile in the Twentieth Century: Thomas Mann, Bertolt Brecht, Vladimir Nabokov

It is common to dub the Spanish Civil War a "dress rehearsal for World War II." It is less common to conceive of the Spanish war's literary victims as models for the famous exile writers of this century—Thomas Mann, Bertolt Brecht, and Vladimir Nabokov—whose experiences span a wide temporal and geographical spectrum. However, the lack of evidence that German or later Russian authors, or for that matter Hungarian or Polish writers, read and assimilated the work of Spanish intellectual émigrés does not rule out the potential for common points of departure. The case study again serves as my methodological tool in the attempt to understand the literary representations of the European malady of the thirties and forties, an infirmity which followed the Spanish model of 1936 to 1939. Exile was one of the consequences of that malady, and as such it became another form of sickness with its own complications and symptoms.

What follows is a discussion of three non-Spanish writers who were afflicted by exile and whose cases tell us something about the patterns of exile writing itself: the propensity for testimony and autobiography along with all the problematic manifestations—moral discourse, obsession with memory, displacement of the subject, and marginality. (There are also patterns that are specific only to one author.) It is my contention that these issues appear and reappear in writers forced to leave Spain as a result of the war or who chose to do so regardless of literary influences. Again the tension between specificity and collectivity, the fact that exile refers to both a person and an experience, intrudes into the search for clearly delineated categories. Yet the case studies which occupy this chapter share common historical ground: Europe in the wake of an overwhelming totalitarian threat, the very same threat which sparked the writing of so many Spanish intellectuals of the same period. That the eyes of the world were on Spain in the mid- and late thirties is no less an indication of a shared European experience. And although the workings of history seem less unwieldy than those of literature, no literary critic would deny that Mann, Brecht, and Nabokov on the one hand, and Spaniards such as Max Aub, Luis Cernuda, and Juan Goytisolo on the other, share an experience which has had a profound effect on their writing: exile.

Thomas Mann

The collective experience of exile was perhaps as important a determining cultural factor in the Germany of the thirties and forties as it was in Spain at about the same time. Weimar, with all its artistic pluralism as well as the social and political turmoil which led to its downfall, was not unlike the Spanish Second Republic of 1931 to 1936. The intellectual trajectory of certain writers from romantic subjectivism in the pre-Nazi years to political commitment with the rise of fascism, as was the case with Thomas, Heinrich, and Klaus Mann, Hermann Broch, and Bertolt Brecht among others,[1] had its Spanish parallel in the reorientation of Alberti, Aub, Sender, Dámaso Alonso, and others who, regardless of exile, had to endure not only the material difficulties but the existential trauma brought on by a social and political conflagration. German anti-Nazi exile writers living in the United States were forced to come to grips with a social dilemma even though their aesthetic priorities may have resided elsewhere; and in Spain the upholders of "pure poetry" caught in the web of Ortegian vanguardism saw their own texts transformed by exile and the environments of different lands. In both cases the cultural aftermath of war rendered the continuation of an intellectual process nearly impossible. Exile had the effect of splitting not only the groups and movements but individual writers whose former existence was as removed aesthetically from present reality as it was geographically.

Thomas Mann is one of the most paradigmatic cases: his intellectual itinerary ranged from the subjectivism of his first novels to his testimony before a U.S. congressional committee on behalf of his fellow German exiles. His case is equally revealed in one of his most important works written in Los Angeles during the final years of World War II: *Doctor Faustus*. Mann's celebrated novel is rich in philosophical and ideological complexity, yet it becomes even more elaborate when examined within the context of exile. While not autobiographical in any strict sense, Mann himself suggested that *Doctor Faustus* contains autobiographical elements in the portrayal of Serenus Zeitblom, Ph.D., who is somewhat of a facsimile of the author. The first person narration, with all its shifts in perspective within an all-encompassing I, gives the work autobiographical qualities. The narrative of *Doctor Faustus* seems to beg the question: 'whose autobiography?' The literary and ontological problems of autobiography are of crucial concern to Mann for he, a German, is writing the story of German decadence at a time when literally all is lost, including his own way of life. He chronicles the fall of Adrian Leverkühn through the eyes of Zeitblom, whose almost mystical identification with his protagonist mirrors the relationship of the author of *Doctor Faustus* to the fallen subject of its discourse. Clearly the relationship between Zeitblom and Leverkühn is one of the work's most penetrating problems, as the author himself seems painfully aware when he begins the chapters of Zeitblom's story with discursive words on the ways in which the perspectives of Leverkühn and Zeitblom overlap. As in an autobiography, subject becomes object and vice versa.

Mann frames his novel with the following initial sentence by Zeitblom, the narrator: "I wish to state quite definitely that it is by no means out of any wish to bring my own personality into the foreground that I preface with a few words about myself and my own affairs this report on the life of Adrian Leverkühn" (p. 9). The ironic tension of these words, particularly in the excessive denial ("quite definitely," "by no means," "any wish"), grows with every chapter until it becomes possible that the very opposite is true: that Zeitblom speaks to recount his own experiences. His reading of a life so close to his own forces the reader to interpret Zeitblom's rendition as a reflection of his own life through the trials of Adrian Leverkühn. Zeitblom writes the life of his friend with a "trembling hand" (p. 243), and in the most suspenseful moments, such as Adrian's dialogue with the devil or the death of his beloved Echo, takes time to relate the emotional difficulty of recreating these scenes (pp. 214–15, 460). It is also essential to the work's unfolding that Zeitblom often interrupts his narration with comments on the nature of biography. He assures his readers that, in spite of what they may interpret as evidence to the contrary, his work is not a novel but a truthful portrayal of a life.

> Have I said enough? This is no novel, in whose composition the author reveals the hearts of his chosen characters indirectly, by the actions he portrays. In a biography, of course, I must introduce things directly, by name, and simply state such psychological factors as have a bearing on the life I am describing. But after the singular expressions which my memory leads me to write down, expressions of what I might call a specific intensity, there can be no doubt as to the fact to be communicated. (p. 268)

These words are typical of the exile writer's ambivalence about the truthfulness of his or her testimony and about the conversion of that testimony into a fiction. In *Doctor Faustus* the ambivalence takes the form of double-edged irony: that Mann's work is fictional and not biographical is evident, yet at every stage of the writing biography seems to enjoy a privileged position over other substructures such as parody (of *Faust*, or Nietzschean philosophy) or the historical novel. Zeitblom's lamentations over being unable to re-create fully Leverkühn's life, a fact made more frustrating, he declares, by the nature of language itself ("How many writers before me have bemoaned the inadequacy of language to arrive at visualization or to produce an exact portrait of an individual," p. 443), are indications of Mann's own distance from his subject. His wish for "compensation and atonement" (p. 463) at the loss of his land, as well as what he sees as the fall of western civilization, is as vain as Zeitblom's insistence on the biographical reality of his account. Thus the beginning sentence of the work ironically disclaiming any interest in writing an autobiography may be read as Mann's own self-conscious denial of the very same activity.

Linked to the issues surrounding biography and autobiography is Zeitblom's intention (if not obsession) of documenting the story of his musician friend. He sees the text he is writing as a moral duty, an obligation whose fulfillment, as painful as he describes it, is an absolute necessity: "I lay before the reader a testimony to my good faith in that I give space to the theory that I make difficulties because I secretly shrink from the task which, urged by love and duty, I have undertaken. But nothing, not even my own weakness, shall prevent me from continuing to perform it" (p. 35). While the actual place of Zeitblom's writing is not a distant land, his state of mind is most certainly that of an inner exile, and his need for testimony is the wish of every exile to account for a lost experience in hopes of some sort of vindication. And, as in many novels of Spanish exile, the narrator's present constantly intrudes into the recording of those memories. As Zeitblom dutifully marches to the end of his task, the bombardment of his land, his sacred culture, is taking place before his eyes and ears, a situation which he laments on more than one occasion: "Meanwhile we have experienced the destruction of our noble cities from the air, a destruction that would cry to heaven if we who suffer were not ourselves laden with guilt" (p. 168). The interruptions of present politics render Zeitblom's obligation a difficult one, yet at the same time they lie at the heart of his project. Just as his own ramblings on his text's genesis and its intentions belie their seemingly marginal place within the development of Leverkühn's life, the ongoing destruction of Germany breaks into the narrative of its own unfolding. Mann, a real exile, participates in the paradox, as does Zeitblom, by recreating his own destruction, his exile.

Bertolt Brecht

Besieged with the annihilation of everything he considered of value, Mann's years in exile were characterized by the futility of his attempts (like those of Spaniards living in Mexico during the Civil War) to be of some help in the repatriation of the refugees. The United States became not only the most attractive refuge for German intellectuals but the battleground for the polemics of German exile as well. One of the most influential and charismatic participants in these fiery yet inconsequential debates was Bertolt Brecht, who was, along with Mann, a figure of German and world letters. Yet, like the endless Mexican *tertulias* in which Spanish intellectual émigrés accused one another of ideological and tactical errors which led to their sorry fates, the "somewhat sterile complexities of exile politics" among the Germans contributed to the weightlessness of émigré life.[2] Brecht's case shows that he was well aware of his own amorphous political condition after his rejection of all available social and existential postwar alternatives, including Stalinist Russia, a revolutionary state which all his cohorts and critics expected him to embrace. Brecht's exilic trajectory is extensive and emblematic of what many Spanish leftist intellectuals (like Alberti and José Bergamín, who was exiled twice) had to endure in Europe in the wake of World War II. From fascist Germany in the mid-thirties, Brecht fled to Denmark, then Sweden and Finland; from there he traveled to North America after the frightening turns taken in the Soviet Union, and finally from the reactionary atmosphere in the United States aroused by the proceedings of the House Committee on Un-American Activities, he returned to Germany. Unlike Mann, Brecht's enduring participation in politics, and his conviction that the tensions between social and aesthetic practice would eventually be overcome, made him all the more resentful of the "sterile complexity" of his exile.[3]

Yet in spite of his social commitments (or perhaps, as he would have preferred, because of them) Brecht was above all an aesthetic innovator. If exile was not a direct cause of his so-called alienation technique in theater, it certainly contributed to it. Distance for Brecht was a necessary ingredient, not only for the creation of a dramatic work but for its reception. He argued that close identification or immersion into a work's thematic development leads to political and aesthetic passivity and the illusion that the work of art is an accurate representation of the world outside it. Distance of time and place, and a subject removed from the reality of the spectator, allow for reflection—a rational assessment of present conditions within a historical process which has little to do with the aesthetic one.

But such typically Brechtian coherence, logic in the face of wartime insanity, is doomed to the scrutiny of Brecht's own theatrical practice. In *Mother Courage* and *The Life of Galileo*, two plays written in exile during the war, the exceptions to the Brechtian precepts render the eternal tensions between theory and practice all too apparent.[4] While both plays are not allegories in the traditional sense, they do call for allegorical connections to the devastating social problems plaguing Europe during Brecht's exile, especially in the light of his theoretical essays, which, in Brecht's special case, must stand against and with his dramatic works. In this sense *Mother Courage*, whose delightfully sympathetic protagonist serves to question, if not subvert, Brecht's proscription of any emotional identification with a character (a distance if not created by exile, certainly fostered by it), may be interpreted as a reading of his own essays on dramatic function. In like manner the various metaphorical levels of *Galileo* (disguised references to Hitler's coming to power and to Brecht's own banishment) place the very concept of distance into question: the space between writer and text, the time of writing and the period of the work, spectator and actor, the land of the writer and that of the work, theory and practice. All the relations between these unlike qualities are analogous to the relation between writing and exile.

The identification of specific exilic themes in Brecht's plays is a difficult critical task perhaps because of his dramatic theory which questions the easy parallel between a theme in a work and a burning contemporary issue. Such is not the case, however, with his poetry, texts which in many instances openly contradict Brecht's own views on literary representation. The poems dealing with forced separation from a land are significant examples. Here Brecht's words, like much poetry written in exile no matter what place or time, evoke the melancholy sentiments of a man stripped of a former existence. In the tradition of Ovid, Brecht's lamentations belie the philosophical precision and collective understanding of the world which he called for in other writings. In some poems he seems aware of that very contradiction, as in the following lines from "To the Danish Refuge."

> Tell me, oh house between the sound and the pear trees:
> Does the old slogan, "Truth is concrete,"
> Which the refugee locked in time between your walls,
> Survive bombings?
> (*Poemas*, p. 185)[5]

The concreteness of the political situation which brought about Brecht's exile, as opposed to the lack of such tangibility in the actual experience of exile, is the subject of these lines. It is not unlike the dilemma of many Spanish left-wing refugees from fascist tyranny, such as Rafael Alberti who wrote in 1939, almost immediately after his departure from Spain,

> Me despierto.
> París.
> Es que vivo,
> es que he muerto?

Es que definitivamente he muerto?
    Mais non . . .
    C'est la police.
(*Poemas del destierro*, p. 33)

(I awake.
Paris.
Am I alive,
have I died?
Have I definitely died?
    But no . . .
    It's the police.)

For both Brecht and Alberti the commitment to philosophical materialism is questioned by the condition of exile. For Brecht the problem is particularly acute considering his attempt to devise an aesthetic theory based on dialectical materialism, as the questions he asks in another poem, "Thoughts on the Duration of Exile," attest: "Don't nail anything on the wall," "Why do you need to plant another tree?", "Why review another grammar?", "When do you think you'll return? / Do you want to know what you really think?" (pp. 156–57). In these lines the poet's own exilic condition brings on a series of ambivalences, questions not only on his own being but on his former convictions. "Truth is concrete" is a typically Brechtian dictum which, according to a Spanish translator, was scratched by Brecht himself on the walls of his Danish refuge close to the Sound (*Poemas y canciones*, p. 185). During the exilic years in Denmark and Sweden not only did Brecht yearn to maintain the political, social, and aesthetic vitality of a concrete truth (a truth which seemed more open to question with every year in exile), but he doubted his very own concreteness. His questions were both rhetorical as well as authentic quandaries about his relationship to an ever more alienated world. The yearning for truth thus brings on its opposite: enigma and ambivalence.

Like many exile poets of the Spanish Civil War (Abellán, IV,

13–108), Brecht carries on a poetic dialogue with a tradition of exile literature, especially the exilic elegy. His poems are filled with juxtapositions between a present geography and one left behind: "beyond the Sound and the forests" (p. 154), "the tranquility of the Sound does not deceive us" (p. 160), "my native city, how did I find it?" (p. 186). The Sound itself, a constant presence in Brecht's exile poetry, is an echo of the mythical waters of exodus whose perpetual movement betrays its own immutable appearance. But the intertextual dialogue among other exile figures is most evident in a poem he calls "Visit to the Poets in Exile," a gloss of which appears below.

> When between dreams, he entered the exiled poets' cabin, next door to the abode of the exiled masters, he could hear gay talk and laughter. Ovid appeared at the door and said whispering, "It's better not to sit down just now. You have not died yet. Who knows? You may return without anything having changed except you." . . . But more down to earth and worn, Villon approached him and asked, "How many doors does your house have?" And Dante, grabbing him by the arm, took him aside mumbling, "Friend, those verses of yours have many flaws: you must think that all is against you." . . . "If you get to trial, find yourself a shyster lawyer," shouted Euripides, "because he'll find a loophole." The laughter had not yet died down when from a dark corner, a cry was heard, "Hey, you, do they know your poems by heart?" "And will those who do be spared the persecution?" "Those," said Dante quietly, "are the forgotten. Their works will be destroyed along with their bodies." The laughter ceased. No one dared to look. The newcomer had grown pale. (pp. 165–66)

Each quotation attributed to the exile figures is a paraphrase of that poet's story of exile; and each second person address further marks a poetic dialogue both within each figure and among the group of dead literati. Ovid's concern for dying at home, Dante's attention to poetic imperfections, Voltaire's admonition against poverty (not quoted here), and Euripides' playful suggestion that the visitor find himself a shyster lawyer are all indications of specific exilic histories, stories past and present within the poet's dream. The lines also suggest that the poet is following in the footsteps of the exile poets by writing a similar story. The final crescendo (laughter) ironically gives way to silence, that tense split second which follows self-conscious humor. The "forgotten," Dante says, as if to create a fourth level of his universe well below or at the margins of his *inferno*, are those whose words and bodies have disappeared without a trace; not even memory, as unreliable as it is, can attest to their existence. Brecht, in exile yet still alive, has entered Dante's world prematurely; thus his fate is itself a question. The poet's prospects are surely dim, especially in the face of another all too familiar adage which seems to inform every line of this poem: "All those who enter here, abandon hope."

The gloominess of Brecht's portraits of exile, however, is by no means the keynote of his writings from Denmark. Unlike most masters of the exilic elegy, Brecht posits laughter as a weapon in an atmosphere whose deadening solemnity vitiates against mirth of any type. In "Visit to the Poets in Exile" it is Heine who advises the visitor, "Mix in a few jokes here and there" (line 19); and Brecht's own works, whether written in exile or not, testify to his having heeded his predecessor's remark.

Nowhere in Brecht's exilic corpus is parody and the burlesque as a defense against exile more manifest than in one of his lesser known works, *Dialogue of the Refugees*.[6] Perhaps better than any of his other writings, this text synthesizes the problems surrounding the language and motivations of exile literature even though its parodic structure is something of an exception among exilic works. Its two characters are themselves burlesque imitations of political émigrés who lead pathetic lives away from the battleground of a previous land. Again the distance which Brechtian epic theater calls for is not as apparent here as in his plays, for at the outset he situates his dialogue in war-torn Europe with several references to the Führer and the Duce as well as to the ss and

Dachau. Yet these readily identifiable names appear within an exchange between two strange men perfectly unsuited to their surroundings. Their speech is unfamiliar and semantically (also at times syntactically) removed from a conventional thought process. They refer to a passport as "the most noble element of man" (p. 7), a phrase every bit as exilic as it is ironic. One of the characters states that the modern is outdated, both choose a certain bar for their conversations because of its inhospitable atmosphere, and a seemingly philosophical discussion of liberty is based on an example of the freedom (or lack of it) enjoyed by Swiss mountain guides (pp. 88–89). The genre of this work is uncertain. Not exactly a traditional philosophical dialogue in the classical Greek tradition, yet something like it, this text is also different from theater and narrative, even though there are certain elements (stage directions, props) which link it to that genre.

The characters, Kalle, a worker, and Ziffel, a physicist with a good command of politics, philosophy, and literature, weave in and out of the crucial issues of their day in an effort to relieve themselves of the pains and sorrows of exile, sentiments which are themselves objects of parody. Brecht satirizes the behavior of exile in a manner similar to the humorous accounts of Spaniards living in England during the forties by Esteban Salazar Chapela (*Perico in London*). Exile allows both writers to mock a variety of movements, political and aesthetic, with special emphasis in Brecht's case on the Third Reich. Everything is open to ridicule, including the speakers themselves as Brecht's unlikely pair (the intellectual and the worker) come together in the most likely of places (the train station), since they are the only individuals in town who speak German.

Beyond the satire of exilic behavior, this text captures a central problem in exile literature: the writing of life. Ziffel is writing his memoirs and having a difficult time of it, as he confesses to his worker-foil, who is content to allow his life experiences to stand alone. Brecht interrupts the dialogue with fragments of Ziffel's text as the intellectual reads and elucidates his own interpolated texts. At one point Kalle, the worker, ingenuously declares, "I thought that one only writes one's memoirs at the end of one's life," to which Ziffel responds,

> I don't have a clear view of anything, nor do I possess the art of nuance, but I do fulfill the first condition as well as any man on this continent, that is, I have probably come to the end of my existence. This is not the best place to write, because I need cigarettes, and here they are difficult to find because of the blockade. . . . But something else worries me more. No one would be surprised if an important person proposed to tell his contemporaries of his life, his opinions, his wishes. I have precisely that intention, but I am a person without importance. (pp. 23–24)

Not only does Brecht suggest the reason for the outpourings of exilic autobiographies, he expresses the dilemma of the recording and the assessment of a life. As I have been suggesting, exile gives rise to the sense of a life's end; it deceives its victim into perceiving his or her life as a book with structural coherence. Ziffel, on the other hand, seems to become faintly aware of the deception while he writes "without the art of nuance," and without the guide of a unifying principle. Well before the completion of the dialogue, Brecht mercifully allows his character to abandon his project, though his parody of "the important man's memoirs" continues. These German exiles (Brecht included), not only in this strange text but in the rest of Brecht's works written away from his dying land, all come to the realization that exile is a death sentence; that is to say, it is linguistically an utterance of finality and existentially a punishment whose severity does not fit the crime.

Ziffel's and Kalle's ridiculous ramblings in the midst of a horrendous political situation further indicate exilic pathos. Yet within the literary figure of pathos there is always a thread of empathy, an unwritten realization that the circumstances leading to the undesirable condition are (or could be) shared by writer and reader. Unlike the grotesque, whose repulsion creates distance, pathos seems to stir an unspoken desire to draw the participants in the artistic work together—another frustrated attempt to regain the wholeness which exile dissolves. Ziffel and Kalle are examples, for their proximity to Brecht himself, another pathetic German exile, opens the possibility of a readerly comparison. It is this window to comparison which allows for the most un-Brechtian of artistic effects: empathy.

Vladimir Nabokov

The likeness and unlikeness between character and writer, and the inquiry into this very relationship in *Dialogue of the Refugees*, is reminiscent of the themes and concerns of another familiar exile figure, Vladimir Nabokov. Ziffel and Kalle are every bit as absurd as the myriad of intellectuals, politicians, and misfits who populate Nabokov's works, people who also share the plight of many Spaniards living in unfamiliar territory and whose inability to adapt has been the object of much literary satire. Sympathy for these lost souls is inevitable, even in a writer like Nabokov whose keen sense of distance between his narrators and characters at times belies that note of sympathy. That Nabokov felt the victimization of Russian writers fleeing from the Revolution, Stalin, or fascism is manifest in his letters and autobiography in spite of the separation he fostered between himself and his fellow exiles.[7] The issues treated in his novels and stories are indications of this reluctant hint of sympathy, which is especially apparent in his creation of the immortal Timofey Pnin, a character much like Ziffel in his sheer absurdity.

Nabokov is well known in the United States for his ability to debunk North American culture by setting one of his émigré intellectuals loose in its wilds: the case with *Lolita* as well as *Pnin*. The latter is the most representative. Numerous devices offset the protagonist from the American mainstream of university professors: wordplays (not only with Russian and English malapropisms, but the very ridiculousness of the name Pnin as it sounds in English); the almost slapstick entanglements which Pnin (and the reader) must suffer; and Pnin's absolute ineptness at understanding the function of certain objects as well as the concept of function itself. Yet along with these distancing elements stands the narrator's relationship to the character. Also an exile (but a smoother one than Pnin, far more successfully assimilated into American culture), his discreet presence in the beginning of the novel grows blatant toward the end when the reader discovers that the narrator, "an Anglo-Russian writer" (p. 117), is Pnin's replacement after the latter unjustly loses his teaching post. Nabokov's indictment of American intellectual life is at the same time self-criticism, not only through his insertion of the Anglo-Russian narrator but by the textual self-commentary which structures the work. As Pnin is about to leave town the narrator arrives and stays at the house of one of the contributors to Pnin's misfortune, a Professor Cockerell who entertains his guest with delightful and accurate imitations of the Russian's behavior and speech. "I must admit that Jack Cockerell impersonated Pnin to perfection. He went on for at least two hours showing me everything—Pnin teaching, Pnin eating, Pnin ogling a co-ed, Pnin narrating the epic of the electric fan" (p. 156). What ensues is a paraphrase of the narrator's account of Pnin's exploits in North American academe (pp. 156–58). In these pages Nabokov rewrites his own novel, and in so doing opens Pnin's story to moral questioning: the exilic ethical dialogue which includes not only the narrator (who feels a hint of guilt at admitting that Cockerell's imitation is magnificent), but the narrator's readerly analogue—you and me.

Timofey Pnin's past is also open to question as it intrudes into the present (a trademark of Nabokov's writing), highlighting one of exile literature's most dominant subgenres: the retrospective. Nabokov's glimpses of his own past are disguised, however, by the trappings of texts whose concern is not so much the re-creation of the past as it is the fusion of past experience with the present of writing. *Pnin* is no exception nor is Nabokov's exilic autobiography, *Speak, Memory*. In *Pnin* the psychological underpinnings of the character are in many ways determined by a past irreconcilable with the present. A similar situation exists in *Speak, Memory* where the narrator (a good imitation of Nabokov himself) gropes for images, smells, and people of a former life through a language which resists its re-creation. The gap between the past experience and the present of the text is the unconnected distance between the homeland and the new life. Historical continuity and the smooth transition between chronological stages is a privilege enjoyed by those who stay at home.

As dissimilar as the two works seem, *Speak, Memory* informs the historical dimension of *Pnin*. The structural unity of Nabokov's autobiography is open to question not only because the author elaborates on autobiographical issues, but because *Speak, Memory* is a compilation of retrospectives written at various times in Nabokov's life with little or no intention of publishing them as an autobiography. While *Pnin* (written during the interim between the two editions of *Speak, Memory*, originally titled *Conclusive Evidence*) makes frequent use of the flashback, the autobiography may be read as an inquiry into the flashback itself and its relation to the notion of literary time. Like the Spanish exile writer Jorge Semprún in his *Autobiography of Federico Sánchez*, Nabokov steps beyond the flashback as an informative and psychologically explanatory device. The I of *Speak, Memory* and the protagonist of *Pnin* often have a hard time distinguishing between present and past (as in the appearance of Pnin's Baltic aunts in the audience of the Cremona Women's Club, p. 23). Pnin's past defamiliarizes his present in ways which render his own existence (the former one as well) a mystery, "a helpless fatigue . . . detaching him, as it were, from reality" (p. 17). The interior monologue of Pnin's "spiritual son," Victor, is an example.

> Ancestral portraits darkened the walls of the vast panelled room. Otherwise, it was not unlike the headmaster's study at St. Bart's School, on the Atlantic seaboard, some three thousand miles west of the imagined Palace. A copious spring shower kept lashing at the French windows, beyond which young greenery, all eyes, shiv-

ered and streamed. Nothing but this sheet of rain seemed to protect the Palace that for several days had been rocking the city. . . .
Actually Victor's father was a cranky refugee doctor, whom he
had never much liked and had not seen now for almost two years.
(p. 70)

The most revealing mark of this passage, beyond the artful blend of
times, places, and characters, is the ellipsis, a gap made all the more
distant by its silence. As the narrator invents a Victor who is himself
engaged in the activity of inventions, a cacophonous voice intrudes
into the unreality of the situation (the reality of writing) with the word,
"actually."

These temporal and spatial switches displacing the text from a recognizable milieu are emblematic of the dominant theme and device of
Speak, Memory. With nearly every scene of his life Nabokov inserts a
subverting word, a disclaimer, a parenthetical remark, or a reflection
on his own writerly task, all of which bring attention to the text itself
not as a frivolous aesthetic exercise (although Nabokov seems to assure
us that there is not much beyond this in his works) but as an urge to
open his life to the scrutiny of writing. The result is a reflection on
writing itself as well as on the ways in which his text swallows him,
metamorphoses him, and takes his new species into another world.
When he speaks of his first poem he allows himself a digression (not
the only one of *Speak, Memory*) in which he expounds upon the nature
of poetry.

But then, in a sense, all poetry is positional: to try to express one's
position in regard to the universe embraced by consciousness, is
an immemorial urge. The arms of consciousness reach out and
grope, and the longer they are the better. . . . the poet feels everything that happens in one point in time. Lost in thought, he taps
his knee with his wandlike pencil, and at the same instant a car
(New York license plate) passes along the road, a child bangs the
screen door of a neighborhood porch, an old man yawns in a misty

> Turkestan orchard . . . all forming an instantaneous and transparent organism of events, of which the poet (sitting in a lawn chair, at Ithaca, New York) is the nucleus. (p. 218)

It is indeed ironic that in a book titled *Speak, Memory* the author should speak of his own activity as "an immemorial urge," a desire to grasp simultaneously a variety of diverse events, times, and places in one almost mystical climactic thrust. Yet this irony is the mainstay of Nabokov's autobiography (and other exilic autobiographies, such as Semprún's)—the desire to reach simultaneity of experience through writing. As Nabokov is well aware, writing the experience, the memory, destroys the real object of that memory and replaces it with an experience of another kind. All that is left of the original is a trace, a piece of what once was or may have been.

Collecting and recollecting are the motifs of *Speak, Memory* just as entomology (or more precisely, lepidopterology) seems the driving force behind Nabokov's life. One could very well juxtapose these two phenomena (recollecting and lepidopterology) as the main activities of the writer's exilic life, for exile calls for a new taxonomy, a process of naming and renaming of things and people that seem constantly to fly from the clutches of memory. What makes Nabokov's exilic nomenclature unique among the exiles is the intensity of the process—a passionate need to capture the memory along with the butterfly, to name it and thus possess it as part of his belongings, his text. At the risk of falling victim to one of Nabokov's pet peeves, Freudian psychology and all its pseudoscientific and therapeutic strains, in *Speak, Memory* he appears as the classical anal-retentive personality (in this case an exilic one). He takes great joy in describing his one hundred exploits capturing butterflies not only in the wilds of nature but at his desk compiling, categorizing, and accumulating more species and names. This life contradiction is, in a linguistic sense, another manifestation of the irony of Nabokov's text: its tightness, its carefully chosen vocabulary, its precision in contrast to the escape of its very words from the net of signification as they wander aimlessly into exile.

The futility and arbitrariness of exile are as apparent in Nabokov's political stands as in his writing. Nabokov might have been the first to declare that politics never had any specific aim other than the vulgarity of material interest. He remains, not only in *Speak, Memory* but in the ideological content of his fiction, repelled by revolutionaries and fascists alike and is equally uncommitted to bourgeois liberalism. Nabokov was an elitist and branded himself as such. Even more appalling to lovers of social equality is the fact that his elitism is more of the feudal variety than the intellectual one. In spite of his account of his father's heroic death for the cause of Russian liberalism, his political tastes lay elsewhere, nostalgically at the heart of a land whose aristocratic elegance and charm are frequently the evocations of his autobiography. Nabokov is a member of a particular group of exiles who never consider themselves full-fledged participants in their own culture (Joyce is an example along with Conrad, and Blanco White, Cernuda, and Goytisolo in Spain). Distance was one of his trademarks from the moment he was born, as *Speak, Memory* suggests not only through the peculiarity of his upbringing (his father's taste for anything British) but through his resistance to assimilation of any kind.

Perhaps it is the anomaly of Nabokov's case and his impatience with easy categories which might save him from his own elitist cultural and political pretensions. At every point in his exile, especially in the United States, he defended his fellow intellectuals cast from their homes for whatever political reason against the marginality in which the host culture (along with the one at home) insisted on placing them. *Pnin* is a case in itself, but there are many others: the flesh-and-blood figures of *Speak, Memory* (chapter 14) and the cultural misfits of his fiction, constantly at work in their respective émigré newspapers, journals, and publishing houses which fold almost as soon as they appear, like those from the Spanish Republic in exile scattered around the Western world and forgotten. In some ways Nabokov himself was a victim of exilic marginality, in spite of the acclaim he enjoyed in the United States. He had his share of quarrels with those very literati who thought so much of him—the Cockerells of North American English departments. He bemoaned the indifference of the literary establishment toward his Russian works. And his friendship with Edmund Wilson, the guru of that very establishment in this country, turned into a feud tarnishing Wilson's shine as a critic and "expert" on Russian literature (Karlinsky, *Nabokov-Wilson Letters*, pp. 3–25).

The Nabokov-Wilson falling out, although steeped in intellectual egotism on both sides, is indicative of a larger issue, both political and literary. It reveals the ways in which exile writers must depend on facile readings of their cultures for success in the new land, creating one more in a long line of exilic dilemmas: how to face the stereotypes, the criticism which stems from lack of understanding and previous indifference, as well as the praise that comes from the same source. Nabokov chose to subvert the conventional wisdom, as his own works such as *Lolita* and *Pnin* attest. Yet at the same time he was painfully aware of the forgotten Russian writers of his own generation, those who matured in a democratic period of Russian history immediately before the Revolution—a political arena in which Nabokov's father was an important participant and which Edmund Wilson chose to ignore. These writers (Mandelstam, Amnensky, Bely and others) are mentioned in the correspondence and occasionally appear as characters in his fiction. They stand as metaphors of oblivion and what Nabokov himself could have become, and they are akin to the myriad Spanish exile intellectuals of the Civil War who share the dilemma. Like Nabokov, Spaniards such as Juan Goytisolo and Jorge Semprún have fared well amidst the Parisian literati who treat them as token renegades from a barbarous land. But what of the Pnins and Sebastian Knights of Spain wandering around the world with a tale that no one will hear?

Whether it originates in the wake of the Russian Revolution, the pogroms, the Nazi regime in various parts of Europe, the death camps, or the Spanish Civil War, exile constantly reminds us of one of its most salient effects—marginality. The literary and linguistic trappings of exile are manifestations of that same phenomenon: the spatial and temporal borderlines of one's own existence, the slipperiness of language as a rendition of that existence, the ostracism, the oblivion, the silence, and along with all these detriments, the joyous subversion which occurs at the intrusion of the marginal into the center. Even such a canonical figure as Thomas Mann, a writer whose importance spans two centuries, seems to question his own canonization in *Doctor Faustus*. Brecht's Kalle and Ziffel make their way into Germany's center, dislocate it, and bring it along with them into exile. And Nabokov, ironically the most committed of the three to the defense of his class of neglected exile writers, engages in the subversion of his own words and concepts. The "sterile complexities of exile politics" are indeed every bit as pathetic as the situation of the exiles themselves. But one more feature of the exilic experience serves as the beginning of my rescue attempt of Spanish émigré writers: the fecundity of exile language.

Writing the Lives of Spanish Exiles

4 The Intellectual Diaspora of the Civil War

In early April 1967 Manuel Andújar, one among many intellectuals and fiction writers forced into exile in 1939, set foot on Spanish soil after a long stay in Mexico. Andújar's trajectory began from his native Jaen when he traveled to Madrid and then to Barcelona where he was a journalist during the war. In 1939 he followed many of his countrymen into Vichy, France, only to find himself in a concentration camp at Saint-Cyprien, which he described in his book, ironically titled, *Saint-Cyprien, plage*. Sixteen years after his exile, with the aid (and the impediment) of distance in both time and place, Andújar recalls his trip from the war-torn Old World to Mexico aboard a ship called the *Sinaia*. He writes in "Crisis de la nostalgia" ("Crisis of Nostalgia"):

> Erase un viejo barco, de larga y amarga historia. Cuentan de él que cobró ancianidad y una pátina sombría en la brega de transportar, durante muchos años, míseros creyentes de las costas norafricanas a la peregrinación sagrada de La Meca. Capas de mugre y sudor, de rezos y leyendas habíanse adherido a sus maderas y planchas, dábanle un aire correoso, como la piel tostada de los profetas del desierto. (p. 105)

> (There was once an old ship with a long and bitter past. They say that with age and many years of transporting wretched and struggling North Africans on their sacred pilgrimage to Mecca, the ship developed a dark patina. Layers of filth and sweat, of prayers

and legends, had clung to its boards and gangplanks, which had given it a leathery glow like the bronze skin of prophets in the desert.)

Strangely enough, these words are taken not from a novel, a short story, or personal memoirs, but from an essay in which the author is more concerned with the exposition of a historical and cultural problem affecting modern Spain than with the evocation and re-creation of a specific moment in his own life or that of his compatriots. Overall this essay is marked by a scholarly tone which eventually overpowers the fictional quality of the beginning words. At the same time the traces of a parable are felt throughout this text, for there is a fictional quality which tends to diminish the distance of Andújar's discourse from Andújar himself. He refers, for example, to what the Spanish exiles living in Mexico came to regard as the second discovery of America ("Crisis," p. 108). Veiled comparisons between Columbus and his men to voyagers aboard the Sinaia serve as a motif to enhance Andújar's exploration of the cultural and ethical ramifications of the second discovery, both a re-creation of and a reaction against the first. Like a good Spanish liberal, he points out that Spain is itself the product of an uneasy amalgam of East and West, as the allusion to Muslim culture in the beginning images suggests. Andújar's concern is to place Mexico in its rightful place in relation to Spain, that is, Republican Spain free of feudal, religious, or material hierarchies or totalitarian principles: "Contribuimos a un mestizaje cultural. . . . Aquí estamos y así somos. En México, para España" ("Crisis," p. 119; We contribute to a cultural crossbreeding. . . . here we are in Mexico, and that is the way we are, for Spain).

After his return to Spain Andújar reprinted the essay as the concluding section of a longer piece on the effects of exilic "mestizaje" or crossbreeding of Spanish Republican and indigenous cultures. The addendum is indeed appropriate, in spite of the time lapse, for in both texts he plays a double role: that of an intellectual whose roots lie firmly within the ground of the generation of Miguel de Unamuno, and an eyewitness. This latter role also comprises two dimensions: literally a voyager on the Sinaia cast out of his land by a war, and metaphorically a sailor on Columbus's new ship. The voice of both the intellectual and the eyewitness is that of a *nosotros* whose condition, regardless of the nostalgia and loss, will eventually become a triumph, both historical and ethical. At several significant junctures Andújar refers to the recording of history, as he affirms the need to transcend the gathering of statistics to arrive at history's poetic essence, a factor which yields to the drama and "pulp" ("Crisis," p. 108) of individual lives. The primary sources of the "first" discovery of America (Columbus's and Cortes's letters, Bernal Díaz's chronicles) are not unlike what Andújar writes, even though the eyewitness account of the latter is clearly secondary to the stated intention of answering an old question within a new context: What is Spain in the light of exile in Mexico?—a question much in keeping with Unamuno's concept of "intrahistory." The tension of Andújar's essay resides precisely in the disequilibrium (perhaps contradiction) between the abstraction of history and the individual participant in that history.

The textuality and literariness of the varied accounts of discovery and conquest of the New World, as far removed as they are from the stories of exile experiences in the twentieth century, may stand as models not only for the ways in which poetic devices and concepts intrude into the recording of history in general, but for the overlapping literary and historical structures common to exile texts. It has been argued, for example, that America was not discovered but invented by the chroniclers of discovery.[1] In like manner Andújar has argued that for Spain to exist again after its destruction in 1939 its citizens living both within and without will have to invent it. In light of the comparison it is revealing to subject the works of the many essayists of Civil War exile not only to conceptual scrutinies but literary ones. The keys to a structural understanding of Spanish exile literature (or perhaps any exile literature) lie precisely within that testimony, even when the subject matter calls for intellectual distance and objectivity.

Andújar is considered a talented writer of the contemporary Spanish novel and he elegantly hides the testimonial nature of his essay; yet the role he plays as an exile with a tale to tell adds to the elegance of the prose. Similarly, the most interesting essays (from a literary point of view) on Spanish Civil War exile are from the exiles themselves. The diaspora sparked by the war of 1936 to 1939 was above all an intellectual one. The proliferation of writers, professors, painters, sculptors, actors, architects, and scientists among the million or so who left is by no means proportionate to the number of these professionals within the population at large at the time of the departure. It is thus a natural consequence that many of these intellectuals left written evidence of their experience in exile, even in the essays that do not deal directly with the Spanish exodus. The postwar essays by thinkers such as José Gaos, María Zambrano, and even Américo Castro are not properly understood without the consideration of their exilic contexts. Vicente Llorens declares (in *Aspectos sociales de la literatura española*) that Castro could not have written *España en su historia* (*Spain in its history*) had he not left Spain (pp. 14–15), an affirmation echoed by José Luis Aranguren (*Crítica y meditacíon*, p. 139). The well-accepted designation of those Republican Spaniards residing in the Spanish-speaking world as *transterrados* (the transplanted ones) is attributed to the philosopher José Gaos in an essay on Spanish adaptation to Latin American culture. He argues that, because of a common language, as well as certain shared values, the *transterrados* were able to continue their work away from Spain without the serious hardships most exiles had to endure ("La adaptación," p. 177). Yet Gaos's notion of *transterrados* is as much an indicator of his own ability to continue where he left off as it is of the community of intellectuals living in Mexico City. And it is María Zambrano who writes passionately and convincingly (in "Los intelectuales en el drama de España") that the loss of the Spanish Republic to fascism produced a common language of resistance among the intellectuals during and after the war. All three of these essayists speak as members of the community of Spanish intellectuals living outside of Spain.[2]

At the downfall of the Second Republic the exiled intellectuals, both as individuals and as a group, were in a state of limbo. Some interrupted their academic and literary careers in order to devote themselves to the defense of democracy. As a result, the discourse on previous concerns seemed to many irrelevant to the new situation. It is no wonder then that the many essays written immediately after the war were well in tune with the concerns of the so-called Generation of 1898, specifically the Generation's antirationalism and its attention to geography as a factor in the consciousness of a nation. As Andújar's essay on the "Crisis of Nostalgia" shows, Unamuno makes an important appearance in the attempt of the Spanish exiles to reach a historical and philosophical understanding of their own dilemma. In spite of the well-documented influence of José Ortega y Gasset in the essays of these exiled thinkers, it is Unamuno who stands out as the group's spiritual mentor.

Unamuno's concept of *lucha* (struggle) in *Agonía del Christianismo* (*Agony of Christianity*), a work written in exile during the dictatorship of Miguel Primo de Rivera, serves as a springboard for exiled essayists such as José Bergamín and María Zambrano, perhaps due to the importance Unamuno gives to the place in which he writes his essay. In the introduction the Spanish philosopher situates his discourse within the political context which gave it birth. Military tyranny, he states, confined him to the isle of Fuerteventura, and then, thanks to French aid, he was able to take refuge in Paris where *Agony of Christianity* was first published. Exile in Fuerteventura, he goes on to say, is what provided him with the material for the text: "mi íntima experiencia religiosa y hasta mística" (p. 21; my intimate, even mystical religious experience). Thus, like many exile writers, Unamuno's objective is to translate that vital experience into a text.

In keeping with Unamuno's essays, introspection, both cultural and historical, characterizes Bergamín's philosophical reflections in *En el pozo de la angustia* (*Pit of Anguish*). The *Pit* is Bergamín's search for literary and spiritual roots; he invokes the spirits of Calderón, St. Teresa, and Don Quijote in his synthesis of Christianity and social revolution. While Bergamín does not allude to his personal exile, the fact that he wrote *Pit of Anguish* almost immediately after he was cast from his land, and the many references both to Unamuno and to an exilic fall from grace (Dante, the notion of eternal purgatory), suggest that the experience of exile allowed Bergamín to conceptualize a universal fall into his existential abyss. His notion of *hombre de acción* (man of action) is in certain respects a vindication of his life in exile and a search for the lost home, as he makes it clear that his uneasy synthesis of religion and revolution comes from Spanish sources. Similarly Unamuno reads the landmarks of Spanish civilization such as the *Quijote* and Velázquez's painting of the crucifixion (in *El Cristo de Velázquez*) as affirmations not only of his own ideas but of his geographic identity.

In like manner María Zambrano searches for the emblems of a national consciousness in her *Pensamiento y poesía en la vida española* (*Poetry and Thought in Spanish Life*), also in keeping with the writing of the exiled intellectual David García Bacca and his conversion of Antonio Machado's poetry into an ontological theory. In the collection of essays written by Zambrano during and after the war, *Senderos* (*Paths*), she begins her search for a philosophical tradition in Spain emphasizing the tension between action and contemplation, as does Bergamín in his *Pit of Anguish*. According to Zambrano the necessity of playing a role in the "drama" of the war relieved that tension for many intellectuals, only to arise again in exile.

> Este mismo colapso y de mayor longitud se produjo entre los intelectuales, que dejaron de serlo para ser hombres. . . . Sufrieron esta crisis los que por su contextura humana, por su capacidad moral, estaban llamados a resucitar en su condición más tarde. (*Senderos*, p. 47)

(This same collapse of a longer duration arose in intellectuals who ceased to be so in order to become human beings; the people who suffered this crisis, due to their moral and human capacities, were called upon to rise again in their human condition later on.)

Later she states,

Pero se trata también y más hondamente, de realizar en lo intelectual la revolución que se realiza en las otras zonas de la vida. Se trata de decir lo que tanto se sabía y nunca se dijo . . . de dar vida y luz a todo lo que necesita ser pensado, a la cultura nueva que se abre camino. (p. 50)

(But it is also a matter of realizing intellectually the revolution which is realizing itself in other aspects of life. It is a matter of saying what was well known and never articulated, . . . of giving rise to everything that needs to be thought and to the new culture on the threshold.)

These ideas appeared frequently, in various contexts and forms, in the myriad of literary and political journals published by Spanish Republican exiles in places such as Mexico City, Buenos Aires, Paris, and Toulouse. In the journal founded by José Bergamín, *España Peregrina* (*Pilgrim Spain*), writers such as Juan Larrea, Corpus Barga, Tomás Navarro Tomás, and Augusto Pi y Suñer, put together a sort of manifesto not long after the conclusion of the war in which they bombastically pledged to continue the intellectual and moral battle in which they were driven to participate. However, the grandiose and elevated tone of the manifesto ("triumph of the universal cause of Spain," "subordination of our individual lives to superior values"; Abellán, III, 32) unwittingly hides the precariousness of the authors' condition and is typical of the linguistic overcompensation of the exile who not only has an ax to grind but a life to vindicate.

If, in fact, there are points of convergence among the essayists who had supported the Republic and who were forced into exile as a result, what can be said of the structural features of that convergence? As Zambrano's essays as well as the exile manifesto suggest, there seems to be a need to speak in a common language, a unified voice: "no se trata de un testimonio individual, sino de todo un pueblo" (*Senderos*, p. 56) (it is not a matter of an individual testimony, but of an entire nation). Not surprisingly, the feature which stands out in these essays almost as a common bond among a monstrously dissimilar group of texts is the voice of a *nosotros*. It is a voice which, if not always articulated directly through an omnipresent we, as in Andújar and Zambrano, often unmasks its collective nature by suggestions of shared experiences, both political and literary. Juan Marichal's discussion of the intellectual exodus of 1939, "De algunas consecuencias intelectuales de la Guerra Civil Española," ("The Intellectual Consequences of the Spanish Civil War") is an indication of how a scholarly essay on exile may become contaminated with literary devices when the writer is an embodiment of the consequences. As seemingly detached as the Harvard professor appears in his text, he relies on experience as the catalyst for his principal ideas. As the son of Republican exiles, he recalls that during the war, when he was an adolescent, a peasant told him the reason for the conflict: " 'Sabes, nosotros luchamos por la libertad del mundo' " (p. 82; You know, we are fighting for the freedom of the world). With these ingenuous yet penetrating words, Marichal makes his main point: that for the first time in the history of modern Spain, a Spanish problem had become a universal one. The only we in the essay is uttered by the peasant-protagonist, yet his voice includes that of Marichal and provides the critic with the moral weight of his argument.

In like manner Manuel Durán, another Spanish War outcast of the same generation as Marichal, and a poet in his youth, employs the first person plural throughout an essay on "La generación del 36 vista desde el exilio" ("The Generation of 1936 Viewed from Exile"). The title is significant, for Durán makes no pretense of objectivity. His is a view from the inside, not only that of a member of the generation, but as one who has firsthand knowledge of exile. He begins his discussion with a question which ironically serves to make his stand (and his angle) perfectly clear: " 'Transplantados son mejores.' Eso decía Gracián de los españoles en el *Criticón*. ¿Nos hubiera consolado la frase si la hubiéramos conocido o recordado mientras nos dispersábamos por los caminos de Francia o nos preparábamos para embarcar hacia América?" (p. 193; "They are better transplanted." Gracián used these words in the *Criticón* to characterize Spaniards. Would this judgment have consoled us had we known or remembered it as we were scattered throughout the roads of France or as we prepared to embark on a journey to America?) Durán's point is not new. He reminds his readers of what they already know, that the wounds opened by a bloody civil conflict are still sore and the writer is himself living proof. Yet Durán's *nosotros* also makes an attempt at reconciliation, not with the enemy, of course, but with those who stayed in spite of their uncomfortable position within Franco's order. For this reason Durán's attempt to synthesize inner and outer exile is all the more compelling, especially in the light of a we which draws together all the forces of dissent.

Considering the long duration of Spanish Civil War exile, however (two generations as well as a younger group of banished and self-banished dissidents from the Franco regime), another crucial question comes to mind: to whom are these essayists referring with the word we? To themselves as a community of exiled intellectuals, to all Spaniards, to a hypothetical reader who stands in solidarity with the author? Is it merely a scholarly *nosotros* which serves as a distancing substitute for *yo* (I)? Surely, as Ortega y Gasset reminds us, the historical circumstances of each writer as well as his or her intellectual milieu provide at least part of the answer; but the consideration of the structure of exile is equally revealing. Exile, regardless of its historical moment, makes for a variety of losses and reciprocal gains or attempts to compensate for those losses. There always seems to be another community ready to take the place of the lost one: the society of the new home or an accompanying group of outcasts. Thus exile renders the group which comprises we an ambiguous concept and in the last analysis distances the word from its referent. The groping nature of the Spanish essay written in exile after the war, with its incessant and difficultly identified *nosotros*, testifies to the slippery nature of the language which exile fosters.

Perhaps the most revealing of the many essays on the consequences of Spanish exile is that of Francisco Ayala, "¿Para quién escribimos nosotros?" ("For Whom Do We Write?"), not so much for its ambivalence (Ayala's expository writing rarely lacks lucidity) but for the fundamental problem he poses. Any writing, whether from exile or not, sets off a dialogue between writer and reader, even if the writer poses as a self-contained entity (or writer-reader).[3] Ayala's treatment of the issue in the light of the intellectual diaspora of the Civil War renders an already complex problem even more complex. He states that exile, however trying, presents an opportunity for Spanish writers to transcend what he considers a hackneyed problem: the being and destiny of Spain, a theme which has now become unworthy of the obsessive attention it has received among the exiles. Ayala urges his fellow banished writers to grow with the experience. If the audience has shifted then the writer must accommodate the text to a new public, which is, ideally of course, comprised of citizens of the world. The accommodation of a writer to a public may seem to some (perhaps to exiles more than to others) an apology for writerly prostitution, yet within an exilic framework what seems like accommodation is essentially compensation for a loss. A writer in exile must face the loss of a former readership and compensate for it by imagining a new one. For an exile the problem of the reader is a primordial one, both sociologically and aesthetically. The exile's potential reader is as amorphous as the condition itself. Toward the end of his essay it becomes clear that Ayala's *nosotros* no longer comprises merely the narrow group of exiles from Civil War Spain but the human family. Yet in spite of his lucidity, Ayala's solution to the problem is dubious: "¿Para quién escribimos nosotros? Para todos y para nadie" (p. 21; For whom do we write? For everyone and for no one). The paradox solves nothing, yet its very contradiction is emblematic not only of the exile writer but, as Ayala's main point seems to be, of any writer.

It is ironic that of all the intellectuals discussed thus far, from Andújar to Ayala, it is these two whose expository texts are most in keeping with the tone and precision of academic discourse, even though they are the ones whose total literary production leans more toward fiction than exposition. When they write about exile Zambrano, Durán, García Bacca, and Marichal repeatedly make disguised and undisguised attempts to bridge the gap between literature and criticism due, at least in part, to both the subject matter and their own conditions of banishment. But by far the most representative critic with a pen in both camps at once, especially when he discusses exile, is Vicente Llorens. By profession Llorens remains clearly within the ranks of academicians. A disciple of Américo Castro in Spain, he was able to continue his academic work after the war at the University of Santo Domingo in the Dominican Republic. He lived yet another exilic experience when the dictatorship of Trujillo sent him to Puerto Rico and eventually to the United States where he became professor of Spanish literature and civilization at Princeton and later at Stony Brook.

Llorens's *Liberales y románticos*, on the intellectual emigration of early nineteenth-century Spanish writers to England, is a landmark in Spanish studies, not only for its erudition but for the profundity with which it treats literary problems. Exilic literary tensions become the mainstay of Llorens's later work with his interest in the exiled poet and his former professor, Pedro Salinas. Within the large corpus of writing on Spanish Civil War exile, Llorens engaged in one of the few attempts (along with that of Claudio Guillén) to deal with the language of exile on a theoretical level. In "El desterrado y su lengua" ("The Exile and his Language"), as well as in the other essays which make up the collection titled *Literatura, historia, política*, Llorens traces the points at which a variety of dissimilar exile texts meet, using Ovid's *Tristia*, "Elegía del destierro" by the nineteenth-century poet Enrique Gómez, and Unamuno's *Romance del destierro* as examples. Llorens's criticism highlights a certain literary frustration, not only that of the writers he discusses, but that of the critic himself who finds his own terminology inadequate to deal with his subject matter. At many points in *Literatura, historia, política* Llorens falls short of taking his own penetrating observations to their full consequences. In these essays one detects the scholar's urge to close the gap between himself and his own discourse.

Llorens's frustration is most clearly manifest in one of his unacclaimed yet most interesting works, *Memorias de una emigración* (*Memories of an Emigration*). Germán Gullón calls this book of memoirs a strange text, given that Santo Domingo is scarcely worth mention in comparison to the other cultural centers of Spanish exile, such as Mexico City or Buenos Aires (Abellán, IV, 278). Yet it is precisely the theme of insignificance which stands out most clearly in this work when read within the context of Llorens's own observations on exilic writing. In *Memorias* Santo Domingo may be read as the mythical place of exile; it is as much a literary figure as it is a city, the capital of half an island. It is a site whose very name, La Hispaniola, as well as its historical importance in the discovery of the New World, is suggestive of the textual quality of reality, in this case a deeply ironic reality as Llorens affirms throughout his memories. For a European, Santo Domingo promises the exotic pleasures of a Caribbean island, and for an exiled Spanish intellectual, the city becomes a penal colony cut off on all sides from a former time and place (like Ovid's Tomis and Dante's Inferno). In addition, Santo Domingo is paradoxically a place of return to an earlier period of Spanish life.

Llorens, both a European and an exiled Spaniard, testifies to the ambivalence of his own position on the island with the writing of a text which has no genre. *Memorias* is a book of personal anecdotes and character sketches, political exposition, intellectual history, literary history, literary criticism, art criticism, and even sociology in a detailed discussion of the consequences of exile on the Spanish family. The text's resistance to definition reminds one again of the letters and chronicles of the Spanish explorers, narratives whose seemingly fantastic stories are guided by a reality which lacked a corresponding language. Llorens's denouncement of Trujillo, for example, is dependent upon a more familiar reciprocal figure—Franco—just as the chroniclers described the inhabitants of the new land in terms of the only corresponding entities on the Iberian Peninsula—the Moors. One could read Llorens's work as a collection of short narratives, given the anecdotal quality of elements like the dialogues between the characters and the disjointed nature of the text's outer structure. The chapters seem to possess their own inner coherence without the benefit of a unifying outer structure. As a whole the text comprises many genres, and its vacillation is a telling reminder of what the author himself wrote about the exilic condition in *Literatura, historia, política*: "la patria deja de corresponder a una realidad geográfica" (p. 26; the homeland no longer corresponds to a geographical reality).

As mentioned earlier, Llorens's *Memorias* also puts into question, as many autobiographies and books of remembrances do, the very notion of importance and, by extension, any hierarchical order. Not that Llorens sets out to demolish the systems of authority which dictate what is important and what is not, but the nature of his enterprise inevitably opens the issue of authority to special scrutiny. In the prologue he writes almost apologetically of his intention to record his exile in Santo Domingo: "Mi insignificancia me impide tomar la pluma para entregarme a ejercicios insignificantes, extraña sensación hablar como testigo presencial" (p. v; My insignificance inhibits me from wielding the pen in service of insignificant exercises, a strange sensation to speak as a present witness, *sic*). The figurative quality to these words does not abate in the body of the text, where one finds the typically exilic interplay between distance and closeness and a certain repetitiveness, if not redundance. Llorens stresses his own insignificance in the writing of an insignificant text and meekly justifies his "narcissistic exercise" by referring to himself as a "testigo presencial," a witness who is present. The effect of the passage, however, counters the author's emphasis on his own insignificance as well as on the fact of his having been present in the events and situation he will describe. The very writing of the text throws his doubly stated unimportance out of balance, and the time and place of the writing (New Jersey and New York in the early seventies) cannot account for what the author defines as a presumptuous undertaking. Thus authority becomes insignificance and vice versa. The tension between the prologue and the main text is the paradox of the work: Llorens's problem is the difficult, perhaps impossible, reconciliation of the political, existential, and conceptual significance of the concept of exile with the insignificance of an individual exile, the exile of flesh and bone.

Scholarly essays written for a relatively small audience, like those of Vicente Llorens, are admittedly not the stuff of great literature, and to deal with them as literature is perhaps to ignore the informative and elucidating qualities which are their primary reasons for being. Yet it is also true that the relationship between the discourse of literature and the discourse on literature is a tenuous one. In literary criticism's wish to open the door to literature, it cannot help being contaminated by literariness and thus becomes conscious of its own ambivalent task—to elucidate something which escapes lucidity. In the criticism of exile literature this relationship seems to expose itself, especially in the cases of scholarly discourses which themselves claim the condition of exile. The critic's exilic situation and his relation to the text under discussion is also crucial (in spite of formalism's insistence to the contrary), for the exile's attempt to deal with that situation is itself another text which, as these pages have argued, follow previous models. The literature of exile brings into play a variety of texts: those of literature and criticism, of fiction and reality, of history and the recording of history. And in many ways it is this intertextual weaving which is the mainstay of literature, whether in exile or not.

5 Literature of Testimony

Santos Sanz Villanueva observes in the concluding paragraph of his categorization of exile narratives that there is another group of texts worthy of mention: the testimonial narrative. He attributes the preponderance of such texts to the exile's need for personal liberation, yet he does not develop this suggestive idea. Instead, he simply casts the testimonial narratives aside by asserting that they are of little literary importance or interest. They lack imagination, he states, and it is imagination which sets literature apart from other types of writing (Abellán, IV, 181–82). In my view, both the distinction Sanz Villanueva makes and his assumptions about the nature of literature simplify the issues involved in exile texts. It is precisely the literature of testimony which leads to the naked structure of exile, a structure which, when embellished, branches out in many directions. The tensions between what happened and what is written, between the I of the writing and the I of flesh and bone, are the very ambivalences which often arise in purely literary works. It is revealing, therefore, to inspect the texts that claim no literary significance other than the telling of a "true" story and to deal not with the truth of that story but its telling.

The plentiful books of memoirs by Spanish exiles of 1939 serve to illustrate a need for recovery and compensation, as well as the independence of those memories from the actual experiences. Writers of books of remembrances (political, literary, personal, nostalgic) occasionally let slip the hidden contradictions of their own discourses. As lawyers have warned on more than one occasion, eyewitness testimony is in reality the most unreliable, even if the most credible to a jury. Yet the reigning contradiction in the book of memoirs as a genre is perhaps not so much between two or more versions of reality, as it is in the tension between reality and its rendering. The wish to re-create the facts for posterity is the central urge of the text. Vicente Llorens's memories of the Dominican Republic, although couched in academic discourse, are no exception. Yet Llorens, ever mindful of the workings of literature, seems aware of his own distance and at times even flaunts it. It is the less self-conscious texts, written by people whose literary insignificance is closer to reality than it is for Llorens, which expose the tensions and discrepancies of exilic writing in ways that are at times brutally clear.

The political memoir, especially when it appears in exile, cannot hide its own strategies no matter how strained the attempt to do so. The very word strategy refers to both a textual structure and to politics. Memoirs by politicians, members of parties, or participants in political events describe actions taken, and the writing is not only the proof of that action, but its justification. In the case of an exile, the writer often has a cross to bear as well as a story to tell. The text of the memoir, or the memory of the memory, is thus closely allied to the exile's persona, a moral persona which stands in contrast to his or her reputation within the community of those who stay. The memoir is a reading of the self within a certain situation. Yet often the distance between the writer and his or her own reading betrays the original strategy, and the urge to justify, to make counteraccusations or tell what really happened, backfires.

As Paul Ilie has observed (*Literature and Inner Exile*, pp. 85–87), the re-creation of the events during the war and after in Ramón López Barrantes's book of memories (*Mi exilio*), gives rise to a variety of issues, both literary and political. Ilie observes that López Barrantes's text is representative of exilic ethical discourse, especially in its insistence on the moral superiority of those who refuse to go back to their country, even when the regime makes it possible. Yet what Ilie does not pursue is the vacillation of the argument, not only as a linguistic structure but as a political statement. It is true, as Ilie points out, that the self-deprecating tone of López's text in the light of his own return to Spain indicates a consistent argument about the unethical nature of the return. Yet it is also true that López writes his story as a type of self-vindication.

Ramón López Barrantes was a high-ranking administrator of the treasury during the Republic and had close contact with financiers and politicians. In his exile in Paris at the moment of the official end of the war, he made the polemical decision to turn over what was left in the Spanish National Bank under his control to the representatives of the Franco government. He saw at the time a need to show the new rulers of Spain the inscrutable good faith of the losers, a symbolic act which he hoped would be repaid in kind. This was López's fatal mistake, his "claudicación." The error reappears as a motif in the story in the form of the author's ultimate decision to return to his homeland, for once again he gave in to the forces which were subjugating him.

Yet the way López structures his story belies his own moral self-deprecation. *Mi exilio* reads like a picaresque rendering of a life, as if it were gospel truth with a scattering of comments on certain incidents as the story develops. The objective of the picaresque is to justify a life, which is also the intention of López's text. Given the events in the story, the reader is led to believe that the author is not nearly as unworthy as he seems to believe, that in spite of the immoral consequences, the act itself was honorable. In addition, the author argues that if he were again in the same situation he would not act differently —further material for ethical pondering. The main problem arises in the use of the word "claudicación"—bungling, giving in, retrenchment in the face of adversity—which is the dominant motif of the memoirs. Was the mistake purposeful, or was it merely the result of the author's lack of understanding of the situation? The culminating section, itself titled "Claudicación," is filled with ironic bitterness, as the author tells of the shabby treatment he received from those who considered him a traitor. As a Republican he points out the contradiction in the word "traitor" when it was he and others like him who remained loyal to the freely elected government. He maintains, however, that he made a mistake and that his exile is the "penitence" for that mistake (pp. 368–80). As in the picaresque, the moral discourse seems to question its own moral authority. One wonders if, in the long run, López Barrantes has not posed his own exile as an embodiment of a universal fall.

Coupled with the eyewitness description of the political entanglements in *Mi exilio* are the numerous literary devices which intrude into the faithful recording of events. There is even a self-referential dimension to the text in which the author alludes to the unfolding of his own memory, a trademark of exile literature. The author also relies almost as much on fiction to tell his story as he does on fact. He reverses the roles of Don Quijote and Sancho, for example, by referring to himself and his crew of bankers as vulgar Sanchos and the lowly militiamen who stayed in Madrid to defend their city as idealistic and noble Quijotes (pp. 123–24). He goes on to speak of the defense of Madrid as a "gesta" (gest) reminiscent of a medieval epic story. Yet the effect of these literary touches counters the motivating need to justify his acts at a highly trying time in his life. A reversal of the commonly accepted Cervantine duality questions its moral presumptions, and the anachronistic comparison of the events of Madrid with a medieval "gest" adds a touch of the ridiculous to a serious subject.

One of the most revealing of López's aesthetic twists is his comparison of his capitulation to the Franco regime by handing over the Republic's funds with the famous postbattle scene painted by Velázquez in *Surrender at Breda* (p. 184). López's portrayal of his own acknowledgement of defeat is a climactic moment in his text, since it is the tragic flaw that will lead to further mistakes. He seems far more concerned with the political and economic details of the situation, yet the mere mention of the Velázquez painting allows for a variety of images in conjunction with his difficult situation. It remains unclear who López believes his counterpart is in the painting: the Marquis of Spinola (the Spanish victor) or the Dutch commanding officer who graciously kneels before Spinola as he surrenders. It is likely that López represents the latter. But if that is the case, the Marquis of Spinola, his elegance, his magnanimity, his noble objection to the Dutchman's humility considering that he fought valiantly, is clearly not an accurate representation of Francisco Franco. On the contrary, the comparison is a grotesque one, for Franco was anything but magnanimous at the conclusion of the war. López's oxymoronic (and perhaps unwitting) comparison between Spinola and Franco is bitterly critical of the dictator and ultimately leads to a similar comparison between himself and the vanquished Dutchman—the bungler and the noble warrior who fought a good battle.

López Barrantes's dialogue with his historical and literary tradition (at the level of any educated Spaniard) reveals its own ambivalence in the final paragraph of *Mi exilio* in which the onetime Republican official quotes an exiled nineteenth century Spanish poet at the moment of the latter's return to Spain: " 'Bendita, ¡oh Patria!, seas que me has dado / . . . asilo / para morirme en el vivir honrado / que es el secreto de morir tranquilo' " (p. 380; Blessed are you, oh Homeland, for having given me a refuge to die honorably in life, which is the secret of a peaceful death). López cites these verses as the final stroke to his book of memories. The citation is intended as a self-reading, and as such it is an affirmation of López's moral satisfaction and sense of peace. Yet its effect is anything but settling, considering the previous words of the same culminating paragraph: "Diré para terminar, parodiando, que a mis soledades voy y de mis soledades vengo. Porque me encuentro en la vejez en el peor de los exilios: el que desfondado se impone uno mismo dentro de su propia Patria." (I shall say in conclusion, parodying [Lope de Vega], that to my solitudes I go and from my solitudes I come. Because in my old age I find myself in the worst of exiles: the self-inflicted bottomlessness of living in one's own country.) The image destabilizes the tranquility of the poet who returns to die in the land of birth as an elephant returns to the burial ground. López remains an outsider in his own land due to the choices he made. The land no longer has the ability to satisfy the exile's urge to return, to pacify the wanderer with geographic and nostalgic charms. As José Bergamín observed (in *El pasajero peregrino español en América*) "distance is intimacy"; yet the paradox of the distant closeness of exile is "alarming and unsettling" (pp. 69–70), a further step into the "pit of anguish."

López Barrantes is as interesting in his memoirs for his biting self-criticism as for his literary flare, not uncommon among those insignificant men and women who left a record of their departure. His text also testifies to the almost inevitable ambivalence of that recording. In marked contrast to López Barrantes's self-exploration stand memoirs which make not the slightest attempt to question the moral rightness of their own former actions. Yet even these evince certain exilic patterns of writing. A case in point is Valentín González, the famous El Campesino (the Peasant), a once loyal Communist who, with the aid of the Trotskyist novelist and exile, Julián Gorkin, wrote the story of his exploits during and after the war in *Yo escogí la esclavitud* (*I Chose Slavery*). The work is steeped in polemics, as are many political memoirs, and for the cognoscenti, El Campesino's inside analysis of the Soviet Union's participation in the war and its role as a haven for many Spanish exiles, including the author, lends a certain immediacy and directness to an otherwise complex political problem. The Spanish peasant who rose through the ranks of the Republican army with astounding acts of death-defying bravery tells his story with a great deal of energy and conviction, for his purpose is, as he says at several points, to expose the political and moral crimes of the very people whom he supported, the leading members of the Communist Party. He was duped, he declares throughout the work, by an idealistic yet practical facade disguising a maniacal attempt to subjugate its members and nonmembers to its own dogma and brutal practices. The penalty for not giving in was confinement or death. After the Spanish Civil War El Campesino's troubles started in Russia where he claims he was not docile enough to continue in the Russian army. He eventually breaks with party principles and denounces the politics of Stalin only to land in a Russian work camp. His escape from the camp is as fantastic as the deeds he was said to have accomplished in Spain. He tells us in several versions of his memoirs that he promised the nurse in the work camp who had fallen hopelessly in love with him that he would sleep with her if she arranged for an extension of his stay in the infirmary and eventually a release from the camp. Needless to say, she accepted (pp. 260–61).

The Campesino in exile seems to follow the model of a Campesino who became a legend in Republican Spain, the material for an epic Hollywood film, as Gorkin seems well aware. The implicit ridicule contained in López Barrantes's allusion to the medieval sagas of bravery corresponds in El Campesino's memoirs to Gorkin's novelistic structuring of the peasant's life, complete with a prologue which explains the moral and political lesson readers may draw from the story as well as the typical disclaimer of any transcriptional tampering. The text reads almost like Cervantes's explanation of the narrator's relation to Cide Hamete Benengeli. Yet in spite of Gorkin's insistence to the contrary, the situation of the discourse of El Campesino's life distances the supposed author from the experiences he narrates, as the eye of Gorkin, a Trotskyist and militant anti-Stalinist, intrudes into the life of El Campesino. Clearly the tension of this work does not lie in the psychology of exile or in the banished victim's search for selfhood, but in the situation of the writing. One further question stands constantly in the shadows of the work: whose memoirs are recorded, those of El Campesino (the legend), Valentín González (the person), or Gorkin (the transcriber with a political ax to grind)? The answer is as paradoxical as it is exilic—all of these and none of these.

Whether written in the self-critical vein of López Barrantes or in the manner of El Campesino's action-packed saga of disillusionment, Spanish Civil War memoirs from exile are often painful texts even though they may serve as the only asset that remains. Perhaps the most agonizing manifestations of these autonomous yet intimate memoirs are those which deal with life in prison camps. The Spanish refugees who fled to France collectively experienced the ultimate effects of exile, since in the land of liberty, fraternity, and equality they found another form of the tyranny they had been trying to escape. Exiled from fascist Spain, as they crossed the border they suffered inner exile from fascist France, this time the ostracism of the internment camp. In the many texts written as a result and a reminder of this experience, the dominant sentiment is that the second exile is not only worse than the first, but that it intensifies the first. The condition of exile here is considered absolute, immutable. Since the political situation of Europe in the early forties resembled, in large-scale, that of Spain in the mid-thirties, exile, in spite of its individual and specific nature, became a universal experience. Jews, Poles, Communists, refugees from other war-torn countries, and other antifascist resisters suffered identical fates. And even in the prison camp diaries, chronicles, and memoirs, regardless of the author, the portraits of lives in particular and life in general remain introspective. The universality of the experience is almost taken as a given, common knowledge which needs no elaboration. The survivors of the prison camps often structure their experience around a first person, a subject whose surrounding world is so awesome and powerful that the very continuing existence of the I within it is a triumph. The memory itself becomes proof of a victory, indeed an ironic concept in the light not only of the loss of Republican Spain, but the all pervasive loss which exile represents. The exilic need for compensation, like the Jewish concept of atonement, is again the motivation for texts which seem to deny the very possibility of compensation, given the gravity and horror of the situation.

The Spaniards who suffered and survived stand as an example of the universality of an experience which Jews like Elie Wiesel have written about with all too glaring precision. Alemosio Raposo, Lorenzo Andreu, Vicente Fillol, Isabel del Castillo, and A. A. Bravo Tellado are human beings who have little in common other than the time they spent in French prison camps from 1939 to 1945 and the fact that they were able to publish their testimonies of the experience. It is telling that each of these individuals' documents seems concerned with the significance of the name of its author. The following passages are only three among numerous indications of this concern:

> Lector: Esta obra ha sido escrita por un humilde obrero. No busques en ella afán literario. Confórmate con veracidad y honradez. (Raposo, *Memorias de un Español*, p. 5)

> (Reader: This work was written by a humble worker. Don't look for any literary inclination in it. Be satisfied with veracity and honesty.)

> No quiero decir mi nombre ni quién soy. ¿Para qué? ¿A quién interesa? Soy uno de tantos a quienes la guerra civil española cambió el rumbo de sus vidas. Pero de la vida, a veces, hay que dejar testimonio, y yo voy a hacerlo (Fillol, *Los perdedores*, p. 5).

> (I do not want to tell my name or who I am. For what? Who could it interest? I am among many whose life was changed by the Civil War. But at times one must leave a testimony of one's life, and I am going to do it.)

> Pero la vida de un hombre cualquiera, se dirán las gentes apresuradas y escépticas, no merece la pena conocerse. . . . [Sin embargo] como la vida de un hombre, por poco que la vida de ese hombre signifique, es en todo caso una novela, el Diario de ese hombre no resulta en absoluto pueril ni desdeñable (Ros, *Horas de angustia y esperanza*, pp. 13–14).

> (But some skeptics and people who hasten to judge will say that the life of a common man is not worth knowing. . . . [But] since

the life of a man, however insignificant that life may be, is, in all cases, a novel, the Diary of that man cannot be the least bit puerile or despicable.)

Many exilic testimonies seem to be written "with a trembling hand" (like that of the narrator of *Doctor Faustus*)—the humility of one who is unsure that it is appropriate for him or her to speak. Most assert that their voice is one among many, that they represent a collective experience (a hidden we) which, in the last analysis, is the real object of their discussion. Yet again the paradoxical nature of exile, its collective significance coupled with its individual nature, mirrors another typically exilic irony: the contradiction between the text and its content. The exile declares, "I should not write, yet I write," an assertion which appears in various forms even among those writers whose significance (political or literary) is beyond question. In the case of prison camp remembrances, hardship, pain, and horror seem to be the justifications, yet at times the authors of these testimonies focus on those very justifications. There is an underlying awareness that their lives have undergone a fundamental change, so much so that their past seems unattached to their present. As the exiled Teresa Pamies, a Catalan feminist and communist, says in her memories of the war, *Cuando éramos capitanes* (*When We Were Captains*), "Imposibles me han pareceido las palabras que pronuncié hace treinta años. . . . Palabras insólitas por ingenuas, injustas a veces. Las he leido como si no fueran mías, pero lo fueron" (p. 11; The words I spoke thirty years ago have seemed impossible to me, strange and ingenuous, at times unfair. I have read them as if they were not mine. But they were). Thus in order to capture that life, those words, the exile must capture them (like Nabokov's butterflies) in the text of a memory. The theme of death is also pertinent, not only to prison camp testimony but to other exile texts, because the writer tends to speak of him or herself as one who died, then came again to life to record the event—a death which perpetuates itself and continues in exile.

The exilic memoirs of experience in prison often focus on the inner motivations of the writing, just as an exile seeks to explain the activity (the crime) which set off the banishment. For the reader such introspection might seem odd considering that any experience in prison is reason enough for writing. In fact, prison notebooks or diaries almost constitute a separate genre with its own conventions. One of those very conventions seems to be the author's need to justify himself or herself with a text. Many times the effect of this need is a dialogue between the writer and the text. This essential separation and distance characterize almost any fictional work.

The prison camp testimonies that brand themselves such, the ones whose intentions are, at first glance, purely political, give way to other texts, literary ones which seem to dwell on that essential split between a glaring reality and the attempt to transcribe it. The numerous internment camp poems and narratives written by Spaniards who lived the experience (Max Aub's *Diario de Djelfa* [*Djelfa Diary*], Celso Amieva's *Almohada de arena* [*Pillow of Sand*], Virgilio Botella's *Así cayeron los dados* [*The Way the Dice Fell*], Manuel Andújar's *St. Cyprien, plage* [*Beach at St. Cyprian*], Agustí Bartra's *Cristo de 200000 brazos* [*Christ of 200,000 Arms*] or Sender's *Crónica del alba*) are in many ways readings of the "factual" accounts of that same experience. In the literary texts irony as a rhetorical device seems to have a double-edged quality: the irony of the text and the irony of life (war, politics, societal contradictions). The fact that, as many of the real prison diaries relate, the captors are themselves captive is an example: the French prison keepers are the prisoners of the Germans; the Senegalese who were exploited for military purposes during the war by both the French and Germans are described as the slaves of European power, as are the Arabs of Max Aub's *Djelfa* and Andújar's *St. Cyprien*.[1] The intellectuals thus convert the experience into a reading of the world, in this case a world prison. The possibility that the remembrance of the concentration camp, whether it be a poem or a diary, is merely an addendum to another text, the text of life, is the unstated theme of the exilic prison memoir.

Perhaps one of the most gripping embodiments of the intertextual weaving of testimony and literature is Agustí Bartra's novel, *Cristo de 200000 brazos*. Bartra, another poet and survivor of the French camps, concentrates on the literariness of the memoir as a particular type of writing. The structure of the novel is based on the reconstruction of eyewitness accounts of life in prison: diaries, notebooks, and oral histories, including that of the first person narrator. The narrator acts as the mediator between the experience and its recording. At times he quotes from the diaries of his fellow inmates, at others he retells stories which were told to him. The text keeps turning back on itself as the narrator constantly interjects, "me contaba que" (he related to me), or when he makes it clear that he is rewriting one of his friend's letters, filling in the gaps, inventing a coherence that may not exist. The self-reflexive dimension of the work also reveals itself in the epilogue in which the narrator expresses one of the only hopes he has left: that someone will turn his notebook into a creative account of life in the camp:

> En este carnet se cuentan muchas historias que me he inventado para contarme a mí mismo en horas de desaliento y soledad, otras que me han sido narradas y otras todavía que he vivido. . . . Dudo que nunca me sea dado aprovechar lo escrito aquí para una obra que pueda ser el testimonio palpitante y conmovedor de uno en quien no olvidar es la central militancia de su alma. . . . ¡quién sabe si alguna vez llegaría a tener la fuerza serena que se necesita para objetivar creadoramente lo vivido! (p. 121)

> (In this notebook there are many stories I invented to amuse myself during my hours of solitude and discouragement, others which have been told to me, and still others which I have lived. . . . I doubt that I shall ever have the gift to take advantage of what is written here to create a work which could be the palpitating and moving testimony of one for whom the struggle against forgetfulness is the central battle of his soul. . . . Who knows if

one day I might have the calm strength one needs to objectify what I have lived!)

Later the speaker says that his consolation is that someone may do just that, write a creative work on his experience. Bartra thus takes that fatal leap from narrator to author, for the text itself is living proof of the narrator's hopes; it has been transformed from a fiction into a tangible object, the book uncomfortably held in the reader's fingers. The question remaining here, as in the unadulterated books of memoirs, is—is this a creative work, as the narrator wills, or is it the real version of life in a prison camp? In the final analysis this is the crucial question which the literature of testimony asks, especially when it is posed in a land that seems to have lost its reality: Exile.

6 Exilic Autobiographies

As the most interesting theoretical work on autobiography has shown, the very existence of autobiography as a literary genre is nebulous, considering the almost infinite ways in which an author's life intrudes into his or her text.[1] The guiding factor in the designation of a work as autobiography is the proximity of the writer to the I of the text, a factor which poses a variety of questions about the nature of writing. Even the most naive autobiographies, those which on the surface show little awareness of these questions, often cannot avoid the problem of the self and its double or its textual representation. The all-pervasive issue of a life which yearns to be transformed into a structure, an organic whole, becomes the dominant element in the autobiography's evolution.

Exile and autobiography are integrally related not only in their resistance to definition, but in their closeness to two other concepts—birth and death. As many exilic texts have shown, exile stands alongside death not as a copy or reproduction but as a distortion, a conscious rendering and alteration of death. In exile a life ends, yet it continues; the effect is that the self is split by a notion of temporality which allows the present self to inspect and to re-create the former one, to give it a new birth. Autobiography is just that, a rendering, a recreation of a self made possible by an essential split. And although not all autobiographies contain or even hint at an ending—a death—the notion of beginning and finality is always implicit, if only in the very necessity for a commencement and an end to the text. The autobiographer is faced with a difficult task: the uniting of the birth and death of a life with those of a text. All of these issues are brought to light by both exile and autobiography, and the efforts of Spaniards who sought to record their lives and their journeys as a consequence of the Civil War are vital proof of their complexity.

The issues of insignificance and authority also make their way into autobiographies of Spanish exile; these texts seem to beg the question —what makes a life worth telling? For example, readers are inclined to choose the life of Rafael Alberti over that of Cecilia de Guilarte, though both wrote autobiographies in exile. Guilarte shared Alberti's need for testimony, yet in the case of the woman writer the satisfaction of that need unfortunately will not go far beyond the testimony itself, since as a person and as a writer she remains unknown even in Spain. In her autobiographical novel *Nació en España* (*Born in Spain*), however, she seems as aware as Alberti (in his *Lost Grove*) of the crucial and problematic link between herself and her text. She speaks, as does Alberti, as a participant in important cultural and political events, yet unlike Alberti her voice takes on a collective quality, perhaps due to her own relative insignificance.

The texts of Alberti and Guilarte show that all the burning literary issues surrounding exile and autobiography are, in the last analysis, no more crucial to literature than to life: authority, collective significance, individual fame, birth, death, re-creation of past experience. Perhaps the most penetrating explicator of these issues is Salvador Otaola, though he never wrote an autobiography in the strict sense. In his three main works (*Los hombres*, *El cortejo*, and *La librería de Arana: historia y fantasía*) he probes the very relationship at hand: literature and life, autobiography and the real human being who writes it. *La librería de Arana* (*Arana's Bookstore*) in particular may be described as an inquiry into the nature of autobiography of Spanish Republican exiles living in Mexico City after the Civil War. *La librería* is most apparently a personal testimony of life among the exiled intellectuals, the significant ones along with the forgotten, most of whom seem to be writing an autobiography or a book of memoirs. Otaola weaves reality with literature through the portraits of a handful of men and women (including himself) who made up that milieu: Max Aub, José Ramón Arana, León Felipe, José Moreno Villa, Manuel Durán, Francisco Pina, José de la Colina, Paulita Brook, and others.

The nebulous unity of this seemingly discursive work is based on the life of a bookstore owned and operated by the exile poet, José Ramón Arana. The bookstore is a place where the exiles, in all their vanity and pathos, congregate to discuss issues of all sorts, mostly literary. The store seems to tell its own story as it begins its life walking from door to door and square to square. The traveling salesman and owner, Arana, trudges along loaded down with books in search of customers until he eventually acquires the capital for a real store. The motif of the wandering bookstore appears throughout *La librería* in the form of the dynamics and constant activity of the people involved in it, both buyers and sellers. In many ways the movement of and within the bookstore represents the exilic search for a new residence. The objective and concrete nature of cultural production is laid bare in *La librería*, since in exile one of the necessary ingredients in the dissemination of culture is absent—a buyer. In this traveling bookstore, whose existence is thoroughly dependent on the initiative and drive of a conscientious businessman (Arana), the buyers are ironically (and pathetically) the producers. The incestuous nature of the situation, its cultural isolation, the absence of an intellectually nourishing community outside the bookstore is the sad tale that the bookstore seems to be telling about itself through its owner.

Yet what saves Otaola's portrait from pathos and self-deprecating despair is not only the self-conscious humor with which he caricatures the bookstore along with its patrons (something he learned from Ramón Gómez de la Serna), but the explicit and implicit concern for the consequences of exile on writing. One of the most provocative conceits of *La librería* is the association of the making of a book with giving birth, which is also linked to the problematic beginning of an autobiography. Labor, delivery, blood, sweat, pain, anger, joy, pride, and all the other consequences of pregnancy are all too familiar to birthing mothers and writers. Otaola reserves this image for his depiction of Francisco Pina, who, for a variety of reasons, is painfully aware of what it is to "parir un libro" (pp. 295–97; birth a book). The analogy is especially pertinent to exile writing and to autobiography. The pains and sorrows of exile (a commonplace in the exilic elegy) become explicitly temporal: a period of gestation ends in the reproduction of a text which is the re-creation of a self. Of far more existential and literary complexity than the typically postmodern association of the pen with the penis, ink with semen, etc., the concept of birthing a book (mother-child) opens up the act of writing to a variety of literary and vital issues and suggests that there is an autobiographical dimension to the writing of any text.

Whether Otaola wishes it or not, the mothering of texts, from conception and birth, through childhood and adolescence, to independence and death, is his most gripping metaphor, and it is emblematic of the very text he is writing. It is interesting that Francisco Pina's biography of Charles Chaplin serves as the central example of Otaola's analogy, for the fact that Pina's work is itself another person's life underscores the tension between the text's dependence and independence from its author. When and to what extent does the child-text begin to have a life of its own? Otaola's particular interest in autobiography furthers the mother-text image and reveals one of exile literature's most enduring problems—the reproduction and continuation of a life and the autonomy of that life from its creator, the motherland.

Permutations of the theme of autobiography appear almost unwittingly in Otaola's work. He discusses, for example, the autobiography of one of his friends, an exile painter and writer, Juan Renau, whose memoirs (titled *Autopsy*) are filled with vivid, perhaps even excessive, depictions of seemingly insignificant details. As proof Otaola quotes extensively from the text as he remembers reading passages out loud to his exile compatriots of the bookstore. What he accomplishes, in a sense, is the re-creation of Renau's autobiography, the rewriting of his friend's text, a deed made even more significant by the fact that the autobiography was not published at the time. Thus, in some ways, its birth never took place. Otaola then performs the birthing act, as if by proxy, and thereby adds further distance to the relationship between author and text. In one instance Otaola reintroduces the mother-text image when he says of Renau, "Yo le animaba convencido de que estaba presenciando el parto de un buen libro de memorias" (p. 37; I encouraged him convinced that I was witnessing the delivery of a good book of memories.) Although the issue of the real publication of the text is not part of Otaola's described scenario, as it was in the case of Pina's biography, the reader intuits that very difficulty from the theme of forgotten lives and forgotten texts and the broader issue of the oblivion of exile. In many ways the literature of exile is composed, at least in part, of texts that never were, aborted and forgotten.

As a tribute to autobiography, Otaola states with his characteristic good humor that what interests him both in *La librería* and as a general literary problem is "una vida cualquiera contada con salero, con su miaja de gracia. . . . Sólo se les puede pedir llaneza y corrido estilo (p. 167; any random life narrated with spice, with a touch of wit. . . . One can only ask for humility and a flowing style). This seemingly modest request is deceptive and reminiscent of the work of Otaola's literary mentor, Ramón Gómez de la Serna, whose autobiography, *Automoribundia*, is a perfect example of Otaola's precept (in spite of Gómez de la Serna's fame) as well as a manifestation of the exilic tensions and patterns of the genre. Just as significant, in my estimation, is the fact that few critics who have studied Spanish exile literature consider the inventor of the *greguería*[2] an exile, since the bulk of his work was written prior to a departure which had little to do with politics. But such conventional wisdom leaves itself open to myriad questions, not only about the criteria for the categorization, but in the general definition of exile as a purely political phenomenon. If Gómez de la Serna was not in exile, he was certainly a displaced Spaniard in

Argentina. And his decision to leave was clearly influenced by the political situation of Spain in 1936.[3]

As Otaola points out, autobiography as a genre is relatively uncommon in Spanish literature (*Librería*, pp. 173–74), and Gómez de la Serna's two-volume story of his life stands as an interesting exception. I would add, however, that a dearth of autobiography is by no means the case in the literature of exile from the peninsula. The life of José María Blanco White is a noteworthy example, in addition to those published after the Civil War (Alberti's *La arboleda perdida*, José Moreno Villa's *Vida en claro*), including the plethora of books of memories and diaries which are, in effect, autobiographies in the making.[4] *Automoribundia* is of interest (as are many autobiographies) because of its organization of a life which has two dimensions—one at home and one away. Contrary to what one might expect, these two parts are not so much symmetrical as they are reciprocal. Gómez de la Serna's life in Madrid, childhood experiences, adolescent encounters (as in "Por qué fui bautizado como humorista," (pp. 154–57; Why I was Christened a Humorist) seem to determine the flow of the rest of the text. The shift from Spain and all it represented for him (life in Madrid, the Café Pombo, the *greguería*) to an unfamiliar land is barely detectable, yet it is this very change of direction, both in the life and in the narrative, which allows for the scrutiny he subjects himself to. There is a dependent textual relationship between the two parts of his life; childhood and adolescence are the bases for later experiences and writings, and the period of Argentine displacement allows for the reexamination of those encounters and texts: "ver en perspectiva todo lo que se tuvo abrumadoramente encima" (p. 615; to see in perspective all that had oppressively descended on me). At the crucial juncture between home and exile Gómez de la Serna pauses, if only for a second, to reflect on the arbitrariness of his new situation: that before the departure, he was an emigrant, and after, an immigrant—a purely relational distinction far more within the realm of language than reality.

Quizás es más señor, más residencial, más de puertas adentro lo de inmigrante, pero lo romántico es ser emigrante, que quiere decir el que se vino porque se fue y no como inmigrante, que parece ser el que se metió dentro y parece que no vino. (p. 614)

(Perhaps immigrant is more respectable, more residential, more homebody, but emigrant is more romantic, for it means the one who came because he left, not like immigrant, who seems to be the one who slipped in and it looks like he didn't come.)

In many ways it is the tension and lack of definitive distinction between the first and the "second stage of life" (p. 615) which characterize the rambling re-creation of Gómez de la Serna's life: not so much a division of life into two segments as the absence of continuity or a thread of unity. Exile makes for an uneasy transition, a broken flow which undergoes an attempt at reunion through writing. But the text's attempt to recover the continuity of life is many times a frustrated one, and this very frustration frequently becomes another object of the text's discourse.

In the self-proclaimed autobiographical novel by Cecilia Guilarte, *Nació en España*, one of the characters talks about the changes in perception of one's own life after having experienced exile:

Creí que la vida empezaba de nuevo, aquí. ¡Qué tontería! ¡Como si la vida no fuese un hilo desde el principio hasta al fin, que sólo una vez se quiebra! ¡Empezar de nuevo, cortar el hilo por donde convenga! Y luego, ¿dónde anudar su punta mutilada para seguir tirando, para continuar viviendo? ¡No, no! Es un hilo desde el seno tibio de la madre hasta el frío abrazo de la tierra que se cierra entre nosotros. (p. 220)

(I thought life began again, here. What a joke! As if life were not a thread from beginning to end, that it is broken only once! To begin again, to cut the thread anywhere! And then, where to tie the broken point in order to keep pulling, to continue living? No, no!

It is a thread from the warm breast of the mother to the cold
embrace of the earth which is tied between us.)

The mother-text concept appears once again, this time as an umbilical
cord between two lives, two lands, two texts. The severing of the cord
is the exilic break which is paradoxically an attempt at integration.

Birth is indeed an important concept in autobiography since the
writing may stand as a rite of passage from nothing to something. Exile
intensifies the difficulty of recording that passage, for the involuntary
departure mirrors the forced act of coming to life. In the case of one
who leaves of his or her own will, there are always influences, situations, and events which initiate the process. The exile moves from one
life to another without being entirely in control of the forces which
catalyze the transference. The irony of the situation is that the act of
writing the autobiography is a voluntary one—a self-engendering deed
which counters the involuntary nature of birth. This self-birth is thus an
act of exilic rebellion, another compensation, this time for the loss of
free will.

Constancia de la Mora's *Doble esplendor* (which she translated as *In
Place of Splendour*), an autobiography of a Spanish aristocrat turned
communist, is a manifestation of the voluntary and involuntary dimensions of exilic experience. She describes, for example, her own birth in
vivid detail: "Hacía frío aquel día de enero de 1906 en que yo nací"
(p. 11; It was cold that January day of 1906 when I was born).
Throughout the book the author's privileged perspective (as well as her
social class) is in doubt, just as the novelistic structure of her text
—history mixed with everyday experience—stands in an uneasy relationship to what the reader might intuit as the reality of her life (beyond
what she relates). In her enthusiasm to write history she analyzes and
describes events which she did not witness, thereby taking control of
them. Yet her authority naturally becomes problematic, for these renditions are as unreliable as hearsay. The weather on the day of her birth is
an example, as are her many analyses of the political and military

strategies of the Republic during the war. Similarly, Gómez de la Serna makes a great deal out of the fact that "me nacieron" (p. 15; they forced me into birth), although his text is far less prone to relate events which he could not have experienced firsthand. Both of these exilic autobiographies, however, stand as protests against the strings which pulled their subjects into exile as well as against the arbitrary circumstances which led to their births. The act of protest furthers the autobiographical tension between the intended accuracy and the subjectivity of the text.

In one of the most original treatments of autobiographical birth, Rosa Chacel's *Desde el amanecer* (*From Dawn*), the author declares with great conviction that she was not born involuntarily, that indeed she was not only aware of her birth as it happened, but that she willed it. "Yo rechazo esos tópicos vigentes de nuestros días como 'me trajeron al mundo sin consultarme,' 'Yo no tengo la culpa de haber nacido'. . . . Siento el principio de mi vida como voluntad" (p. 11; I reject those declarations in full force these days like 'they brought me into this world without asking,' 'It's not my fault that I was born'. . . . I consider the beginning of my life as will). Chacel's autobiography is, in effect, an exercise in self-control; she states at the outset that she will only include the first ten years of her life, and she proceeds to relate them with utmost precision, as if she were making a performance of her own memory. Chacel's work is in some ways an antiautobiography, precisely because of the seeming accuracy of the events and the tone of unquestioned authority. Implicitly she refuses to fall into what she likely feels is an autobiographical trap: the standard apology for an unfaithful rendering of a life caused by the pervasive deceptions of memory. Yet this unflinching dedication to accuracy is a further example of compensation, perhaps overcompensation; for the picture that Chacel paints of herself as a child is not of a girl in possession of free will: there are her stern parents, the austerity of life in Valladolid, her religious inclinations. Even in her first ten years of life she creates a world of illusions (Zorrilla and romantic freedom, her "erotic-aesthetic" fantasies, p. 95); and this creation is not unlike the one she embarks on seventy or more years later, her autobiography, a text written from a place as distant and exotic as Rio de Janeiro—a place name which sounds oxymoronic when utered in the same breath as Valladolid.

As *Desde el amanecer* shows, autobiographies written in exile evince a nostalgic prose, which is perhaps the first quality one might think of in conjunction with an aesthetic of exile. The concept of nostalgia is a problematic one and it reveals itself in a variety of ways in the life-texts of authors in exile from Spain after the Civil War. Nostalgia is, in essence, a reading of the past based on selective memory. The medieval Spanish poet, Jorge Manrique, expressed it as well as any contemporary author when he suggested, in his *Coplas por la muerte de su padre*, that there is nothing worse than the present. Life is a constant deferral of a fleeting present to a future, which leads to something that ironically seems better: death.

The title of Gómez de la Serna's autobiography, *Automoribundia*, is illustrative of this conception of time and death. Since the exile's future seems to have been stripped away, all that remains is death itself, especially since, as I suggested earlier, exiles tend to perceive their condition as the end of a life. Nostalgia, then, is the thought process of a new system of deferral, not to the future but to the past. That the past is not only better, but irretrievable, is the motivation for the nostalgic lament. Unlike the deferral to the future in which there is at least the possibility of resolution and integration, the exile yields to the past knowing that this act is futile. In addition, memory underscores the lingering possibility of an inaccurate reading of times gone by, and as such exposes the artificiality of the nostalgic re-creation.

Nowhere is exilic nostalgia more apparent than in the autobiographies of banished poets (except, perhaps, in their own poetry). In the cases of the numerous Spanish poets who left Spain as a result of the Civil War, much of the poetry written after the departure is filled with nostalgic evocations of their own experiences of exile. Pedro Garfias, Alberti, Emilio Prados, Concha Méndez, Rafael Dieste, Juan Rejano are several among many examples.[5] Although not all of these poets wrote autobiographies in the strict sense, much of their poetry in exile has autobiographical touches; and in the cases of the poets who did attempt to re-create their own lives in prose, the link between the life stories and the poetry is crucial. The two most important (or most accessible) autobiographies are Rafael Alberti's *La arboleda perdida* and José Moreno Villa's frequently cited *Vida en claro* (*Life Clearly Told*). Alberti's *Arboleda* is perhaps one of the most revealing of documents about the social and cultural life of Spain in the first half of the twentieth century, and for this reason the author of *Marinero en tierra* saves his nostalgia for crucial moments, poetic surges which add an almost spiritual element to the documentary flavor of his work. In the same vein Moreno Villa describes not only his own life in the famous Residencia de Estudiantes, but that of fellow poets and friends who were as important as he (or more so) to the history of Spanish literature (Lorca, Guillén, Ortega, among others). Yet his work is confessional in many aspects; it is this confession which brings on nostalgic resignation, not an uncommon feature of his poetry as well as that of Alberti and other poets in exile.

Nature hovers in and above the texts and the lives of these two Andalusian poets, and it lies at the root of their motivations. Alberti's grove is not only the title of his life story, it represents his loss. The initial chapters of Moreno Villa's memoirs describe in great detail the two doses, as he calls them, of his early life, the two ingredients which together define his later existence—the sea and the countryside. As poets both are held to the conviction that nature signifies, and in their autobiographies the lost geography of a former time indicates what they represent as human beings. It also serves as the unifying thread of their texts. And as exiles they become aware of their own desperate attempt to find this thread, this system of signification.

The life-texts of both poets are not only nostalgic, they are explorations into the traps of nostalgia. Alberti evokes memory in the preliminary words of each chapter; Moreno Villa describes the associations of the objects and scenery of his house in Málaga with the themes of his life: "Veo ahora, de repente, que el cuarto de mi padre daba al mar y que el de mi madre daba a la catedral" (p. 7; I see now, suddenly, that my father's room faced the sea and that my mother's faced the cathedral). Thus the associations of his father with a voyage and his mother with spiritual strength become parts of his own being in a poetic imitation of a Hegelian synthesis: "debo tener un poco de sal marina y algún arbotante catedralicio" (p. 9; I must have a bit of sea salt along with the flying buttress of a cathedral). Even from Mexico Moreno Villa seems well aware of his own need to signify. The immediacy of the situation of the writing, which resonates in the opening deictic, "I see now, suddenly," underscores that typically exilic place of writing, a view from the inside that exists alongside an overriding awareness that the viewer is not within but without the land of his description.

The signifying process of exile is also part of Moreno's scenario, as he seems to question the very system of associations he has created: "hay una tendencia en los hombres en convertir en símbolos ciertas observaciones. . . . ello me atrae, pensar un poco en estos hechos con que principio" (p. 7; there is a tendency for man to convert certain observations into symbols. . . . this attracts me, to think a bit on the facts with which I begin). The genre of autobiography allows for Moreno's self-awareness, for had he written a poem on these very associations the tension between reality and writing would be subsumed into a totally artificial world. Moreno's typically exilic vacillation between here and there, reality and language, becomes even more apparent as the need for a faithful re-creation of situations and events leads him away from the Hegelian beginning of his text: the sea and countryside, ship and cathedral, cannot contain all the parts of his life which he must record. The loose threads rebel against the binary opposition which he himself defines as the essence of his life. In effect, Moreno's autobiography has led him, along with his text, further into exile.

Alberti's case is similar, but his autobiography differs from Moreno

Villa's. His own importance as a poet overshadows his autobiography. He is one of the principal members of the Generation of 1927, and perhaps even more significant, is one of the few of that generation able to give living testimony to a crucial time in Spanish history and culture. Alberti the historian thus informs the role he plays as the re-creator of a lost grove. Throughout the narrative of his life memory is his primary tool in the performance of both roles, as the beginning pages of *La arboleda* suggest. Memory is the theme of these pages and the body of the text yields to it as Alberti recalls his own beginning words at several crucial junctures, just as he recalls his lost grove. In the following excerpts from the pre-text of his autobiography, Alberti explains the significance of the title.

> En la ciudad gaditiana del Puerto Santa María, a la derecha de un camino, . . . había un melancólico lugar de retamas blancas y amarillas llamado la Arboleda Perdida.
>
> Todo era allá como un recuerdo: los pájaros rodando alrededor de los árboles ya idos. . . . Todo sonaba allí a pasado, a viejo bosque sucedido. Hasta la luz caía como memoria de la luz, y nuestros juegos infantiles durante las robanas escolares, también sonaban a perdidos en aquella arboleda. (p. 9)

> (In the city of Puerto Santa María in Cádiz, on the right side of a path, . . . there was a melancholy place filled with white and yellow Spanish broom called the Lost Grove.
>
> Everything there was like a memory: birds flying about trees that had already disappeared. . . . Everything sounded like the past there, like an old and forgotten forest. Even the light emanated like the memory of light, and our childhood games when we played hooky also sounded lost in that grove.)

The poet then turns to the possible end of his grove.

> Cuando por fin, allá, concluido el instante de la tierra, . . . seamos uno en el hundirnos para siempre, . . . quién sabe si a la derecha

de otro nuevo camino, . . . me tumbaré bajo retamas blancas y amarillas a recordar, a ser ya todo yo la total arboleda perdida de mi sangre. (pp. 9–10)

(When we're all there at last, after the final instant of the earth, . . . and when we are one in our burial, . . . who knows if at the right side of another path, I'll lie down in white and yellow Spanish broom to remember, to be all of myself at last, that total lost grove of my blood.)

These passages are representative of the prose poetry of nostalgia, yet they also mark the self-conscious resignation of nostalgia—an attempt to re-create the world in terms of the past, knowing that the past itself is the result of another re-creation. Alberti seems well aware that he writes the memory of a memory (as in the remembrance of a light which is itself "like a memory"). He suspects that there is no origin of his *arboleda*, and that the final moment may present itself as another lost grove: "Y una larga memoria de la que nunca nadie podrá tener noticia, errará escrita por los aires, definitivamente extraviada, definitivamente perdida" (p. 10; And a long memory of which no one could ever take notice will wander written through the wind, definitively misplaced, definitively lost). These are the final words of a beginning, and as such they will reappear in the text only to expose again their finality, as in the culminating rendition of the construction of the poet's house, his "new grove," outside of Buenos Aires (pp. 319–24). The "definitive" nature of the loss is at least open to question, if not contradiction, by the very existence of the text. Admittedly the real grove is lost, yet it never seemed to have a concrete existence, being always a memory. As Alberti recreates his grove in Argentina, in France, in Italy (and in all the places of his exile) according to the memory of the one in Puerto Santa María, and as he continues to write the lost grove at this moment (parts of which occasionally appear in *El País*), a question looms in its shadows: how can one lose something that was already lost?

The literature of nostalgia is often regarded as naive and reactionary, yet the life stories of Moreno Villa and Alberti question that designation. They are ambivalent about their pasts, perhaps because they are in exile, or it may be due simply to their own individual inclinations toward introspection. But in either case, their textual re-creations of nostalgia hardly represent a statement against progress or, for that matter, an unstated wish to turn back the historical clock. I suspect that their self-awareness comes from the exilic tendency to defamiliarize the former land and to question the very historical process which shapes it. The autobiographies of Moreno Villa and Alberti are self-conscious textualizations of memory, and as the authors record their lives by turning them into histories they become aware of the tension between the real events and their re-creation. It is not that Alberti and Moreno Villa deny the concrete nature of those events—that they actually took place; it is that their concreteness is lost in the recording and thus is subject to close scrutiny. Poetic devices in these prose texts notwithstanding, the two life stories seem to assert that the relationship between poetry and life is paradoxically close and distant. Although both poets speak relatively little of politics in their autobiographies (surprising, in light of their commitments to the defense of the Republic), a different political content emerges from their texts—a statement questioning the absolute and immutable nature of past experience, a statement on the politically and linguistically interested nature of history itself.

In *Arboleda* and *Vida en claro*, and in many of the other autobiographies of the Spanish Civil War, the link between the writer and the land is perhaps the primordial motif within an array of significations and associations which, like life itself, seem to have no unity, no thread, no link. The all-important connection between the self and the earth (its people, its memory), however illusory, is, as Cecilia Guilarte suggested, another umbilical cord which, when severed, sends us into exile and endows our bodies with the independence we cherish and lament.

7 A Novelistic Autobiography or an Autobiographical Novel?

Autobiographies traverse many genres: essays, poems, novels. Some texts deal with autobiography as an inherent problem in the nature of writing itself. In addition to the prison camp testimonies in the poetry of Aub, Bartra, and Amieva, mentioned earlier, and the verses of Moreno Villa, Juan Rejano, Manuel Andújar, and Pedro Garfias, with their theme of exilic experience, the novels of Spanish exile also exhibit autobiographical tendencies. Whether or not a novelist re-creates his or her own life in the form of a character in a novel is perhaps a moot question. The abundance of autobiographical novels written by Spanish Civil War exiles and designated as such by the authors themselves is difficult to deny; such abundance is not typical of the Spanish narrative as a whole.

Arturo Barea's three-volume epic, *La forja de un rebelde*, is autobiographical in every sense of the word and has suffered critical neglect for that very reason.[1] Ramón Sender's series of nine novels, *Crónica del alba* (*Chronicle of Dawn*), is another example, since the protagonist, Ramón Garcés, and the author are as similar as their first names suggest. Esteban Salazar Chapela's *Perico en Londres* (*Perico in London*) and a lesser known, but no less interesting, novel by Arturo Esteves, *Búsqueda en la noche* (*Search in the Night*), as well as *El exilio interior* by Miguel Salabert, are all autobiographical novels, according to the stated intentions of each author.[2] Cecilia de Guilarte's *Nació en España: novela o lo que el lector prefiera* (*Born in Spain: Novel or*

Whatever the Reader Prefers) along with a similar text by Silvia Mistral, *Exodo: diario de una refugiada española* (*Exodus: Diary of a Spanish Refugee*), are two more cases. Each of these novels makes little or no attempt to hide the fact that the creator is interested in reproducing him or herself through the writing. The problem in each case is perhaps one of the most fundamental problems in the apprehension of literature of any sort: the inevitable difference between self and creation, that eternal gap between writer and text.

For those of us too sophisticated to enjoy anything else, the most interesting cases of autobiographical self-production are those that allow the necessary space between the writer and the writing. Yet even the writers who seem convinced of their own successful (that is, accurate) self-rendering cannot seem to avoid the self-consciousness: Lopéz Barrantes and El Campesino are examples. Jorge Semprún's political autobiography, *Autobiografía de Federico Sánchez*, by all estimations falls into the self-conscious (that is, interesting) category; yet the author's determination to stay out of the realm of the novel, or better yet, at the margins between fiction and reality without ever giving in to either, testifies to the inevitability of the gap. His *Autobiografía* traces the life of Semprún's other, Federico Sánchez, the name assigned to him by the Communist Party of Spain during the frustrated struggle against the Franco regime from the late forties to his expulsion from the party in 1964. The text is filled with expositions of political problems, mistaken strategies of leftist opposition, errors in logic and tautologies formulated by those who considered themselves the vanguard of the antifascist battle. Anecdotes, re-creations of conversations and debates, character sketches of real politicians, descriptions of meetings and demonstrations, all contribute to the political appraisal of a real historical situation by one who participated in that history and carried out the very policy he now bitterly defames.

Yet Semprún's concern is not only with the blindness of a political party but with his own failure to see. It is this very self-deception which adds literary and quasi-novelistic elements to the text, without which the *Autobiography* would have been another work entirely. Semprún is the son of Republican exiles who continued his parents' struggle against fascism by joining the French resistance, for which he spent time in a Nazi internment camp. He is an exile three times removed from the powers which cast him out: first, as an accompanying member of a family of exiles, second, as a survivor of a German concentration camp at Buchenwald, and finally, as the victim of expulsion from a party whose principles he upheld for over twenty years.

Not unlike Constancia de la Mora's historical account of the Civil War through the recreation of her own life, Semprún's autobiography serves as a historical document of party politics. While the former reads like a wartime epic novel worthy of comparison with those of Barea, Sender, and Aub, the *Autobiografía* has all the trappings of a postmodern literary text, much in keeping with some of the more experimental works of the Latin American boom such as *The Death of Artemio Cruz*. In Mora's and Semprún's autobiographies the tension between fiction and nonfiction becomes the texts' focal point: in the former unwittingly and in the latter self-consciously.[3] Mora vacillates constantly between the first and third person points of view even though the text's structure depends upon the first person for virtually all of the events and circumstances of the narration. Yet this first person often becomes omniscient in analyzing simultaneous events, judging the moral and political worth of characters, and offering a view of Spain, not as much from outside as from overhead. Mora's narrator, herself, gives us all perspectives at once and makes sense of it all. Semprún's vacillation, on the other hand, appears as the subject of the text's very discourse. The narrator addresses Federico Sánchez in the second person and at the same time offers his own perspective through a first person. Thus the *yo-tú* is the essential split voice of the text, which manifests itself in a variety of other ways: Semprún-Sánchez, Communist Party official-dissident member, exile from the party-exile from Spain. While Mora vacillates between an extremely personal one-woman perspective and that of an objective all-knowing authority, Semprún offers his testimony in an ongoing dialogue with himself. The result of both of these shifting perspectives is yet another manifestation of the ambivalences in exile literature.

Not surprisingly, the narrational split between the I and You also appears in an autobiographical novel written in exile by Segundo Serrano Poncela: *Habitación para hombre solo* (*Room for a Solitary Man*). While Semprún's autobiography is constrained by a need for political vindication, *Habitación* centers on a theme common in its day: alienation in all its manifestations—political, social, cultural, existential, and psychological. The work is based on a series of separations, the initial one being the protagonist's break from his native land. This split leads to the division in perspective between a *yo* and a *tú*, and its textual strategy is similar, if not identical, to Semprún's. As the former Communist Party militant divides himself into two so that he can address himself as another person, Serrano's *tú* serves similarly as a ploy in a dialogue between the author and his created self in the text. The notion of textual duplication and repetition is a central one in *Habitación*, which begins with the words, "Todas las mañanas se parecen y tú repites la misma escena desde hace tiempo" (p. 5; Every morning is like the previous one, and you repeat the same scene as you have done for some time).

Although the similarities between *Habitación* and the *Autobiografía* are plentiful, the latter is unique in its literary categorization. *The Autobiography of Federico Sánchez* is indeed a difficult text to categorize, unlike Serrano's, which is clearly a novel. Semprún plays with the various possibilities of his work's classification. In addition to the obvious conception of the text as a political autobiography, the second person narration endows the discourse with a psychological dimension, a type of self-exploration reminiscent of confessional literature. Yet Semprún's confessions are always tempered by counteraccusation, typical of exilic moral discourse and emblematic of the author's own paradoxical condition. His former unflinching loyalty to the party is the proof of his good faith, but it is also the very sin he confesses. Much of

the autobiography is a political treatise analyzing the mistaken positions of the party during the long aftermath of the Civil War. However,
the almost excessive elaboration of those erroneous arguments at a
time when they no longer matter further testifies to the ethical uneasi-
ness with which Semprún views his past allegiance to the party.

In keeping with the *Autobiography*'s nonconformance with any genre
is the constant implication that the text is a quasi-novel, or a novel
which is not a novel. Unlike certain works of literature which have
been characterized as anti-novels or texts that parody the conventions
of the genre and thereby draw attention to themselves as works of art,
the story of Federico Sánchez draws attention to the world outside the
text with an implicit understanding that all the events, people, and
circumstances of the narrative have direct corresponding entities in
reality. Semprún's stated intention is: "evidenciar por escrito lo evidente"
(p. 190; to evidence in writing what is evident). Yet the reader cannot
but wonder about that seemingly redundant phrase, given the fact that
these extra literary entities enjoy all the traits of fictional creations.
Federico Sánchez himself is the foremost example. His very name is a
fiction, a designation used to hide his real identity. By the same token,
the necessarily clandestine nature of Federico's behavior throughout
his life suggests that his very existence (like that of many exiles) is
illegal. He is a member of the resistance at one point, a member of an
outlawed party, the owner of a forged passport, and a dissenter within
the party. All of these disguises lead to textual deviations from the
genre of autobiography. Ironically, Semprún's text exposes the literariness of the real world, for he does not wish to transform it or even
manipulate it; on the contrary, he merely offers a commentary on the
world's artificiality.

In one instance the autobiographer grapples with the ambivalence of
his own activity by referring to the tempting possibility of converting
his text into a full-fledged novel: "Si estuviera escribiendo una novela,
en lugar de hacer un relato meramente testimonial . . . sin duda
aprovecharía esta ocasión de lucimiento literario" (p. 182; If I were

writing a novel, instead of a merely testimonial narrative . . . without doubt I would take advantage of the literary luster this moment offers). The remainder of the paragraph renders the hypothesis a reality, as the author crosses the limits of the genre of autobiography, a transgression which is emblematic of Semprún's enterprise from start to finish. The subjunctive ("si estuviera") becomes the elliptical phrase for a sequence of verbs in the conditional, all of which serve as the temporal referents for the hypothetical situation. If he were writing a novel, he states, the details in his scenario would be a character on his way to an important political meeting, a universe enclosed in a train while the Danube scurries along outside, a luxurious meal served in the restaurant car, secretaries, interpreters, Communist Party officials, including the old matron of the antifascist struggle, Dolores Ibárruri—*La Pasionaria* herself, "mother of all Spaniards." The passage ends with, "pero no estás escribiendo una novela" (p. 184; but you are not writing a novel).

The ironic denial of any fictional dimension to the text continues with Semprún's need to trace his own intellectual and political development as a proponent of an ideology to one of its skeptics. His break with the party and its tenets, the work's main theme, calls for a series of references to his previous works. One in particular, *El largo viaje* (*The Long Voyage*), is a novel about a character caught in the midst of the ravages of World War II Europe. *The Long Voyage*, then, refers to an autonomous text as well as to the autobiography itself, the sixth chapter of which has the same title as the novel. The disclaimer which structures the autobiography, the rejection of any novelistic interference, falls apart by his own manipulation of the previous text within his life story. Semprún not only rewrites his novel, but, in effect, continues it, as the viaje becomes a linguistic journey which, unlike the novel, will not end with the last sentence. As the narrator suggests at one point, "como si *El largo viaje* todavía no hubiese terminado, como si todavía estuviese por hacer, por escribir, . . . libro futuro" (p. 241; as if *The Long Voyage* had not yet finished, as if its writing were still pending, . . . a future book).

The *Autobiography*'s resistance to easy categories, in spite of the title, is reminiscent of another text written in exile from Russia, a land far removed from Spain yet similar in the cultural importance exile has played in this century and in other stages of its history. I am referring again to Nabokov's *Speak, Memory*, an autobiography that reads like a novel or a novel which poses as an autobiography. The motif of memory, the ever apparent catalyzing force of much exile literature, is central to both works, for in many ways Semprún's political autobiography and Nabokov's life story are not only explorations of past experience; they are inquiries into the ways the past reappears in the present. Clearly, Nabokov lacks Semprún's desire for political vindication, yet the manifestations of exilic remembrance are common to both texts: constant shifts in place, the intrusion of the present into the past and vice-versa, and as a consequence, the confusion of one for the other, moral questioniong of past behavior (both the subject's and the society's), compensation and overcompensation for the loss of certain objects and situations, the frustrated attempt to deal with the imperfection of memorabilia as copies of real objects and situations, all in conjunction with memory both as theme and as vehicle.

The place of *Speak, Memory* is itself the object of discourse as it is in Semprún's autobiography. In both, concrete places recalled, named, and described by the authors lead to discourses on the very notion of place and its problematic evocation through memory. The Russian butterfly which Nabokov describes in dreamlike detail crosses the Bering Strait, flies over Alaska, and ends its journey in Colorado in an allegorical re-creation of the author's own restless life (p. 120). In the same vein, yet without Nabokov's propensity for metaphor, Semprún's discussion of the place of writing is integrally related to the theme of memory. Streets and buildings in Madrid (as in the constant reference to Bahamonde 5), along with Santander, Prague, Moscow, all have dual existences, like the author himself: one in reality and another in memory. Remembrance seems to overpower the narrative of Federico's life as it leads to associations which do not follow the thread of a particular anecdote or a political argument. The multiple places of exile seem to merge; Madrid recalls Paris, and Paris moves to Moscow with the Communist Party. At other times the northern coast of Spain along Santander and the Basque country suddenly appears as a lost paradise in the middle of Madrid while Franco lies dying, a fact which itself leads to the memory of yet more places.

While Nabokov evokes several places at once, Semprún creates a seemingly unending chain of locales with the parentheses of his memory. Lengthy parenthetical interruptions are in fact among the autobiography's most dominant stylistic ploys,[4] so much so that at times the inner narrative erases the outer one, questioning its own insignificance. In many ways the entire autobiography is a series of parentheses within the frame of Dolores Ibárruri's initial speech denouncing the excess of intellectual activity within the party, particularly that of Semprún and his friend and ally, Fernando Claudín. In keeping with Semprún's parenthetical structure, La Pasionaria's speech is itself the contents of a parenthesis within the proceedings of a party meeting, as the beginning sentence and the title of the first section indicate, "Pasionaria ha pedido la palabra" (p. 7; Pasionaria has asked to be recognized). The effect of the many inner structures of the life story is that of a *mise en abîme*. As an interruption to Ibárruri's words the author recalls the tense day before July 17, 1959, the date planned for the General Strike intended as a protest and response to Franco's national holiday to commemorate the uprising of July 17, 1936. But the interruption is itself filled with digressions: the first contact with La Pasionaria, Kleber Street in Paris, recollections of old friends, a severe critique of the language used by the party, including the author's own political writing, a passage of which he incorporates into the text (p. 37). The inner journey of his life continues throughout the work along with the constant reliance on memory as the self-perpetuating catalyst of the trip. The voyage ends at the beginning, Ibárruri's denunciation, which thunders in the narrator's mind (and text) and drowns out all the other voices which have contributed to the stimulation of his memory:

"Intelectuales con cabeza de chorlito" (p. 284; scatterbrained intellectuals), she declaims, as Semprún is left at the end of his life-text with nothing but an echo of an insidious phrase.

Parentheses of memories are worthy devices of an exilic thought structure, for a life of exile is indeed parenthetical. The interruption brought about by a forced displacement changes the conventional acceptance of parentheses as enclosures for something tangential to the main current of an argument, a description, or a story. In exile the parentheses of a new life take on an unforeseen importance; in the development of the life as a whole the life within the parentheses becomes autonomous. While the previous existence serves as a frame for the life within, it is that very frame which dominates the inner life. Exilic parentheses also question the function and feasibility of the closing marker (the end parenthesis), for the continuation of the outer structure cannot proceed as if the interruption never took place. The return from exile to the original condition, or the continuation of life as it was, is impossible even when there has been a physical homecoming. Both the land and the subject have changed, regardless of the subject's haunting obsession with the preservation of origins. Semprún's case makes this wish painfully clear.

> (sí, desierta, así recordabas la playa del Carraspio, como si la imagen de tu memoria fuese una de esas postales desvaídas de comienzos de siglo . . . pero no te queda ninguna fotografía de esa época, ninguna huella material, todo ha sido borrado, aniquilado, por la guerra civil, por el exilio, sólo te quedan las fulguraciones de una memoria cuyos personajes son cada día más jóvenes, a medida que tú mismo te acercas al horizonte penumbroso de la muerte. . . .) (p. 272)

> (yes, deserted, that is how you remember the beach at Carraspio, as if the image of your memory were one of those faded turn-of-the-century postcards . . . but you do not have any more photographs of that time, no material trace, everything has been erased,

annihilated, by the Civil War, by exile, all that remains for you are the emanations of a memory whose characters grow younger each day as you yourself approach the dim horizon of your death. . . .)

Semprún's obsession with origins stems from an urge to preserve the privileged status of the former life, yet exile frustrates that desire. The space between the closure of the exilic parentheses and the beginning of the continuation of a former life becomes blurred. Exile has created a role reversal not only between the old and young, as the above passage indicates, but also between the dominance of the outer existence and the incidental nature of the parenthetical one.

In the final analysis the intrusions and interruptions of various types of discourses, such as parenthetical notations, summaries of political arguments and counterarguments, emerge from Semprún's own conception of his life and his autobiography as a dialogue with himself as well as with his country, his peers, and former comembers of the party. Perhaps the most telling indication of how he conceives the text of his life is the motif of *autocrítica* or self-criticism, a term charged with psychological, existential, and political significations. Within the political spectrum of the autobiography self-criticism is a familiar concept to those who have participated in leftist politics. Especially for the intellectual, but for others also, it assumes a tension between one's own beliefs and the uncontrollable influence of the society at large: the ideology of the ruling structure versus the counterideology of the leftist or progressive individual. Self-criticism also involves a good deal of internal searching and questioning of one's own behavior in the light of class pressures. The political uses and abuses of the concept are the objects of parody in Semprún's text. At times he seems to take the notion of self-criticism seriously enough to structure his life-text around it. In fact, the autobiography itself is an undoing and outdoing of the Leninist notion of self-criticism.

In the initial stage of *La autobiografía* Semprún recalls the relationship he had with one of the more active members of the Party, El Tano, a metal worker who listened attentively at meetings. At times Tano was impressed by the narrator's facility with language, his ability to relate abstract concepts to the concrete situation of the class struggle in Spain. But on other occasions Tano became frustrated at not being able to understand a particualr point. He once cried out at Semprún, " 'Te voy a hacer tu autocrítica . . . ¡no eres más que un intelectual!' " (p. 14; I'll do your self-criticism for you . . . you're nothing but an intellectual!). Here begins a series of references to the concept of self-criticism throughout the text. Tano's accusation contains the various facets of self-criticism's uses in the autobiography. Semprún satirizes the unlearned yet earnest worker with his ridiculously paradoxical use of the term and thereby parodies the concept itself as it appears in classical Marxist-Leninist political theory. Yet, as it becomes increasingly evident with the unfolding of the life story and with the fact that the party's Central Committee, including La Pasionaria, has made precisely the same remark, Semprún has gone beyond the limits of parody. The unconscious irony in Tano's words later echoed by Pasionaria (that the activity of self-criticism is undertaken by someone else, another self), is the conscious irony of the text. Semprún, through the multiple levels and stages of his exile, has become double, a binomial self engaging in a dialogical exchange (criticism and self-criticism) between its two parts. What makes Semprún's use of the concept problematic, if not contradictory, is that, unlike the harmonious synthesis which ideally comes about through the process of self-criticism (a Marxist-Hegelian synthesis of opposites) the effect of the internal dialogue, like that of exile, is further fragmentation. The words contain not only their binomial opposite but their resemblances, metonomies which lead to other associations, like the parentheses within parentheses. In like manner Tano is not so much Semprún's opposite as his other, an entity engaged in an activity similar to that of Semprún. While self-criticism seems to lead somewhere in the Marxist-Leninist sense, in Semprún it leads the subject further into a labyrinth of exile.

The stated autobiographical intentions of Semprún's text and the playful rendering of his life through a fictional apparatus indicate the ways in which fictional structures inform the exile's attempt to testify to the life he or she has lived. Yet they also arc indicative of certain structural patterns of exile literature in general. Many exile writers are faced with the dilemma of re-creating their own exile both as a response to their banishment and as a work of fiction. The initial break from the land gives rise to a need to recover a lost identity and thus re-create the former self in a frustrated struggle against oblivion. Their texts must, therefore, remain in the middle ground between real events and created ones without ever losing sight of either. The works of Max Aub (as we shall see), as well as Barea's *Forja*, Sender's *Crónica*, and Serrano's *Habitación* are textual embodiments of these agonizing problems. As Serrano tells us from his *Room*, to write on oneself is a difficult task, especially from exile.

> Nada más difícil que escribir sobre sí mismo, tan difícil como la autovivisección. Cuando el propósito es recrear la novela de la propia vida, el esfuerzo cuesta vida y resulta peligrosamente incompleto. . . . Sólo Dios (¿dónde está?) se encontraría en condiciones de escribir sobre cualquier acontecimiento de su vida, desde el tiempo absoluto, pero Dios no escribe novelas ni autobiografías. Se miente cuando se dice: tal fue mi pasado. . . . La imaginación es el mejor sustituto de la memoria. (p. 146)

> (There is nothing more difficult than writing about oneself, more difficult than self-vivisection. When the intent is to create the novel of one's own life, the attempt is of vital cost and the result is always incomplete. . . . Only God [where is He?] could find himself in the condition to write on an event in his life, from an absolute time, but God doesn't write novels or autobiographies. It is a lie to say: that is how it was in my past. . . . Imagination is the best substitute for memory.)

This passage is emblematic of any tortured attempt to write an autobiography, including Semprún's, yet it is even more telling when placed in its exilic context. The separation which self-writing seems to call for, a separation resulting from the desire for unity of the I of the self with the I of the written page, is not unlike the condition of exile. Exile is, in a sense, a precondition for writing. Serrano's term, "self-vivisection," is reminiscent of many of the exile texts discussed thus far, from Nabokov's *Speak, Memory* to Gómez de la Serna's *Automoribundia* (or self-killing), Simón Otaola's autobiographical autopsies, and Guilarte's severing of the umbilical cord. Self-vivisection is likewise an apt description of the annihilation of Federico Sánchez by Jorge Semprún and vice versa.

My characterizations of exilic memoirs and autobiographies are clearly within the relatively recent predisposition to read literary texts as disquisitions on their own systems of artifice, a tendency even more recent in Hispanic studies than in other fields. Indeed, an elaboration of the condition of exile and the apprehension of how that condition is manifest in language leads, perhaps inevitably, to the recognition of the problems in the recording of lived experience. So much so that the recording itself becomes the ultimate focal point. Yet it is also clear that the patterns of exile literature lead outward as well as inward. As the essays, memoirs, and autobiographies of banished Spaniards show, reality remains the point of exilic departure, and as the departure takes place, reality itself becomes tenuous. It is not so much that exile writing transforms reality but that the process of faithful reporting of exile comes under close scrutiny and questions the apprehension of the real world. Thus in the most extreme cases, such as Semprún's autobiography, the work takes on the majestic task of transforming a world which has already been transformed by exile, an attempt to imitate not the reality of the world but its artifice. In like manner memoirs of exile are, for the most part, remembrances of people, things and circumstances which were already recollections at the moment of their re-creation in textual form.

It is interesting that in one of the few attempts to analyze metafiction in Spanish literature, Robert Spires (*Beyond the Metafictional Mode*) speaks of a category of writing for the kind of texts under discussion in the previous chapters—"reportorial fiction" (pp. 8–9). The problem is, however, that in Spires's groupings of literature, metafiction and "reportorial fiction" are at opposite ends of the spectrum. What his graph fails to account for, as do most attempts to categorize literature (even the more interesting ones), are the cases in which the act of writing takes the text beyond whatever category (genre, mode, historical period) it occupies. "Reportorial fiction" is a perplexing category, for the very name is contradictory, unless it is metafictional by definition —the report of a fiction. Not only would one be hard-pressed to find anything in literature that comfortably falls under this heading, its conception, according to Spires's categorical scheme, is tautological. "Reportorial fiction" is the foil he needs to contrast his real concern, which is metafiction.

The modern critical disdain for realism, of which Spires's study is yet another example, emerges from formalism's distaste for the consideration of historical, political, or social concerns in literature.[5] The antipathy is perhaps self-defeating, for it could logically be applied to novelists in the vanguard of what Spires calls a "movement" of metafiction: García Márquez, Vargas Llosa, Fuentes, as well as the self-exiled Spaniard, Juan Goytisolo, all of whom exhibit intense political concerns in their writing. But even in the more naive texts, the ones which claim no literary profundity or even talent, such as the memoirs and diaries of exile (Antonio Ros, Constancia de la Mora), the tensions involved in the faithful reporting of real experience tend to reveal themselves in spite of the author's wish to avoid those problems. Essays, memoirs, and autobiographies written from a place labeled Exile often cannot help but bring into question the precarious situation of the writer as one who must "take hints, follow leads and be a restless nomad until the end comes" (Mazzotta, *Dante*, p. 274).

The Politics of Exile: Max Aub

Ironically, I sense that Max Aub, along with many of his generation (Sender, Andújar, Ayala, and other Republican intellectuals who played a role in the political development of the war), would not appreciate the amplitude of my category of exile or my unwillingness to exclude certain writers from the discussion. For Aub politics is the essence of exile. Yet at the same time his exile branches out in a variety of directions. In many ways Aub is the embodiment of the Spanish Civil War exile writer, for his life and literary corpus were determined by some sort of banishment at nearly every stage. The designation of him as an exile is not the least bit problematic, for not only does he fit most, if not all, the descriptions, his exile is multifaceted, as most exilic experiences are. A Paris-born Jew whose father was German and mother French (surnamed Mohrenwitch), Aub moved to Spain at age eleven. Instead of pursuing a university career as he wished, he followed the dictates of his father by helping him in the family business and accompanying him on his sales trips. These jaunts took young Aub through many different parts of Spain and led to his own sense of national belonging, even though he was not a full-fledged Spaniard.[1]

The notion of life as trip also characterized his early writing. Heavily influenced by the literary vanguard of his youth (Ortega, Bergson, surrealism), and closer than his Spanish peers to new European aesthetic currents because of his native understanding of French and German, he began to write in a stylized prose whose word associations, dream images, and fantasy were indirectly linked to the land of his travels with his father. International and national politics were a determining factor in his upbringing (an influence missing from his early works), and toward the beginning of the thirties (the years of the Second Republic) he immersed himself in social and governmental dynamics. When the Spanish War began in earnest Aub defended the Republic as a writer and as a cultural attaché in Paris for the Spanish socialist government. At war's end he spent several years in concentration camps at Vernet and Djelfa (Algeria) and in prison in Marseille. His trajectory was typical of many Spaniards not only in the beginning of his exile but in its end: he was able to emigrate to Mexico where he lived until his death (1972), with the exception of two disheartening visits to Spain in the final years of his life.

A Jew, an immigrant with his parents, a Republican refugee, a prison-camp survivor, a foreign resident in Mexico, and finally a stranger in his own country during his last stay, Max Aub, the life, is directly linked to the movements and vagaries of politics. It is a life that testifies to the arbitrariness of both exile and politics, and it is this arbitrariness which stands as his most important literary theme. Yet the distance between literature on the one hand and political life on the other, even in Aub, is a long one. In a literary corpus as massive as Aub's (over thirteen novels, almost as many volumes of short narratives, scores of plays, as well as political, literary, and cultural essays), to find a unifying theme is as difficult, and ultimately as fruitless, as the designation of a guiding principle of his life, or any life. If anything it is this very lack of integration which stands as Aub's central statement, both political and literary. Even in the expository and argumentative essays of *Hablo como hombre* (*I Speak as a Man*), a coherent political ideology is barely discernible.

In a February 1951 letter criticizing the French government for having rejected a request to visit the country, Aub's tone is clearly one of righteous indignation. Yet pathos and absurdity are also ingredients in this text, whose ultimate political stand is by no means lucid. In an attempt to defend himself from the charge that he was and is a member of the Communist Party, the same charge which landed him in a French concentration camp twelve years before, Aub refers to the dilemma in which he finds himself. He is not, nor was he ever a communist, although his file reports otherwise: "Ya sé que estoy fichado, y que esto es lo que cuenta. . . . Es decir, que yo, mi persona, lo que pienso, lo que siento, no es la verdad. La verdad es lo que está escrito. Claro que yo, como escritor, debiera comprenderlo mejor que nadie. Es decir, que lo que vive de verdad son los personajes y no las personas. . . . Yo, Max Aub, no existo" (p. 61; I know that I have been blacklisted, and that that is what counts. . . . In other words, I, my person, what I think, what I feel, is not the truth. What is true is what is written. Of course, I, as a writer, should understand it better than anyone. In other words, what really lives is personages, not persons. . . . I, Max Aub, do not exist). Aub's defense is a discourse not on writing and reality but on the difficulty of articulating the defense itself, considering the impossible situation in which he was accused: an anonymous denunciation, a file that is both outdated (compiled in Vichy France) and a fiction. Ironically, the writer of fiction must resort to reality to combat the tools of his own trade. In a sense, Aub is pursued by the fruits of his own labor.

The writing of Max Aub underscores the textuality of both life and politics. Yet it is significant that Aub is not among the exile writers who wrote political memoirs and autobiographies. The only text remotely resembling a written account of his own life is *Hablo como hombre*, a collection of journalistic pieces and letters dealing with certain incidents in Mexico, Spain, and other parts of Europe as well as his attitudes toward politics and literature. In the strict sense, however, the collection is not an autobiography, nor a book of memoirs, but a collection of essays. It is precisely the conspicuous absence of an autobiography in his vast corpus, and the crucial importance of a specific historical reality, which confirms Aub's interest, if not obsession, with the faithful recording of lives, especially his own.

Aub seems to perceive his life as a compendium, a gathering of many others; the organization of *Hablo como hombre* exemplifies this. It appeared five years prior to his death, and in the light of his poor health during his later years it is not farfetched to assume that the compilation of his previous writing was something of a retrospective, a collection of parts of a life in much the same way as were Alberti's *Arboleda*, Llorens's *Memorias*, and Nabokov's *Speak, Memory*. All these works are fragmentary and make no pretense of presenting a coherent story of a life. What makes Aub's retrospective collection a bit different is its suggestion that a life is a group of texts. The introduction or "Explicación," the only part of the work written exclusively for the collection, makes Aub's intention clear, at least on the surface. The banished writer affirms that he is tired of having others define him, that he would rather allow his texts to speak for him ("como hombre"). The result, he says, is a twisted mass of articles "sin más liga que mí mismo" (p. 9; without any connection other than myself). Following more information about his life and the texts in the collection Aub returns in the end paragraph to his original concern—writing a life: "Lo que más me ha gustado es escribir; seguramente para que se supiera cómo soy, sin decirlo. Creí que lo adivinarían. Una vez más me equivoqué" (p. 12; What has pleased me most is writing; surely so that people would know what I'm like, without telling them. I thought they would figure it out. Once more I was wrong). In essence the introduction of *Hablo como hombre* is both a beginning and an end. It provides the information and interpretive apparatus (a statement of purpose, a political context) as well as a date (May 1967) which places it at the very end of a series of chronologically ordered essays, the final stroke, at least for the moment, of a life.

Aub's practical preoccupation in the essays of *Hablo como hombre* is politics. Beginning with a transcription of his speech as a representative of the Spanish Republic in Paris at the unveiling of Picasso's *Guernica* (1937), through his condemnations of Franco's Spain and reflections on East-West political relations, and ending with an indignant reading of the regime's insidious phrase, "twenty-five years of peace" (1964), Aub traces almost three decades of social life on two continents, and within it the life of a participating observer. Clearly on the left side of the political spectrum, Aub declares the necessity for governments to create a more equitable distribution of wealth through what he calls "liberal socialism" (p. 62). At another point he vehemently criticizes the regime's ties to the United States through military bases in an alliance against Soviet communism: "¿Dónde el honor, dónde la honra, dónde la soberanía que tanto cacareó el *Generalísimo*? ¿No hundió ya bastante a España . . . en la fosa del atraso? . . . ¿Todavía no comprende que está condenado sin remedio en la historia, por todos y por el Dios que predicó exactamente lo contrario de lo que ha llevado a cabo?" (p. 73; Where is the honor, the dignity, where is that sovereignty which the *Generalísimo* crowed so much about? Hasn't he drowned Spain enough . . . in the depths of backwardness? . . . Does he not yet understand that he is condemned in history without remedy by everyone and by the God who preached exactly the opposite of what he has undertaken?) Yet for all its rhetorical flair, a style reminiscent of a long tradition of moral-political oration in Hispanic letters, this passage masks an underlying tension. Like the book as a whole it comprises Max Aub's defense against the charges that brought him into exile. And the best defense, as the saying goes, is a good offense: to use the enemy's tools (sovereignty, God) to make a counterattack. The ultimate effect, however, cannot be what the surface reading of these words would suggest: a clear refutation of an untenable political policy. The outcome is perhaps more devastating, for the very notions of God and sovereignty are put into question, first by the existence of the person who calls upon them, a skeptic, a person with an international and multireligious background, and second by the absence of a community of readers who understand the language, the political issues, and the circumstances. These words resound as in a speech or a political rally, yet there are no listeners. Like a play with no stage, no actors, no funds for production, Aub's text is the speech he never gave. The immediacy of oral language, its supposed purity and authenticity, is exposed for what it really is: just as deceiving and self-contradictory as writing. In the last analysis Aub, the political orator of *Hablo como hombre*, is yet another creation, for as the author affirms in a previous text, "Max Aub does not exist" (*Hablo como hombre*, p. 61).

The Magical Labyrinth

Among the many Spanish exiles determined to bear witness in writing to their own experiences of the Civil War, Max Aub is no exception. His political and literary ideology before the war, however, makes his rendering of the historic event different from most eyewitness accounts. Marra-López rightly points out that the war changed Aub—from a young man grappling with the iconoclastic cultural movements which Ortega defended in his *Dehumanization of Art*, to a seasoned author intent upon re-creating the social and political events of Spain from 1936 to 1939 and the participants in those events.[2] Yet Max Aub had changed well before the war; in fact his assimilation of the aesthetic vanguard of the twenties was only one of his literary influences. The advent of the war merely confirmed certain social and historical inclinations which had been at work in his writing since the early thirties. At the end of the war he had lived through and seen so much violence, chaos, and bloodshed that the espousal of art for its own sake seemed irrelevant (as it did to Sender and Ayala), even though Aub never completely lost touch with some of the ideas and perceptions of the literary and artistic currents of the twenties.

It is significant that Aub began work on what he considered his greatest contribution to peninsular letters, *El laberinto mágico* (*The Magical Labyrinth*), almost immediately upon his departure and even before his experience in prison camp. It is also significant that the association of war with a labyrinth is thematically linked to a painting which Aub greatly admired: Picasso's *Guernica*. In his 1938 speech at the unveiling of the painting in Paris, Aub steadfastly submits that *Guernica* is by no means an antirealist work, that it has everything to do with the "present" reality of Spain. In the words that Aub added to his speech in the collection of *Hablo como hombre*, he prophetically hopes that one day *Guernica* will be transported to its rightful place —the Prado (*Hablo*, p. 13). Like *Guernica*, Aub's *Laberinto* is filled with abstractions and purposeful distortions, yet its reason for being is the Spanish reality of 1936–39. Unlike *Guernica*, however, the *Laberinto* never made such a triumphant return to Spain.

El laberinto is a series of five novels describing the events of the war, beginning with the Republic, following through the military uprising, and ending with the evacuation and fascist takeover.[3] Thus exile marks the beginning of the writing and the final event depicted in the series. The exilic experience tempers the novels and is, in the final analysis, the reason for their being, in spite of Aub's own assertion that he would have written his *Labyrinth* whether he had gone into exile or not. It was the war, he says, which defined him, not exile (Prats Rivelles, *Max Aub*, p. 71). Yet even Aub might have agreed to add the following to his statement: it is the loss of the war, and hence exile, which stands as the series' most vivid image. *The Magical Labyrinth* is a labyrinth of loss, death, insanity, and absence; it is the story of hundreds of individuals who question not only the ultimate reasons for the war but their own places within it. The very notion of place is put into question. Yet unlike the sparsely populated labyrinth which characterizes the works of other post-World War II writers, such as Beckett's *Waiting for Godot* or Borges's labyrinths in his *Ficciones*, Aub's maze is filled with social life: street vendors, soldiers, generals, clerks, intellectuals, women who lose their lives as they walk down the street with their children and gaze at the falling bombs. In some ways the *Laberinto* is the narrative version of *Guernica*.[4]

Each novel in the series centers on an event whose political consequences were far-reaching in the continuing development of the war. *Campo cerrado*, the first corridor of the labyrinth, takes the reader from the advent of the Second Republic to the conflict's beginnings. *Campo abierto* depicts the successful defense of Madrid during the first year of the fighting, while *Campo de sangre* deals with the diminishing power of the Loyalist ranks focusing mainly on the battle of Teruel in 1938. In *Campo del Moro* and *Campo de los almendros* the Republic faces imminent defeat with an anticommunist coup within the left designed to negotiate a settlement with the enemy (*Moro*). And in the final stage Aub re-creates the evacuation of Republicans who feared the ensuing bloodbath perpetrated by the insurgent forces (*almendros*). This seemingly well-ordered and chronological scheme, a social historian's model text, belies the abstract and distorted nature of a world in which order and chronology cannot serve as reliable tools in its reconstruction. Exile has made such tools ineffective, if not useless. The motif of a timeless maze, as much an all-encompassing labyrinth of life as a multitude of seemingly unconnected labyrinths, structures the series. In *Cerrado* the protagonist is caught in a web of events and influences over which he has no control, while in *Abierto* freedom from the maze seems a possibility since Madrid is still part of the Republic. As the war continues, in *Sangre*, the open space (the campo) is once again closed off by further bloodshed and military losses. Toward the final stages of the story the passageways of the labyrinth multiply, making an escape (exile) impossible. The dominant image of *Moro* and *Almendros* is chaos and madness. The constant presence of the labyrinth as a device renders the historical progression of the war an illusion. In a labyrinth there are no stages or chronological developments; time is relegated to an eternal present. The only end is the discovery of a way out, the exilic escape, which is no escape at all.

The motif of the labyrinth has both thematic and structural dimensions in Aub's novels. Direct references to mazes abound, and descriptions of places (in which the confusion of streets or passageways imprisons the characters) mirror the series' seemingly chaotic structure. Aub's history leads nowhere. Links, accurate directional signals to a guiding progression of events, are not parts of the *Labyrinth*, and their absence further contributes to the haphazard world of war and destruction. The only link is the idea of haphazardness itself.

The beginning pages of the first volume, *Campo cerrado*, foretell what is to come in the plot and the structure of the series. Aub opens the series with an evocation of the "toro de fuego" (the bull of fire), an allusion both to Homer (a peculiarly Spanish version of the Daedalus myth) and to a real Valencian town, Viver de las Aguas (a suggestive name but not Aub's invention). Viver still exists and the ritual of the bull of fire is still practiced there. The mystery, terror, and excitement of the bull of fire comprise the initial scene of the *Laberinto mágico* as Aub plays the role of an anthropologist. The narrator tells us that during the town festivities the inhabitants of Viver cover the head of a bull and fasten balls of tar to its horns. At night they set the balls of tar aflame and free the bull in the center of town. The people call out to him and then flee as the bull pursues the voices and his own shadow through the darkness of the streets. The bull of fire, like most myths and rituals, has more than one level of meaning, especially within the framework of a novel: he is the Second Republic, the Civil War, the invading armies (Franco and the Moors he enlisted, the Germans, the Italians). He is also the bull of Picasso's *Guernica*:

> ¡Ya viene! ¡Ya llega! ¡Ya está ahí! Lo llaman, lo desean y cuando la luz, las llamas, la bárbara mole nocturna se abálanza por el callejón, vuélveseles pavor el deseo, como tras un coito frenético y furtivo. . . . Busca ardiente cinco, seis, siete veces su salida inalcanzable. Párase frente a una casa, revuélvese en un callejón sin salida; baladran las mujeres, cían los valientes. (pp. 20–21)

> (Here it comes! It's coming! It's already there! They call it, they desire it, they want it, and when the light, the flames, and the barbarous nocturnal hulk rushes in through the alley, their desire turns to fear, as after a frenetic and furtive copulation. . . . [The bull] looks for an unreachable exit, five, six, seven times. He

stops in front of a house, he goes back down a dead end; the women scream, the brave stand out to challenge him.)

The tension between this bull in a labyrinth—a timeless and spaceless myth on the one hand, the historical and cultural specificity of Spain on the other—marks the ambivalence of Aub's wish to trace the chaotic flow of recent Spanish history.

The motif of the maze appears in a variety of disguises throughout the five novels: endless political debates whose rational solution is never realized (*Abierto*, pp. 512–19; *Sangre*, pp. 155–63); inner conflicts of characters in which every avenue to a resolution is cut off (Rafael López's change from a fascist to an anarchist, Paulino Cuartero's religious doubts); Vicente's search for his lover, Asunción, through the insanity of the streets of Alicante (one of the many plot lines in *Almendros*); and the political intrigues of *Campo del Moro* in which ideological motivations are contradictory, if not absurd. The interweaving of a myriad of characters, some of whom reappear unexpectedly as others fade into oblivion, is itself a labyrinth. The ending of *Campo cerrado* is a partial list of characters, real political figures coupled with Aub's creations, and an explanation of what happened to them after the time span covered by the novel. Not only is this list typical of the exile's weaving of real experience with fiction, it adds to Aub's intentionally chaotic ordering of history. For Aub the past is the story of individual lives connected to one another at random and without a hierarchical order.

The allegorical nature of the labyrinth, its identification with the Second Republic, with Spain, and with the war, reflects a dilemma at the root of Aub's project. The recovery and ordering of the past from the time and place of exile leads to a variety of obstacles which in the end render that recovery impossible. As one of the many narrators of *Campo de los almendros* declares, "también el autor se siente prisionero de sus historias, no sabe cómo salir del laberinto" (p. 427; the author also feels himself a prisoner of his own stories, he does not know his way out of the labyrinth). Aub's concept of history sets him apart from the classical practitioners of the historical novel, such as Galdós, Balzac, or even José María Gironella in post-Civil War Spain. In exile Aub questions the feasibility of dealing with the problems of an entire epoch from an omniscient perspective. The narrators of the *Laberinto* make no attempt to analyze or even speculate about past, present, and future periods of history. Instead of assuming a privileged understanding of social dynamics Aub grounds his discourse in the individual lives of workers, peasants, doctors, politicians, artists, and military officials and their interactions with people in other classes and in their own professions. Understandably, social stratification is at times a motivating force in the behavior of his characters; but the role of these individuals in concrete political and social change is always ambiguous, at times at odds with what one would logically consider their interests, and never serves to illustrate the movement of a historical process. Again, the ambivalence of Aub's "history" of the Civil War stands out: he embarks on an apprehension of a social process and in so doing questions its very existence.

Aub's re-creation of the conflict reads like a collection of anecdotes, diaries, and daily renditions of immediate events without an overall perspective. The titles of his chapters, and certain sections within the chapters, reveal the quotidian structure of his texts: in *Cerrado*, "Vela y madrugada" ("Early Morning and Dawn"), "Mañana y mediodía" ("Morning and Midday"); in *Abierto*, "3 de noviembre," "4 de noviembre," etc.; in *Sangre*, "de once a doce" ("From 11 to 12"), "19 de marzo, 1938"; in *Moro* more dates; and in *Almendros*, "Datos y relatos posibles" ("Possible Facts and Happenings"). Under these headings the author interjects newspaper clippings, historical documents, caricatures of political figures. The following could be the script of a newsreel depiction of events: "Dos horas resisten los facciosos en el restaurante Patria. Pasado este tiempo se rinde la tropa. Algunos oficiales disparan desde los alones reservados" (*Cerrado*, p. 223; The fascists resist for two hours at the Patria Restaurant. After this time the

troop surrenders. A few officers shoot from the reserved dining rooms).
Similarly in *Abierto*, Aub continues to create a sense of wartime
immediacy:

> El general Miaja y el teniente Rojo frente a diecisiete teléfonos.
> "¿Refuerzos? Ahora van."
> "¿Refuerzos? Ahí le envío doscientos hombres."
> "¿Refuerzos? Dentro de media hora."
> "¿Refuerzos? En seguida."
> "¿Refuerzos? Ahora salen."
> "¿Refuerzos? Esperamos medios de transporte."
> "¿Refuerzos? Ya salieron."
> (p. 476)

> (General Miaja and Lieutenant Rojo in front of seventeen tele-
> phones.
> —Reinforcements? They're on their way.
> —Reinforcements? I'll send you 200 men.
> —Reinforcements? Within half an hour.
> —Reinforcements? Right away.
> —Reinforcements? They're just leaving.
> —Reinforcements? We're waiting for transportation.
> —Reinforcements? They just left.)

Indeed, "dar cuenta de la hora" (*Hablo como hombre*, p. 40), to bear
witness to what happened, is what Aub wishes to do in exile. The
quotidian structure of the *Laberinto* arises from the same desire that
compelled many other Republicans to do the same as Aub: to record
their experiences from memory so that the world would not forget. Yet
oblivion (a form of death) is a fact of life, a fact even more agonizing
for Aub than for less recognized writers considering the loss of a reading
public (the audience for whom that historical moment must always be
present). In spite of the *Laberinto*'s urge to engage in dialogue on
political and moral ideas, the most important facet of that dialogue

cannot take place: the one between a voice in exile and a land which does all it can to forget it.

The concepts of memory and oblivion are paramount in the *Laberinto*, as in so many other texts written from exile. For Aub banishment is a disease he must conquer, and one of the tools of this conquest is memory. The struggle to remember is a dominant motif, much as it is in *Federico Sánchez*. Yet in Aub's works memory is not so much a subject of discourse as an ongoing struggle within the text. As in the final section of *Campo cerrado*, several pages of *Campo abierto* (pp. 342–400), list the civilians, most of whom were members of the UGT (the socialist trade union), who defended Madrid against an imminent fascist takeover. Anxious to get on with the story, a reader may question not only why the author included the list, but its length—eight pages of names, addresses, and two- or three-word descriptions of the people whose rallying cry was "no pasarán" (they shall not pass). But in the context of exile and the aftermath of war the list becomes a memorial, a tribute to seemingly insignificant men and women for an impressive, if not miraculous, accomplishment. Aub's homage to the losers, who were winners only for that moment, can appear exclusively from exile. It is in some ways a response to the Valley of the Fallen, that grotesquely large monument frequented by tourists: a cross that protrudes like a phallus above the hills outside Madrid. Standing underneath the cross in the bowels of the structure (built by the forced labor of political prisoners) are the statues of angels with swords, helmets, and enormous hands. Aub's response to these fantastic figures is his list of names of real Spanish citizens, streets of Madrid, and a few words to stress the individuality or eccentricity of the people who correspond to those names. In the same way that *Guernica* commemorates the persons who died in the German bombing of the Basque town, the list is a testimonial, a society's weapon against oblivion and death.[5]

The will to remember is often a common problem for the characters themselves, especially in *Campo de los almendros*, a further manifestation of the desperation, absurdity, and futility which marked the final months of the war. Vicente Dalmases, the young communist who remains loyal to his country and his party throughout the war, is in the final days obsessed with finding Asunción, a symbol of the desired Republic. As Aub probes Vicente's mind, a number of disparate thoughts come to the fore, including a poem by Antonio Machado about the communist general, José Miaja. Here, Aub prioritizes memory not only as a tool in the reconstruction of a person but as an end in itself. Since the character does not have the original text at his disposal, he must invent it. Vicente remembers the general, his thick glasses, his build, the honors he received for having defended Madrid. This remembrance leads back to the one that originally sparked it—Machado: "Un poema de Machado acerca de Miaja. Está viendo la página, el título: 'MIAJA.' No se acuerda de los versos, sí del sentido. . . . ¿Qué más? La memoria, hoyanca (p. 258; A poem by Machado about Miaja. He sees the page, the title: 'MIAJA.' He remembers the gist of the poem but not the lines. . . . What else? The poor man's grave of memory). Given the typically exilic interweaving of reality and fiction in this rewriting of Machado's verses, Vicente's remembrance is a reference to that of Aub in *Campo de los almendros*. The novelist re-creates Machado's text, as does Vicente, with inaccurate fragments of the original, the remnants of a time, place, and a person that no longer exist. Within Aub's text "Miaja" the poem loses its original shape in spite of the wish to preserve it. And Miaja the general is, like his corresponding text, the memory of a memory.

In an addendum to *Campo de los almendros* and to the *Laberinto* as a whole, Aub addresses himself to the primordial problem of the exile writer: the absence of a listener. In these final pages he includes the words of a woman who has read the previous chapters of the series and claims to have witnessed the chaos they portray. Her intention is to add her testimony to that of the author and thus to initiate what Aub wants: a dialogue between the exile and his home. She states at several points that the author, whom she addresses directly as usted, cannot possibly be aware of how horrible it really was (pp. 540–541). The story of her own perils, as she relates it, does not exactly deny those contained in the body of the text, but adds to the confusion of interpreting them. She admits that it is very difficult for her to make any sense out of what happened or "tie things together" (p. 539). This is the challenge Aub offers: to connect the events, to unravel the labyrinth, to remember the links and thus create them, imagine them; it is the task of Aub's reader as it is for Aub. To forget is to allow exile to become a death: "hoy se ha olvidado mucho, dentro de poco se habrá olvidado todo. Claro está que, a pesar de todo, queda siempre algo en el aire . . ." (p. 543; today much has been forgotten, and before long everything will be forgotten. Surely, in spite of everything, there is always something in the air . . .). These words express not only the pathos of loss but the ambivalence of the *Laberinto*. For Aub writing is collective memory; yet through the grid of memory the reality that yearns for its own reproduction becomes weightless, transparent, like "something in the air."

The *Laberinto mágico* embodies a great many of the exilic traits outlined in earlier chapters; yet like all texts, whether written in exile or not, it strays from the group of works which critics most commonly associate with it, such as Barea's *Forja*, Ayala's *La cabeza del cordero*, or Sender's *Crónica*. One of the most unusual features of Aub's writing is his obsession with language, coming, perhaps, from his early surrealist inclinations. His exilic attempt at recovery was, in effect, a continuation of a linguistic battle which had started well before the war or exile. Not a native speaker of Spanish, and estranged from the mainstream of Spanish culture due in part to his European influences and background, he felt a need to become more Spanish than the Spaniards, something which arises in the *Laberinto* with unprecedented vehemence. Thus it is not only language in general which concerned Aub but Spanish in particular: colloquial expressions, verbal taboos, proverbs, sounds, and tones of peninsular speech patterns, along with a variety of regional accents.

In some instances language is more than a tool for Aub; it is the subject of discourse. In a prologue to the entire series the author states that the language spoken and written during the war presents a problem, a "problemilla" he calls it—an ironic designation of something which, in the words that follow, becomes far more than a minor obstacle.

> Problema o problemilla fue desde que la novela ha sido, quiéranlo o no, espejo de lo que vemos y oímos, resolver en metáforas imágenes, iniciales o puntos suspensivos, las palabrotas, ajos, tacos, groserías, juramentos o interjecciones soeces que, a cada dos por tres y sin más valla que la presencia de mujeres, forasteros o falta de confianza entre los reunidos, se nos vienen a la boca a los españoles, . . . vicio que la guerra multiplica.

> (It has been a problem, or a slight problem, since the beginnings of the novel, which is, whether one likes it or not, a mirror of what we see and hear, to mix together in the form of metaphors, images, initials, or ellipses, all the curses, filthy expressions, and four-letter words which come out of the mouths of Spaniards in droves without the slightest hesitation, other than the presence of women, strangers, or the inhibitions of people in a gathering, a vice multiplied by war.)

Although in these words the author refers to the taboo of certain speech patterns, and to the difficulty of mirroring them, this declaration may be extended to Aub's entire enterprise. Each culture has its particular style of desecration, and for Aub, times of hardship such as war have a tendency to replenish that style with varieties of sacrilege, profanity, and verbal debasement. The problem for the author is to recreate that culturally and historically specific manner of speech. Aub's exile and separation from the specificity of wartime Spain makes the problemilla even more of a problemilla. The resolution is to find metaphors, images, initials, or elliptical devices to reproduce the language of the war. In many ways the search becomes a signifying process which is an end in itself.

In another stage of the *Laberinto* (*Campo del Moro*), Aub creates a character who embodies an exaggerated form of the author himself. Manuel Beltrán, a spiritist (*espiritista*) born in France, is unable to rid himself of his French accent, his "acento gabacho" (p. 29) or "froggish way of speaking." At one point Don Manuel is waiting in a line where government workers are rationing coal. He asks the next person in line:

"¿Cree que darán algo hoy?"
"Leche."
El espiritista, que no alcanza los valores reales de la lengua, asegura:
"Esta es la cola del carbón."
"Y están mal ordenadas las letras y sobra el singular."
(p. 208)

("Do you think they'll give any today?"
"Milk!" [In Spain this word is an expletive whose loose translation is "damn."]
The spiritist, who does not apprehend the real sense of the language, assures:
"This is the line for coal" [*carbón*].
"And the letters are in the wrong order [*cabrón*], and there's more than one of them.")

The anagram, *carbón-cabrón* (coal-cuckold), along with the suggestion of the plural, "cabrones," renders the spiritist a victim of ridicule and testifies to Aub's own verbal acumen in Spanish as well as to the self-consciousness of his humor. With the creation of the spiritist Aub laughs at himself, the other Max Aub, newly arrived from Paris and overwhelmed by an unfamiliar culture. Yet the Aub who writes the *Laberinto*, with all its verbal twists, has outdone his fellow Spaniards.

Some critics have characterized Aub's language as excessive and inappropriate to the epic quality of his series of novels.[6] Yet rather than view the linguistic ornamentation and play as a mistake or a defect, it is perhaps more enlightening to consider these elements of Aub's style as further manifestations of a writer in exile. The verbal excess and level of social realism of Aub's novels leads one to a consideration of ludic writing, both in conjunction with and in contrast to his social realism. The *Laberinto* reveals a tension between Aub the popular realist (a modern-day Galdós who records the events of a nation and thereby tells its inhabitants who they are) and Aub the debunker who leaves the recording of reality to others so that he may laugh at it. The latter Max Aub is a hedonist intent upon savoring every word in games of semantic and phonological associations, while the former possesses a single-minded purpose and political conviction. Again we witness Aub's exilic vacillation, this time between seriousness and frivolity. The sobriety of telling the citizens of a nation who they are is incompatible with a style as ornate as the following.

> Picaño, pequeño, cacoquimo. Fofo, astuto, bocón. Malsín, petrañero soplón, fanfarrón, entrometido, espía. Siempre al apaño y amigo del dolo. Traslúcido, con el pelo brillante de mil brillantinas y la cara de polvos y masajes, amo de los limpiabotas. Oloroso de peluquería. A lo que él cree: elegante, de lo más elegante, la raya del pantalón pespunteada para que no haya equívocos. Bajo, bellaco, denunciador por gusto de fastidiar al prójimo, afán de enterado y pura nequicia. El cuello alto, trabilla, las solapas anchas. Farolero, estafadorcillo: de su sastre, de su lavandera, del cobrador del tranvía. . . . Su especialidad: orillear. (*Sangre*, p. 75)

> (Shifty, shirking, little shrimp. Cunning, sponging blowhard. Gabbling, tattling, blustering, meddling spy. Larcenous swindler always out to turn a shady deal. Spiffy: hair flashing from tubes of brilliantine; face pummeled and powdered. Reeking of barbershop. Master . . . of bootblacks. A prince . . . in his own mind! Elegant . . . oh, so elegant. Stitched trouser creases so there will be no mistake. Small, conniving, crafty snitch who delights in doing in his neighbor. Knows what's going on. Starched collar,

spats, wide lapels. Puffed-up petty pinchpenny: with his tailor, his launderer, the trolley ticket-taker. . . . His greatest talent: keeping his ears peeled.)[7]

The object of this baroque description, reminiscent of Quevedo's *Buscón*, is a popular character type, López-Mardones, the petty spy. Many of the sentences lack a verb, and there is a proliferation of adjectives separated by commas and an inner rhythm which resembles the patterns of prose poetry. The imbalance of these words arises from their referent, a type recognized by a reader who has seen or dealt with real López-Mardones during the war. The language that describes him, however, renders him unfamiliar; it obfuscates the character and forces us to concentrate on the words of the description rather than on its referent. López-Mardones, the social type, disappears as he is written away in a language of excess.

The structural, stylistic, and thematic facets of Aub's *Laberinto* also give rise to ideological questions which render the notion of exile a complex one. Banishment, the rejection of an individual by a society, a culture, or a regime, presupposes a political problem, a clash of opposing ideas. In Aub's case the ideological features of his writing are apparent: he opposes the insurgents during the war and abhors the Franco government at all times, and for this he makes no excuses, nor does he hide his political sentiments. As an exile he must stand in opposition and speak in a dissenting voice as his countryman, Picasso, did with *Guernica*. Yet the voice of exile, in Aub's case, goes unheard. It attempts to counter the voice of authority (now the language of the homeland) and to retell the story of the war from the perspective of the fallen (los vencidos), but it loses its coherence and euphony among other sounds: those of loss, absence, memory, time, the problems of a new culture and its relation to the old. From a disconnected place the exilic voice of Max Aub is more than a voice of opposition and contrast; it is a voice speaking from the margins—different, other, impossibly harmonized with the prevailing song of a home that is no longer recognizable.

9 Two Exilic Biographies

The connections between Aub and Picasso do not stop at the novelist's speech at the unveiling of *Guernica* in 1937, nor even at the distortion of social and historical reality which characterizes both Picasso's painting and Aub's *Laberinto*. As the preceding chapter shows, Aub's career began in the midst of the vanguardist aesthetic movements of the first two decades of this century, and his intimate friendship with one of its leaders, Luis Buñuel (as seen in Aub's biography of the filmmaker), is no less an indication that Aub contributed to the surrealist subversions of that time. Yet it is also true that the events during the Second Republic and culminating in the Civil War altered both his political practice and his literary work. The same was true of many members of Aub's generation, such as Ayala and Sender. Unlike many of his former vanguardist colleagues, however, it was Aub whose interest in surrealism, dada, and cubism seemed to persist in some of his later works. His two biographies of invented human beings testify to this almost obsessive interest: *Jusep Torres Campalans* and *Vida y obra de Luis Alvarez Petraña*. The fact that these were written from exile after several major conflagrations (two world wars and a civil one, as well as the attempted extermination of a race) adds some distance and commentary to the motivations behind all the formal experimentation and innovation of these works.[1]

The life stories of Jusep Torres and Luis Alvarez are both parodies and self-parodies of those aesthetic experiments, for they are baffling;

that is, they are consciously structured so that no sane person can receive a clear image of their main subjects. Aub offers his readers no answers in his reconstruction of these strange individuals, yet the suggestions—that they may have been real, that they were great artists whom no one recognized, that their stories are based on the life of the author himself—are many, if not infinite, because each possibility seems to give rise to another one. It is revealing that few literary critics have gone near these biographies, perhaps because they themselves might become unwitting objects of parody.

One of Aub's obsessions that is apparent in both *Torres Campalans* and *Alvarez Petraña* (also illustrated in the *Laberinto*) is the possibility (or impossibility) of converting individual lives into structures and, by extension, creating the interconnections among those life structures. In the *Laberinto* Aub recreates the war with seemingly unconnected bits and pieces of characters, a novelistic technique reminiscent of John Dos Passos's *U.S.A.* trilogy.[2] Like the North American novelist, Aub constantly interrupts the flow of his narrative with brief biographies of characters, even those whose importance to the story as a whole is minimal. Similarly, in the two biographies Aub collects the fragments of the main characters' lives in the form of documents, descriptions of their works, and commentaries on them by friends and acquaintances. The real-seeming nature of the documents is one more of Aub's contributions to the confusion of his life portraits. It also adds to a prevailing concept in Aub's exilic corpus: the notion of life as text(s).

What stands out in these two life stories is the unavoidable uncertainty in the apprehension of a life. Torres, Aub assures us, was a Catalan painter and intimate friend of Picasso who participated in the radical change in art initiated in the first decade of this century, especially cubism. Alvarez Petraña (mediocre in comparison to Torres) was a frustrated poet whose unrequited and cliché-ridden love for a woman named Laura supposedly led him to commit suicide in 1931—an incident the biography leaves open to question. These two biographies may be read as additions to the edifice of the *Laberinto*, since the novels that comprise that series contain many biographies and mini-biographies of real and unreal characters (some seem to fit both categories). The conventional wisdom regarding the real existence of Torres and Alvarez affirms that Aub merely played a trick on his readers, that in fact these two lives are fictions.[3] Such assertions are accurate, yet facile. They tend to close the texts to the very possibilities Aub suggests for them, especially the absolute plausibility of the real existence of their protagonists. Reading *Jusep Torres Campalans* and *Vida y obra de Luis Alvarez Petraña* simply as ingenious inventions robs them of their realistic dimension; for, like many exilic works, they are precisely in the middle between fiction and reality, that is, on the margins of both. With these works, not only does Aub stress the literariness of fiction but the literariness of the world.

Aub seems to have written *Jusep Torres Campalans* with a clear idea in mind, even though the end result is anything but a clear picture of a person. There are few discrepancies in the various accounts of Torres's life, including a text by the painter himself, supposedly collected by Aub. Torres's writing, along with the other documents, follows a relatively coherent pattern. The biography includes acknowledgements expressing gratitude to well-known figures such as André Malraux, Jaime Torres Bodet, Georges Braque, Francisco Giner de los Ríos, and others who collaborated in Torres's resuscitation. Aub also incorporates a cultural chronology, titled "Annals" (pp. 29–96), from the year of Torres's birth (1886) to the year he mysteriously disappeared from the European art world (1914). The chronology includes births and deaths of important people, publications of significant works, debuts, expositions, scientific discoveries, and political events, all of which pave the way for the body of the text which is the biography itself (pp. 97–194). Following the artist's life story, there is an epigrammatic text by Torres which Aub supposedly found in a green notebook (pp. 195–268), followed by a transcription of a dialogue between Aub and the artist (pp. 264–308), and finally, an annotated list of Torres's paintings in chronological order (pp. 309–21).

It is precisely the clarity of Aub's presentation of the "facts" which contributes to the confusion over the character's life. The biographer's scholarly ordering of documents led to the serious appraisal of the painter by art critics and cultural historians. In effect, the art world had discovered a new cubist. Intellectuals and artists in Mexico, where, according to the biographer, Torres had just died, and as far away as New York, were declaring that they had seen his works or that they had had the good fortune of meeting him. As a matter of fact, an exposition of his paintings, in reality the work of Aub, was mounted by Galerías Excelsior in Mexico City in 1958, and in 1962 the Bodley Gallery of New York wanted to exhibit the works to coincide with Doubleday's translation of the biography (Prats Rivelles, *Max Aub*, pp. 58–61).

Aub achieved what he wanted, for on rare occasions have reality and fiction been as closely allied. He out-debunked his former vanguardist colleagues by parodying their own attempts to subvert the bourgeois art world: a typically outrageous surrealistic trick, perhaps all the more outrageous since surrealism's variants (dada, ultraism, futurism) had come to a halt well before Aub's bright idea. The parodic thrust of the biography is apparent not only in the imitation of a scholarly text in which Aub plays the role of editor as much as biographer, but in the actual consequences of the biography's publication. *Jusep Torres Campalans* is a parody in which its readers both wittingly and unwittingly play along: illusion becomes a part of life. The extent to which Aub reveals his own deceit is itself questionable: most, if not all, of the artists and cultural figures that supposedly associated with Torres are real figures, and the confirmation or denial of their relation to him is a challenge to the scholarly reader, as he or she gallantly trudges off to the library in search of evidence of Torres's existence, and perhaps even finds it.

However, the author tacitly gives us hints about the nature of his game in words which recall those of Serenus Zeitblom of *Doctor Faustus*. Aub says in his "Indispensable Prologue,"

Trampa, para un novelista doblado de dramturgo, el escribir una biografía. Dan, hecho, el personaje, sin libertad con el tiempo. Para que la obra sea lo que debe, tiene que atenerse, ligada, al protagonista; explicarlo, hacer su autopsia, establecer una ficha, diagnosticar. Huir, en lo posible, de interpretaciones personales, fuente de la novela; esposar la imaginación, ceñirse en lo que fue. Historiar. ¿Pero se puede medir un semejante con la sola razón? ¿Qué sabemos con precisión de otro, a menos de convertirle en personaje propio? ¿Quién pone en memoria, sin equivocaciones, cosas antiguas?

Escribí mi relación, valiéndome de otros, dejándome aparte, procurando, en la medida de lo posible, ceñir la verdad; gran ilusión. (pp. 20–21)

(It is a trap for a novelist who doubles as a playwright to write a biography. The character has been given, ready-made, without temporal license. For the work to be what it should, it must be linked to and depend on the protagonist; to explain him, perform an autopsy, establish the facts, to diagnose. To flee, as far as it is possible, from personal interpretations, which are the source of the novel; to handcuff the imagination, to limit oneself to what was. To write a history. But can one measure one's fellow human being with reason alone? What do we really know of another, unless we convert him into our own character? Who can subject old things to memory without error?

I wrote my story, making use of others, leaving myself aside, to the extent that such is possible, in an effort to grasp reality; a great illusion.)

In these words Aub hints at a disclaimer by declaring how difficult it is for a writer of fiction to stay within the bounds of a biography. Yet there is nothing in the prologue which contradicts or even questions Torres's existence. On the contrary, his admission of the necessity of sticking to the facts (the illusion of truth) makes the account of his life even more credible. And the word trap refers not to Aub's real disguise but to the disguise he must use to write the biography of a real person: the disguise of a disguise, a device reminiscent of Mann's *Doctor Faustus*. Clearly contrary to *Torres Campalans*'s prankish nature, the German text presents itself as a novel at the outset, yet the problems of the recording of a life are no less apparent and multidimensional. Mann disguises his novel as Leverkuhn's biography which, as I suggested earlier, is a mask of Zeitblom's autobiography. In both the Spanish and German exilic texts there is a tension between the life of an individual on the one hand and the text(s) of that life on the other.

No less problematic is the text of Luis Alvarez Petraña, *Vida y obra*. The strategic use of documents to create a life is similar, if not identical, to that of *Torres Campalans*. Yet in *Alvarez Petraña* the crucial issue is not so much the existence of the protagonist as the authorship of writings attributed to the protagonist. The question of who exists in *Torres Campalans* becomes who writes in *Alvarez Petraña*. The issue of authorship is further complicated by the Byzantine history of the latter's publication. The original edition appeared in 1934, a time when Aub was beginning to question his own vanguardist inclinations and to embrace social and political themes. In exile he published two continuations (1965, 1971) of the biography, since, as he claimed, he had stumbled on more works written by the protagonist of the life work. The reappearance of Luis Alvarez Petraña both as a character and as a text testifies to the incompleteness of exilic life. The fact that in reality the works attributed to Luis Alvarez were created by none other than Max Aub adds another dimension to the biography, a text in which the borders between autobiography and biography are blurred.

In the 1934 edition of *Luis Alvarez* Aub takes the apocryphal to the limits by inventing a mediocre poet along with several of his unpublished texts: a diary recording the anguished love affair leading to his suicide and three poems dealing with the trials and deceits of love. This edition of the biography ends with the poems and letters from Laura (the ungrateful object of Luis's love) to her real lover. Laura's correspondence shows not an ounce of affection for Luis or any regret concerning his desperate act and adds to the pathos of a man unable to escape the clichés of his own sentiment—a love clearly designed as an attempt to transcend his own mediocrity. He is a familiar character in Spanish literature, a frustrated Don Juan reminiscent of *La Celestina*'s Calisto or *Niebla*'s Augusto Pérez. At the same time this initial pre-exilic *Alvarez Petraña* is a literary statement, not only on the self-indulgent aesthetics of the day but on Aub's own earlier writing. The dangers of separating one's life from society and history are embodied in the figure of Luis Alvarez and signal the new social direction which Aub's texts will take.

But Aub did not forget his poet-suicide or his pre-exile writing. Over ten years after the war and far away from the place of Alvarez's birth, the author began a new project: the resuscitation of Luis Alvarez Petraña. The author claims to have come across yet another unpublished text written the same year as the suicide by someone named Miguel Mendizábal, a Spanish refugee of the Civil War whose real name was probably Luis Alvarez Petraña. The text, titled "Leonor," relates the life of yet another individual through a series of character sketches of the protagonist's friends, relatives, and acquaintances. The theme of "Leonor" is, of course, the reciprocity of love, and there are ample similarities between her and Laura, including the name itself and a note at the end (p. 127) suggesting that very possibility. Yet the new text's treatment of unrequited love is hardly the work of a suicidal maniac. On the contrary, Alvarez-Aub playfully creates situations in which Leonor's loyalty to her real lover, this time her husband, is put to the test. Although she remains impeccably faithful, her seductive charm and coyness, coupled with her insistence on chaste friendship with every male she encounters, place that very loyalty into question. They also raise doubts about the authorship of "Leonor."[4] The worn-out phrases and concepts which imprisoned the Luis Alvarez of the first edition become the objects of parody in the second. Aub, fully aware of the pitfalls of his first Alvarez, becomes the author-ally in the new edition. He closes the second version with further loopholes and complications, including evidence suggesting Alvarez's suicide was a simulacrum and that he may have lived as long as 1961 after moving to Mexico for unknown reasons. Thus, after a great deal of speculation, Aub leaves his text open to the most obvious of possibilities: that his writer-character is a model of himself and by extension that he, Max Aub, is the author of Alvarez's works.

The third and final version of *Luis Alvarez* contains a new series of texts as well as the two previous editions. Once again Aub lifts Luis Alvarez from his previous graves as he discovers more of his writings. The new works are prefaced by another diary, this time by Aub himself, describing his stay in a London hospital after suffering a mild heart attack in April 1969. While recuperating he discovers, much to his surprise, that in a room not far from his lies an ailing Spanish poet who claims to be Luis Alvarez Petraña. Alvarez, who by that time must be in his seventies, hands Aub the manuscripts which comprise the final version of *Vida y obra de Luis Alvarez Petraña*: the poet's "last notebook," a short narrative titled "Equivocación," and "María," a monologue of a dancer as she gazes at herself in a mirror. To find a thematic thread linking these texts is the challenge Aub offers to the reader of this third stage of *Alvarez Petraña*. But since the possibilities are so plentiful (unrequited love, death, insanity, fragmentation of the self), the reader is left perplexed. Nothing seems to serve as a unifying motif, other than Alvarez's own life as a writer-lover.

Like the other editions, the final one is filled with notes by the author, declarations by those interested in solving the puzzle, including professors of literature and other authors such as Camilo José Cela. References to real literary journals like *Insula, Gaceta Literaria, Revista de Occidente* also help to create both a sense of academic seriousness and doubt as to the authorship of Alvarez's texts, in the same vein as *Jusep Torres*. Ironically, some pieces of the puzzle fit, yet they do not solve the crucial questions: who is the real author of "Leonor" and certain other texts, what are the reasons for the simulated suicide (if that is what it was), and what is the significance of Alvarez's life and works in the spectrum of Spanish literature? It seems that the more information Aub offers, the less clear is his picture of the poet.

In *Torres Campalans* and *Alvarez Petraña* the real and unreal evidence regarding the lives of two cultural figures is tenuous. Like life itself, the texts amass more and more experience and data with no end in mind other than death. The lifelike quality of both texts lends to the credibility of the figures they engender. The biographies are not written as stories, or life stories, but as a series of documents, anecdotes, testimonies of those who knew them, and most important, their own works. For Aub the writing of a life is the writing of not one text but many, and the unity of these texts consists only in the fact of their having been ordered in some way, molded into a design which the reader can undo and reorder. As with Cortázar's *Hopscotch*, the reader of *Torres* and *Alvarez* is free to skip from text to text, confirming and reconfirming an event, a date, a sentiment, an anecdote. And, as I have reiterated, the life of exile is just that—the collection and recollection of inconclusive evidence, contradictory facts which lead to questions about the apprehension of existence itself.

The political questions embodied in the two biographies are as complex as the confirmation of Torres's and Alvarez's existence. At first glance both texts have little to do with political issues, exile, or even Spain. And although Aub claims that Torres is a Catholic anarchist (p. 125), there is very little in the biographical section of the text which deals with the historical upheavals and events chronicled by the biographer in the "Annals." The absence of a political vision is particularly disturbing considering not only that the two protagonists left Spain at crucial historical moments but that they share certain qualities with the author, in spite of their seeming lack of political conviction. All three are of the same generation and, as artists, participated in the same aesthetic movements while keeping a certain distance from them. Perhaps the most revealing link is that the viewing and reading public did not recognize them. It is this very proximity, the similarity between author and protagonists, which marks the political tension of the works, as well as that of exile politics in general. From a political commitment to democracy and social justice Aub moves, perhaps unwittingly, to another kind of politics: a radical skepticism in which that very commitment comes into question. Aub argues the politics of the nonexistent and forgotten, those unreal human beings who lived through real events. And what makes the argument especially jarring is that his own case falls under the same scrutiny as those of Torres and Alvarez. Like his protagonists, the author lives in two dimensions, fiction and nonfiction. He plays the role of character as well as author. He engages Torres in a lengthy dialogue which makes up a good part of the biography and he does the same with Alvarez. His role as editor-investigator also intrudes into his fictive nonfiction; the story of the investigator's search is as important as that of the investigated life.

It is also crucial to Aub's political vision that the character he creates for himself in both works is one whose social concerns stand out: Max Aub, the exile from the Spain of the thirties, the author of *Hablo como hombre*. The author-character pays lip service to the political questions surrounding his two subjects and stops short of any deep involvement in these issues because of another dimension of his politics—the one which questions how we come to know an individual existence and thereby existence itself. In one of the works attributed to Luis Alvarez, "La equivocación," the autobiographical narrator sums up the unique brand of Aub's exile politics. The narrator-protagonist is a man who witnesses his own burial and describes it through a process of narrative doubling in which he refers to himself as both he and I:

> A lo sumo dígase: *pienso, luego no existo.* El que existe no piensa. Piensa el muerto, el ido, el huido, el desterrado. (¿Qué mejor ejemplo que el mío? Sin contar que nadie sabe que sabe, ni nunca se sabe lo que se cree saber, sino otra cosa. De ahí los listos y los humildes. Siempre me tuve por listo; muerto, humildeo.)
> (*Vida y obra*, p. 210)

(At the most, one should say: *I think, therefore I am not.* He who exists does not think. Those who think are the dead, the gone, the escaped, the exiled. [What better example than mine? Let's not even consider that no one knows that they know, nor does one ever know what one thinks one knows, but something else. That's what the smart and the humble know. I always thought myself smart, and since I'm dead, I'm humble.])

Again death and exile, as well as the persistent exilic self-splitting, make their way into the writing of a man obsessed with his own banishment and his oblivion. The passage testifies to Aub's epistemological questioning—his subversion of the Cartesian formula along with the suggestion that self-knowledge comes about only through exile or death. And perhaps most devastating in light of Aub's political engagement is the possibility that even the real defenders of democracy and justice are ultimately the players of a fictive game.

10 The Blind Chicken

There is a well-known cartoon by Goya titled *La gallina ciega* (Blind-man's Buff, literally The Blind Chicken). A merry group of aristocrats frolic in the peace and beauty of the countryside as they surround a blindfolded young man whose vain attempt to make contact with one of his fellow players is the cause of glee among those who encircle him. The colors of their dainty clothing and earthy complexions blend with the bucolic scenery (a lake, trees, and gentle hills in the distance), which seems to protect them from evil or harm. The immediate picture is one of harmony: everything is as it should be. But is it? Like many of Goya's neoclassical paintings, *La gallina ciega* deals with the relationship between artifice and nature, play and work. And although these genteel people seem at one with their world, they are, after all, engaged in an insidious game of deception and power. It is precisely that tension between seeing and not seeing, freedom and oppression, harmony and the possibility of disharmony which looms over the natural beauty of *La gallina ciega*; and that is exactly how Max Aub chose to read Goya's work.

In many ways it is no wonder that Aub chose this image to designate the account of this first trip to Spain after an absence of thirty years: *La gallina ciega: diario español*. After three decades of dictatorship, economic hardship followed by economic boom, tourism, and the familiar adage, "Spain is different," his homeland had become unrecognizable. The new situation blinded him and turned Aub into a ridiculous, somewhat grotesque old man stumbling his way around a country in search of something forever lost. He was "the blind chicken," and the merry players were his fellow Spaniards, unconcerned with the blind man's dilemma, happy to form part of the imprisoning circle.

La gallina ciega is yet another exilic diary, written with no high literary purpose, no unity other than that of an itinerary. But like many documents of exile, its simplicity masks a series of existential and linguistic problems arising from exilic experience, in this case, the return—the omnipresent yet elusive object of desire. The return is in fact an end, and its realization is the motivation and the definitive marker of many works written from exile.[1] If nostalgia involves the desire for a place that once was but is no longer, a physical return to that place cannot help but bring on a series of irreconcilable conflicts, between present and past, presence and absence, the self and the other, memory and oblivion. The subject of Aub's *La gallina ciega* is precisely this set of conflicts. Although its intention seems merely to record lived experience, its language tends to exceed those bounds.

The author's awareness of the futility of the return and a certain skepticism regarding his own reasons for the trip are apparent from the prologue and in nearly every entry in the diary. Rancor, vanity, wounded pride are among the traits of Max Aub approaching the climax of his life story. His judgments come from frustration, defeat, and from the fact that the return is too much like the end of an existence. But in Aub's case the exile's trip back engenders no disillusionment, for the only illusion is the expectation of finding things as horrendous as he thought they would be, living proof that his exile was not in vain. The defensive tone of *La gallina ciega* is typical of the exilic voice, and the author's awareness of it ironically makes him even more defensive when he asks, for example, "¿Quiere decir que fui a España con la idea preconcebida del estado actual de la península? Es posible. Doy mi palabra que deseaba lo contrario. Sencillamente: no vivía a oscuras; lo que no quiere decir—que diera en el blanco de la razón" (p. 8; Could it be that I went to Spain with a preconceived idea about the present condition of the peninsula? It is possible. I give my word that I wished the contrary. It's simply this: I was not living in the dark, which does not mean, of course, that I always hit the nail on the head). It is precisely this kind of vacillation about his motivations which lends special interest to this diary of return within the wide spectrum of exilic literature.

Like many of Aub's texts, *La gallina ciega* resists generic categorization. It is in fact a diary, but the author is skeptical even about that.

> Este que debiera ser un libro escrito para muchos no llegará a tanto, ni convencerá a nadie; tan desigual. ¿Por eso había de callar? Jamás estuve tan inseguro frente a un manuscrito, . . . Mas la sinceridad no es prenda literaria. Y esto—a mi pesar—quedará en literatura. . . . ¿Qué son estas páginas? Diario sólo hasta cierto punto, porque estos suelen limitarse a anotación de sucesos, reflexión sobre lo inmediato. Interesan en ellos lo inesperado, la gracia del aire; no tiene éste ninguna. (p. 7)

> (This, the book that should be written for many, will not reach such a goal, nor will it convince anyone; as unbalanced as it is. Is that why silence was necessary? Never have I been as unsure of a manuscript, . . . But sincerity is not a literary quality, and this, despite my wishes, will remain as literature. . . . What are these pages? A diary only to a certain point, because diaries usually limit themselves to the notation of events, reflections on the immediate situation. What interests in them is the unexpected, the lightness of the moment; this one doesn't have a bit of that.)

Aub's vacillation comes from the uncertainty of the genre he uses, and it defines the entire enterprise of *La gallina ciega*. Given his propensity to mix the real with the unreal, he is frustrated by the diary as a genre and its proscription of that very inclination. The diary does not allow him an "impresión de conjunto" (p. 8), a synthetic view, and since there is no doubt about the trip's reality, he feels a need to censor certain impressions and events, especially regarding friends whom he wants to protect from political repercussion or simple embarrassment. He attempts to solve the problem by referring to certain people as X or by using initials, yet this strategy only adds further ambivalence and recalls Nabokov's phrase, the unknown quantity of exile. In the preface he seems to apologize for the lack of balance in the diary, yet it is this very imbalance which structures his writing as well as many other of his works in exile.

With *La gallina ciega*, and its ambivalence about its own genre, Aub unwittingly comments on the relationship between the diary as a category of writing and exilic experience. The limitations of the genre are those of life; no grandiose plan with a beginning, middle, and end serves as a guide. The only object of imitation is life experience as it happens. Yet those very life experiences necessarily lead beyond reality and immediacy, for diaries also call for reactions, reflections, intimacy. Thus the limits of a diary are at once wide and narrow. Although the moment is always irretrievable, its very slipperiness leads the writer beyond its boundaries. The urge to catch that moment, to order it with writing, must involve other moments, sometimes not even within the time span of the particular date which heads the entry.

Reality is equally stifling, yet provocative, especially for a writer like Aub who relies heavily on dialogue to create situations. His *Gallina ciega* is no exception: *tertulias* in cafés, a dinner conversation with writers, young Spaniards, or an old friend. But he must reconstruct the event; he cannot transcribe it. At one point Aub abandons all pretense of writing a diary and inserts a short theatrical dialogue whose characters have participated in the previous events—an actor and an actress, the author himself, and two real literary figures: Larra, who died in 1837, and Buero Vallejo, who is still alive. The situation is clearly an invention, but the theme, censorship, is all too real. The author tells us in his typically playful manner that there is a prologue to the work but that he will not transcribe it since he wishes to remain faithful to the realistic obligation which the diary dictates (p. 301). In like manner, when Aub separates a section within a particular entry to describe one of the "characters" in his trip, he reminds us of the structures of his previous novels. These personages, like many in his novels, are real (Américo Castro, José López Rubio, Gloria Fuertes), and as they participate in the drama of Aub's trip they become fictional entities. *La gallina ciega* marks an inversion: the ingredients of his novels saturate his diary in the same way as his novels contain chronicles, diaries, and character sketches of real figures.

The bulk of *La gallina ciega*'s 415 pages deal with impressions of a new Spain, mostly political and cultural. The question most frequently asked of Aub is, "So what do you think of all this?" The interrogative becomes a motif of the work, a spark which ignites a series of judgments, comparisons, and digressions and which Aub does not hesitate to record in an attempt to find a unifying theme of his text-trip. Yet in the last analysis the question bores him, not only because everyone seems to ask it, but because it is a cliché of exile, an object of curiosity among those who do not understand the experience. The question itself becomes Aub's object of commentary as he complains that these new Spaniards are indifferent to the very issues which should preoccupy them. For Aub the question of the new Spain in the light of exile and the Civil War is more than a political issue. It is not only his reason for being, it is the unifying thread of his life-text and another fictional prop.

At a particularly difficult moment for the author, his return to Madrid, the question becomes, "Why did I come back?" As he arrives by night at the city which inspired much of his previous writing, the transformations of the city, in conjunction with the darkness, render the place unfamiliar. The following morning, before daybreak, the author awakens and sets out in the darkness to find the city of his early years. But the search is as futile as the trip back to his homeland.

> Sencillamente no podía dormir porque no podía poner en claro la razón de mi estancia en España, en Madrid. . . . ¿Qué me decía a

mí mismo? ¿Era España esa oscura neblina que iba tiniéndose de no sé qué colorcillo rosado? No sabía qué pensar, no sabía ni qué pensar; solo andaba por las ramas. ¿Qué sentía? ¿Cómo esclarecer mis sentimientos? . . . Si: no era España. No era mi España. Pero lo sabía con certeza de antemano y hacía mucho tiempo. ¿Qué me sorprendía? Me sorprendía no sorprenderme. (p. 179)

(I could not sleep simply because I could not clarify the reason for my stay in Spain, in Madrid. . . . What was I saying to myself? Was Spain that dark mist which was gradually turning to some pinkish color? I did not know what to think, I didn't even know what to think; I was walking alone in the branches. What did I feel? How to shed light on my sentiments? . . . Yes: this was not Spain. It was not my Spain. But I knew this for a fact some time ago. Then what was so astonishing? What astonished me was not being astonished.)

As Spain disappears in the early morning mist, and as Madrid becomes, as he says later, "olvidadiza" (p. 180; lightly forgotten), Aub turns to the self—his own perceptions, his sentiments, his ambivalences—only to find further questions and uncertainties, as well as a new self divided by exile.

Typical of the exilic writer, Aub becomes the object of a psychological split which leads to a linguistic one. The old man wandering aimlessly in search of the Puente de Segovia (the suicide bridge) engages in a dialogue with himself as did one of his early creations, the poet, Luis Alvarez Petraña. The protagonist's pride, solitude, and desperation come under self-scrutiny: "¿Entonces? ¿Degeneras de ti mismo? ¿Por qué tuerces el alma? ¿De qué tienes ansia? Sí: te deshaces en deseos, te consume la furia del amor hacia un pasado que no fue, por un futuro imposible" (p. 179; What then? Do you denigrate yourself? Why do you twist your soul? Why so much anxiety? Yes: you tear yourself up with desires, you are consumed by the fury of a love for an unreal past and an impossible future). In effect, Aub has transformed himself into yet one more character in the labyrinth, a man whose strings are pulled by another Aub, the writer. Yet even this other Aub, the writer of flesh and bone, must suffer an existence as "olvidadiza" as the land of his past. The diary is his urge to capture the moment of return, yet one cannot help thinking, along with Aub, that even this journal will be lost to oblivion, not only because of the pathos of exile, but also because of the nature of the game of writing. As the author himself admits, "Escribiendo olvido" (p. 379; as I write, I forget).

Aub is indeed a paradoxical figure in his *Blind Chicken*, for if writing is forgetfulness and thus a cure for painful memories, why is it that he protests the oblivion into which his homeland has cast him? According to the picture he has painted of himself, would he not prefer to forget (as some exiles have done) and welcome the ostracism of a culture and a regime he considers morally and politically bankrupt? Perhaps an extension of Aub's reading of Goya provides an answer, however speculative. The suggestion of a ripple in the bucolic harmony of *Blindman's Buff* leads to a potential storm, and in fact Goya became more interested, in his later works, in the ripples than in absolute tranquility. His "Black Paintings," for example, are an inquiry into the nature and shades of insanity. Goya's darkness and madness, along with the opposing concepts of light and reason, appear within the diary in the most unlikely places (as in the evening arrival in Madrid) and provide the text with its most pervasive images. The problem with the blind chicken is just that: it does not see what to others is so clear. The result is the insidious beginnings of madness. On more than one occasion Aub relates the errors into which his compatriots have fallen, especially the young ones (their ignorance of a generation of Spanish intellectuals, their resignation, their uncritical acceptance of the consumer society). Yet the necessarily anecdotal nature of these encounters renders him as ridiculous as those he criticizes. He becomes furious, he walks out of a discussion, he answers questions curtly, at times with another question. And, perhaps worst of all, he is aware of how ridiculous he appears, as he observes his own madness. Again, the consideration of two Max Aubs, the character and the writer, is of utmost importance to his exilic writing. While the former protests, scolds, and throws up his arms in desperation, the other sits back and watches. While the former bemoans that few people in Spain acknowledge his existence, the latter writes to forget about it. The task is to forget oblivion.

Yet Aub never distinguishes clearly between the two roles he creates for himself. Aub, the character, announces toward the end of his diary that he is writing an account of his trip, the very text in the reader's hands: *La gallina ciega*. This postmodern touch leads to a self-reading of the work, as the protagonist affirms that his title refers not so much to Goya's cartoon as to the popular Spanish turn of phrase "empollar huevos ajenos" (to hatch someone else's eggs): "Mi idea era que *La gallina ciega* era España no por el juego, no por el cartón de Goya, sino por haber empollado huevos de otra especie" (p. 406; My idea was that *The Blind Chicken* was Spain not because of the game, not because of Goya's cartoon, but because it engendered eggs of a different species). Not only does the additional significance of the title intensify the otherness of exile as the main character becomes the child of the blind chicken, it is ironically an affirmation of Goya's presence within the text. In the following passage, written, strangely enough, for the back cover of the Mortiz edition, Aub continues to deny the cartoon's influence, yet the description of the chicken is so vivid that one cannot help juxtaposing Goya's work to the image of the exile returned.

> No sé por qué se llama así este libro. Se me ocurrió que era bueno, lo puse. ¿A qué se refiere? Goya, sí, pero no al tapiz o su cartón. Ni al juego. Sí a una persona privada de luz, en oscuridad completa—sin perder la vista, pero metida dentro de las tinieblas gracias a una venda o pañolón—anublados el juicio y la razón, incapaz de juzgar los colores, a quien su ignorancia parece discreción, entropecidos los sentidos, a quien todo se le volvió noche, ciego de pasión de orgullo. Sí: España con ojos vendados, los

brazos extendidos, buscando inútilmente a sus compañeros o hijos, dando manotazos al aire, perdida.

(I don't know the reasons for the title of this book. It sounded good to me, so I used it. What does it refer to? Goya, surely, but not the tapestry or the cartoon. Not the game either. It refers, instead, to a person deprived of light, in total darkness—without losing his sight, yet in the dark thanks to a blindfold—his reasons and judgment clouded, incapable of distinguishing colors, a man who sees his own ignorance as discretion, his senses dulled, a man living constantly in the night, blinded by a passionate pride. Yes; with covered eyes, extended arms, searching vainly for friends or the next generation, trying to clutch the air; Spain is lost.)

With the help of the young Goya and the older one Aub has painted another blind chicken, a grotesque one, an animal-like creature who makes both himself and his observers wince at his life spectacle.

The ambivalence between diary and novel, reality and fiction, clarity and blindness, reason and insanity, in the last analysis is the ambivalence between writer and character. For Aub has not therapeutically freed himself of a dilemma by duplicating himself in writing, as the phrase, "escribiendo olvido" (as I write, I forget), suggests. A literary critic concerned with the linguistic and existential ramifications of exile might wish to read Aub's phrase without a pause between the two words; the result—"writing oblivion." In Aub's Spain of mist, confusion, and labyrinths the writer-character has become, like Jusep Torres Campalans, Luis Alvarez Petraña, and all the real-fictional entities who inhabit the Civil War maze, an emblem for ambivalence itself: real within a world of illusion and illusion within a world of reality.

I V

The Poetics of Exile: Luis Cernuda

11 Cernuda's Text of Texts

If exile literature, as Claudio Guillén has stated, follows the patterns of
Ovidian elegies and lamentations, then most of the texts discussed up
to this juncture are concrete manifestations of that critic's axiom; in
some cases, they extend the argument. Pathos and nostalgia are surely
among Spanish Civil War exile literature's most salient trademarks,
and indeed Guillén's observation that exilic literature is predisposed to
"autobiographical conveyance" of the experience has taken up much of
the subject matter of the previous pages. Yet is exile always a cause for
existential grief? Is there nothing advantageous, even joyous, about the
experience? In linguistic terms, is not departure, however uncertain the
return, semantically associated with voyage or the expectation of the
new in contrast to the hackneyed familiarity of the old? As an extension
of elegiac exile, Guillén posits another form of exile literature which
seeks to transcend the experience: "the literature of counter-exile, that
is to say, of those responses which incorporate the separation from
place, class, language or native community, insofar as they triumph
over the separation and thus can offer wide dimensions of meaning that
transcend the earlier attachment to place or native land" ("Literature
of Exile," p. 272). The Ulysses theme, Guillén continues, is representative of counter-exile, for it moves from the fact of separation to
integration and universality.

In like manner, but in a very different context, Julio Cortázar (a
writer whose willing departure from Argentina turned into full-fledged

political exile) tells us in an essay, "Exilio y literatura" (pp. 16–25), that he is tired of hearing about the pains and sorrows of exile, since ultimately they come from romantic and anachronistic stereotypes of the experience. Instead he calls for a recognition of the cultural and expressive benefits of exile, what he designates as "una nueva toma de realidad" (p. 21; a new seizure of reality). Exile, for an aging Cortázar fully committed to political change, is combative. It is a weapon against the regime which ironically uses banishment as its own arm, and it is a way to transform the reality of that regime into a more constructive one. Exile also offers the opportunity for a "re-view" (p. 23) of oneself and of one's culture, a vision from the outside which is part of the "marvelous cultural voyage" (p. 23) of exile. It is above all a process of questioning and reflection.

> Se trata sobre todo de indagarnos como individuos pertenecientes a pueblos latinoamericanos, de indagar por qué perdemos las batallas, por qué estamos exiliados. . . . En vez de concentrarnos en el análisis de la idiosincrasia, la conducta y la técnica de nuestros adversarios, el primer deber del exiliado debería ser el de desnudarse frente a ese terrible espejo que es la soledad de un hotel en el extranjero y allí, sin las fáciles coartadas del localismo y de la falta de términos de comparación, tratar de verse como realmente es. (pp. 23–24)

> (More than anything, it is a matter of questioning ourselves as individuals belonging to a community of Latin Americans, of asking why we lose the battles, why we are in exile. . . . Instead of concentrating on the analysis of the idiosyncrasies, the conduct, and strategy of our adversaries, the first duty of the exile is to stand naked in front of that frightening mirror of loneliness in a hotel in a foreign land, and there, without the facile excuses of localism and the lack of comparable terms, try to see oneself for what one really is.)[1]

Guillén and Cortázar, admittedly within grossly differing contexts, reach similar conclusions after beginning with the same question: in what ways is it possible for exile literature to transcend its own conventions? It is interesting that both (even Cortázar who is obsessed with the building of democracy in Argentina) see something in exile literature which is not only universal but fundamental to literature itself. They stress the inner and outer division exile brings on, a "self-construction" (Guillén, "Literature of Exile," p. 274) which unveils the tension between writer and text. Yet the initial question of both writers is as important as their conclusions, for the nostalgic structure of the Ovidian lamentation paves the way to universal expression. And in spite of the negative appraisal of nostalgia on Cortázar's part, and Guillén's distinction between exile and counter-exile, one wonders if these two forms of literature are not reciprocal. If pressed, both might agree that within the patterns of nostalgia lies the self-questioning which gives them reason to celebrate exile literature. The ambivalences of place, of time, of benefit, of harm, of the lament which leads to joy and gratitude, of the mirror which, contrary to Cortázar, may distort reality by providing no comparisons other than with the image, all these vacillations emerge in exile literature regardless of its attempt at universality. Even those writers who are known for their celebration of exile and triumph over their native lands are ambivalent about that very victory at significant points in their lives and writings.

Luis Cernuda, a man who forged a poetic ideology out of a concept of exile, is an embodiment of both Guillén's and Cortázar's thoughts, for his exilic writing is an attempt at transcendence through concrete personal and bodily experience. Indeed, Cernuda's exile transcends both politics and the privation of the native land. He is a writer who, like André Gide, whom he read and admired, welcomes separation and sets himself apart from the mainstream of society and culture. A rebel, an outcast, Cernuda read himself as an exile well before he left Spain and in exile continues to read his self-book. Yet in being willing to go into exile there is always a price, and that price is the cause of many of

Cernuda's lamentations. Politics and the homeland make their way into his writing and never completely lose their hold. At the level of poetry (the poetic conceit, word relations and associations, rhythm and sounds), the exilic vacillation between the homeland and an elsewhere testifies to the poetic principles Cernuda wishes to convey, poetic principles which are, as we shall see, life principles.[2]

Luis Cernuda was obsessed with departures, both in life, as his autobiography, *Historial de un libro* (*Dossier of a Book*) attests, and in the poetry he compiled into one integral lifework, *La realidad y el deseo* (*Reality and Desire*).[3] He relates in the *Historial* that in 1948, when he was suffering through his last days at Mount Holyoke College before a summer in Mexico, a student had told him that he should forsake the mundane comforts of his job for something more suitable to his existence as a poet. Whatever her motivations, Cernuda felt the student had given him good advice—so much so, that he recalls not only the incident but the woman's very words as somewhat of a moral imperative: "No se quede aquí, no se quede aquí" (p. 932; Do not stay here, . . .). One familiar with Cernuda's poetry could imagine these words (perhaps with a substitution of the *usted* for his archetypical *tú*) as a line of verse from *La realidad y el deseo*. Like an echo, the phrase repeats itself; the stress on the final syllable (aquí) suggests an obsession, an urge, a desire. "No se quede aquí" reveals the restlessness of Cernuda's life as well as his poetry. His speakers always seem to be drawn away from where they stand. His appropriation of a dialogue between student and teacher (in addition to the compelling and haunting nature of the advice) are emblematic of the condition of exile he endures and celebrates from the moment he begins his life and his book of poems.

Like many displaced Spaniards of the post-Civil War years, such as the members of Cernuda's generation of poets (Rafael Alberti, Jorge Guillén, Manuel Altolaguirre, Emilio Prados), Luis Cernuda found it impossible to return to a fascist Spain. What was originally intended as a brief stay in England turned out to be Cernuda's definitive departure from his native land, a land to which he would never return. While his exile was not political in the strict sense, that is, he was never officially expelled nor was his life ever in danger when he was in Spain, his departure was guided indirectly by political motivations. He had sided with the Republic against the Francoists and had gone as far as expressing sympathies with the Spanish Communist Party, because, as he said in his *Historial*, "las injusticias sociales que conocía en España necesitaban reparación" (p. 256; social injustices which I knew in Spain called for reparation). But Cernuda's political allegiances were never a motivating force behind his poetry, as was the case with Alberti. The "reality" of his *Reality and Desire* may have had social dimensions, but social ills and, above all, their reparation never seemed to be of major concern to Cernuda. As a matter of fact Cernuda considered himself useless in the struggle for social change (p. 256). Can one, then, explain the poet's ostracism by those literati who had the blessing of the regime after the war? How also does one account for the frequently vehement, at times repudiative, tone of the depictions of his native land: "España ha muerto" (p. 251; Spain has died); "escribir en España no es llorar, es morir" (p. 220; to write in Spain is not to cry but to die); "mira cuántos traidores / Mira cuántos cobardes" (p. 213; Look how many traitors / Look how many cowards); "toda hiel sempiterna del español terrible" (p. 208; all the eternal bile of the terrible Spaniard); "asqueados de la bajeza humana" (p. 524; disgusted by human baseness)?

That Cernuda was a contaminating and dangerous element according to the Franco regime, and even to the literary establishment of the forties, is not perplexing if one considers the intellectual climate in the aftermath of the Civil War: with few exceptions, the members of the Generation of 1927 along with Cernuda were forced to flee, left of their own accord, or, in the case of Lorca, died at the hands of the insurgents. Yet the situation in Spain at this time does not fully explain Cernuda's acute disaffection for Spanish life. Cernuda's exile is reciprocal, for in some of his texts he plays the role of judge, the official who accuses his land of a crime and thus initiates a process of expulsion. To comprehend Cernuda's rejection of his homeland and, in turn, the land's banishment of Cernuda, one must consider the poet's own moral and poetic code. The life work of Cernuda is, in essence, an elaboration of this code, the verbal manifestation of exile. *Historial de un libro* and *La realidad y el deseo* are the life texts of Cernuda, and they add to the many exilic journeys which permeate Spanish post-Civil War literature.

Dossier of a Book

Poetry, life, reality, and desire are the principal themes of the poet's account of his life, *Dossier of a Book* (*Reality and Desire*). Cernuda's autobiography is, as the title suggests, the text of a text; it is the life of his poetry. Its parenthetical annotation is the title he gave to his complete book of poems, beginning with *Perfil del aire* (1927) and ending with *Desolación de la quimera* (1962).[4] The desire for wholeness manifested in this amassing of his life work under one title, as well as the designation of his life as a book, synthesizes Cernuda's conception of poetry. To write a poem is to write life. His conception is not, however, that a poem imitates or reproduces an experience; poetry is itself experience. In the autobiography the life book of poems is itself a metaphor for the poet and vice versa. For Cernuda writing poetry is a bodily activity. The mainstay of this life writing is the necessary separation of the body from the text on the one hand, and the desire for completeness and integration on the other. In Cernuda's scheme desire is not only an urge for duplication, it precipitates exile in ways that are both unique to the poet and social.

While the *Historial* is at first glance a factual and chronological rendition of the poet's life, it does not lack narrative devices. In the first paragraph Cernuda addresses himself directly to the reader and suggests that in fact there may be more to this "dossier" than meets the eye. He excuses himself for having to relate certain painful life events, but these incidents are parts of the poems themselves, and it is up to the reader to establish the connections between the autobiography and *La realidad* (p. 898). Paradoxically, however, as the reader begins to detect the connections, the distance between Cernuda and his poems seems to grow. Not only has he divided himself into two (author and character), as he does in the poems with the *yo* and the *tú*, his character seems to be driven by a transcendental urge over which the author has no control.

In the *Historial* Cernuda creates a man (himself) who is the guiding force in the development of his own poetry, a man whose poetic vocation reveals itself to him at a young age. Three moments, says the author, determined the flowering of this poet-character: the reading of Bécquer as a child, puberty, and an almost mystical experience that occurred one afternoon on horseback outside of Seville when he was fulfilling his military service. Of that experience, he relates that for the first time in his life he was able to communicate with his surrounding objects, and that at that instant he felt an urgency of expression, a need to convey the experience. As a result his first poems were born, none of which, he takes care to mention, have survived (pp. 898–99). Not only are these opening paragraphs filled with literary devices (the number three, the image of the future poet on horseback, the magical ability of the character to retain the verses of Bécquer, the linking of the sacred and the profane—poetry and sexual awakening), they represent both the character's and the text's rite of passage: a poet is born and baptized and, at the same time, the text has undergone its own initiation ritual. The beginning of the autobiography marks the social split between the protagonist and his world; the difference between the poet and his peers has been realized and accepted. After establishing the uniqueness of the poet, the author can describe the genesis of the poems.

The *Historial* is the story of a man who seems to be in flight from the very moment he is born. It is filled with accounts of movements, changes, and splits all set into play by a natural force which seems to beckon the poet at every turn. At one point in his life book the subject speaks as if he were engaged in a dialogue with himself. He describes the movement of his poetry from one phase to another as a process of "mutation."

> Importa que el poeta se de cuenta de cuándo acaba una fase y comienza otra en su desarrollo espiritual; mientras el poeta está vivo, es decir, mientras no se agote su capacidad creadora, esa mutación ocurre de modo natural, como la de las estaciones del año, nutriéncose de cuanto le depara nuestro vivir. (p. 914)

> (It is important that the poet be aware of when one phase of spiritual development ends and another begins; as long as the poet is alive, that is to say, as long as the creative potential has not run out, this mutation will occur as naturally as the changes in the seasons, nourishing itself with what life provides.)

He reiterates that in his life these mutations were spawned by the repeated journeys from one country to another and by the essential adaptation required for each successive change of circumstances.

The poet vacillates in his adaptation to foreign lands, and that vacillation is depicted in his poetic portrayal of those lands. The cultures which served as his temporary homes (Paris, London, the northeastern United States, Mexico) are pictured in the *Historial* as positive and negative, helpful and harmful, inspiring and boring. The poet's task in each setting is to replace the vacuum of exile with alien influences and texts. Adaptability is marked by the integration and assimilation of a language of foreign poets, as the aliens become allies. For this poet, as for many exile writers, the literature of the adopted land becomes an essential tool in his poetic unfolding. The *Historial* is thus also a reading of foreign cowriters (Hölderlin, Gide, Eluard, Browning, and Coleridge) and an account of the formal search for an authentic poetic voice through unfamiliar tropes and patterns, a prosody which seems odd to Spanish poetic sensibilities. Again the autobiographer stresses the oddity of his poet-character among his peers. He describes the peculiar mechanics that played a part in the construction of some of his poems and the precise ways in which outside influences, especially Hölderlin, paved the way for rhythms that were unique when compared to other Spanish poems of the same generation (p. 927). Given this and other explanations of poetic construction in the light of Cernuda's poetry, it is easy for the reader, particularly the reader-critic, to make the link between character and author. Yet the connection occurs through an intertextual comparison of a variety of factors: Cernuda's own poems, what he says about them in his *Dossier*, Hölderlin, Spanish prosody, and German and British prosody. The readerly task of integration between character and author comes about by separating and comparing texts. The suggestion is, thus, that the poet-character enjoys a myriad of cultural identities.

By the same token, the adoption of a new language is undertaken by one who defines himself as "inadaptado" (p. 937), unsuited to the immediate circumstances. In his remembrance of the unfavorable reception of *Perfil del aire*, the protagonist cites the maxim which advises the cultivation of "that which others censure" and maintains that he has lived this proverb well throughout his life and his poetry (p. 904). He further submits that he has always acted in disaccord with the environment in which he finds himself, an urge he defines aesthetically as well as existentially. He characterizes this spirit of rebellion as a desire to escape from the tedious modes of literary complacency (p. 937). The poet strays purposefully from Spain, from society's norms, from literary norms, and this departure is ironically an attempt at recovery and belonging. His wandering manifests a search both inward and outward, a longing for integration and separation.

> Siempre padecí del sentimiento de hallarme aislado . . . la vida estaba más allá de donde yo me encontrara; de ahí el afán constante de partir, de irme a otras tierras, afán nutrido desde la niñez por lecturas de viajes a comarcas remotas. Y sólo el amor alivió

ese afán, dándome la seguridad de pertenecer a una tierra, de no ser en ella un extranjero, un intruso. (pp. 936–37)

(I always suffered from finding myself isolated . . . life was always beyond where I found myself; from thence the constant desire to depart, to go to other lands, a wish which was nourished by readings about journeys to remote places. And only love relieved this yearning, giving me the security of belonging to a land, of not being a foreigner within it, an intruder.)

In this passage the speaker offsets the suffering and alienation that results from his wandering by the security he finds in his desire to belong. The suffering he describes is a longing to be where he is not. Yet love, the embodiment of this very yearning and anguish, is a reassurance.

The flight of the poet in Cernuda's *Historial* is also prompted by societal rejection. The tone switches frequently from lofty declarations about the search for love through poetry to a defense of the protagonist's own poems in the light of critical disapproval. He answers the charge that his first volume of poems was an imitation of Jorge Guillén (p. 903); his own persecution appears to him in a recurring nightmare (p. 919); he chastises those who believe "El joven marino" ("The Young Sailor") is his best poem (p. 915); and he recalls that the errata of *Como quien espera el alba* were of great consternation to him (p. 931). The unrecognized author of *La realidad y el deseo* is a constant presence in *El historial*, since the references to *Perfil del aire*, "El joven marino," and *Como quien espera* are obviously to real texts. Yet Cernuda adds commentaries by another Cernuda, the poet-character of *El historial*, the one for whom laurels, admiration, and fame are unworthy goals. The Cernuda whose career is unsuccessful (according to the autobiography) conflicts with the one whose object of desire goes well beyond a career. Society seems to have rejected the author of *La realidad*, while a higher force, the force of love, accepts the other Cernuda, the one reproduced in the *Historial*. The protagonist of this life story is a man born of poetry itself: "escribo estas páginas no tanto para ver cómo hice mis poemas, sino, como dice Goethe, cómo me hicieron ellos a mí" (p. 938; I write these pages in order to understand not so much how I made my poems, but, as Goethe says, how they made me). These words refer not only to a creative process, but to Cernuda's very autobiography. Poetry makes the poet just as *La realidad* determines the *Historial*. Cernuda's reversal of the conventional notion that poets construct poetry further affirms the division between himself, the author of *La realidad*, and the autobiographer of the *Historial* who submits, "no siempre he sabido o podido mantener la distancia entre el hombre que sufre y el poeta que crea" (p. 938; I have not always been able to maintain the distance between the man who suffers and the poet who creates). The space between these two Cernudas is a further mark of the ambivalence of exile texts; it is the region in which rejection and acceptance and the dual urge for flight and for the security of the home are one and the same.

The author of the *Historial* ends the story of his poet-character with an anecdote that happened, ironically, during a baptism, perhaps as an urge to return the rite of passage which initiated the text. The baptism is perhaps incidental, reminiscent of the three moments in the poet's life which together represent the epiphany of his poetry. The author relates that after the church celebration the poet's father threw out the traditional *pelón* (coins) for all the youngsters and friends. At that point each of the invited guests, with the exception of the poet's sister Ana, madly began to appropriate as much of the booty as possible. When asked why she did not participate, Ana answered, " 'estoy esperando a que acaben' " (p. 938; I am waiting for them to finish). The poet interprets this gesture as a family trait which has guided his ethical and aesthetic behavior throughout his life: an unwillingness to play along with the world's egotistical banalities and the ingenuous hope that something will be left after the game has ended. The anecdote is also the culmination of the life story, a narrative justification for a life and another moral (as well as aesthetic) defense against the ostracism of exile. The text ends with the words, "character is destiny," reminiscent of the student who told Cernuda, " 'Do not stay here.' " Indeed, these are the words of Cernuda's fate, the force that guides him on an exilic flight to himself.

12 Exilic Reality and Desire

Cernuda's phrase, "character is destiny," is reminiscent of the Freudian dictum, "anatomy is destiny," for in Cernuda's poetry character and anatomy seem to go hand in hand. There is something strangely anatomical about his conception of the life poems of *Reality and Desire*. The force of desire has led him and his poems along their respective paths, and his conviction that he must be true to that desire in spite of the anguish involved is the guiding motif of his work. Critical attention to Cernuda's poetry has centered on the integration of a world view, ideals to which the poet fervently adhered throughout his life, and his life-text.[1] Cernuda and his writing naturally inspire this kind of approach. His conviction that the formal dimensions of a poem should always serve a higher purpose, a goal that is as spiritual as it is philosophical, is realized in all the volumes of *La realidad*, including the early poems. But the synthesis of life and worldview with text is indeed a difficult and nebulous one, because even in the single-minded Cernuda there are inconsistencies, paradoxes, and ambivalences emerging not so much from the contradictions in his life and principles but from his language, a language which is itself nebulous, intangible, constantly turning on itself. In fact, one might say that the tension in Cernuda's poetry emerges from the unyielding nature of his own poetic principles, rules which paradoxically proclaim the plurality of signification. As the poems themselves attest, his words tend to wander from a single meaning in an attempt to reach a poetic nirvana, not unlike that experience on horseback one afternoon in Seville. My reading of *La realidad y el deseo* focuses on three of these recurring and multifaceted words as signposts in Cernuda's exilic journey: desire, oblivion, and land.

Desire

Un desear atávico te atrajo
Aquí, madura la mañana,
Niño ya no, ni hombre todavía.
(p. 340)

(An atavistic yearning brought you
here, in the late morning,
no longer a child, and not yet a man.)

In *La realidad y el deseo* Cerruda writes about the force which set his life and poetry into motion from the beginning of his memory. The numerous metaphorical and metonymical designations of desire, "brisa" (p. 39; breeze), "rosa" (pp. 54, 67; rose), "estrellas" (p. 104; stars), "grito" (p. 114; a cry), "extender la mano" (p. 118; to extend the hand), "una pregunta" (p. 123; a question), underscore the theme's importance as well as the turmoil and conflict it creates. Desire displaces the poet at the outset, for his urge is illicit. Cernuda boldly casts his homosexuality, a condition he never denied, into his book of life poems. Homosexuality defines the nature of his desire as a force unlike that of others and as an object of society's scorn. The poet's need to transgress, however, asserts itself constantly, not as an apology but as a triumph, proof of his own transcendence of the world's banalities.

Por ello en vida pagarás largamente
La ocasión de ser fiel contigo y unos pocos,
Aunque jamás sepan los otros que desvío
Siempre es razón mejor ante la grey.
(p. 324)

(For this you shall pay dearly
the opportunity to live up to yourself and to a select few,
although others may never know that transgression
is always reason enough when confronted by the herd.)

The didactic tone of these lines from "Aplauso humano," typical of many of Cernuda's poems, jars with their message. What in the eyes of the "herd" is deviant and repugnant becomes virtuous in the eyes and words of the poet. Homosexuality is both the reason he will have to pay the harsh price of ostracism and the opportunity to remain loyal to his own nature. It separates him and at the same time renders him complete. The elusiveness of these words, also representative of Cernuda's references to homosexuality ("ello," "ocasión," "desvío," and "razón mejor"), indicates the taboo associated with homosexual behavior as well as the poet's wish to focus not so much on the act, or even the pleasure of the act, but on its motivating force. In an earlier poem, "Dire cómo nacisteis" ("I'll Tell You How You Were Born") from *Los placeres prohibidos*, homosexuality is never the object of description but always a possibility: "tu deseo es beber esas hojas lascivas," (p. 117; your desire is to drink those lascivious leaves).[2]

Cernuda embraces the uniqueness and aberrance of his own desire and the separation it inflicts. Paradoxically, the desire of exile is also a yearning for oneness with a home in which love burns perpetually. The paradox embodied in Cernuda's love taboo is emblematic of the conceptual contradictions in much of his poetry. In *Un río, un amor* desire is a natural force compared to the wind, sea, flowers, clouds, water, and heavenly bodies. The very words of the title, with the repetition of *un*, are a transcription of the object of the poet's yearning, a narcissistic desire of desire. Yet the inward direction of this desire, a longing to find the heart of the heart or the home of the home, cannot lead to a sense of wholeness. On the contrary, its end result is a split: the object of desire needs a subject to realize it and vice versa.

Throughout *La realidad y el deseo* desire is the lens Cernuda employs to view his own present and past experience. The urge to look at himself results in one of the most characteristic features of his exilic desire: an ongoing dialogue between the two voices of love (the *yo* and the *tú*). All of love's trials, the suffering, the losses, the separations, and at the same time the joys and gains, stem from the poet's desire of himself, a want which is, as we have seen in the *Historial*, a pursuit of wholeness and a sense of belonging. The dialogue between Cernuda's two selves is a lovers' discourse whose pronouns affirm both the dependence and independence of the speakers. The linguistic division, however, renders the realization of desire an impossibility. In a sense Cernuda has been exiled to the prison of language. For him, poetry is a celebration of desire, yet the very language of that desire erases the possibility of its fulfillment.

Especially in the later poetry, but in the initial phases of *La realidad* as well, the *yo* hungers for a *tú*. Reflections in shadows, windows, and eyes are pervasive images which provide the scenery for the love dialogue. In a poem which encapsulates the entire enterprise of *La realidad*, "Música cautiva" (p. 472; "Captive Music"), music provides the background for the discourse. The poem is dedicated to "two voices."

> 'Tus ojos son los ojos de un hombre enamorado;
> Tus labios son los labios de un hombre que no cree
> en el amor.' 'Entonces dime el remedio, amigo,
> Si están en desacuerdo realidad y deseo.'
> (p. 472)

> ("Your eyes are the eyes of a man in love;
> your lips are the lips of a man who does not believe
> in love." "In that case, friend,
> tell me the remedy if reality and desire are in disaccord.")

In this text the initial split between the *yo* and the *tú* seems to breed further splits: eyes in love versus lips that do not believe in love, the object of desire (amigo) versus disaccord, reality versus desire. The poet remains captive of his own desire and of his own music, his poetry. The search for a remedy to the dilemma is exasperating; it is the catalyst for the poet's restlessness. The hope of transforming desire into reality is a wish whose result is exile: both the source and the end of the lovers' discourse.

The conceptual conflicts within the realm of desire lead to structural contradictions in Cernuda's poetry. These inconsistencies are further marks of the linguistic manifestations of exile, or the text in exile from itself. In the early stages of his career, Cernuda found in surrealism the aesthetic authority to affirm his own poetic incongruencies. The ideas of the European avant garde offered him a vehicle to avoid simple apprehension of his words, to liberate his language from the constraining forces of meaning. But surrealism went even further in that it provided Cernuda with a partial satisfaction of his wanderlust. The French resonances of the movement, the taste for transgression, and the willingness to allow the text to stray from conventional significations were appealing to this lost Andalusian poet in search of a home. Desire, the reigning force in Cernuda's displacement, was also consistent with the interests of the Parisian surrealists.[3]

A case in point is "Como el viento" from *Un río, un amor*. The word "deseo" never appears yet the existential and linguistic displacement it engenders is typical of the early poetry:

> Como el viento a lo largo de la noche,
> Amor en pena o cuerpo solitario,
> Toca en vano a los vidrios,
> Sollozando abandona las esquinas;
> O como a veces en la tormenta,
> Gritando locamente,
> Con angustia de insomnio,
> Mientras gira la lluvia delicada;
> Sí, como el viento al que un alba le revela
> Su tristeza errabunda por la tierra,

Su tristeza sin llanto,
Su fuga sin objeto;
Como él mismo extranjero,
Como el viento huyo lejos.
Y sin embargo vine como la luz.
(p. 90)

(Like the wind through the night,
painful love or lonely body,
it vainly touches the windowpane;
weeping, it abandons the corners
or at times like a storm
crying desperately
with the anguish of an insomniac
while the delicate rain swirls;
yes, like the wind to whom a dawn reveals
its errant sadness through the land,
its sadness without tears,
its escape without a goal;
like the foreigner himself,
like the wind, I flee far away.
Yet I came like the light.)

The poem is structured upon an asymmetrical equation in which one side is absent. The poet's desire (the invisible side of the equation) unmasks its identity purely by suggestion: the repetition of "como" followed by a variety of images associated with the wind. The wind's power arises from its ability to move, to unsettle the world (as the surrealists wished to do) throughout its travels: "sollozando," "gritando," "tristeza errabunda." The poet ascribes these powers to himself. Even before the final verse, human qualities of the wind ("tristeza," "fuga," "llanto") prepare the way for the poet's identification with it. Like the wind, the poet is a foreigner ("extranjero") and a fugitive ("fuga sin objeto"). "Huyo lejos," he declares, since he must act in accordance with the wind's natural laws. Wind, desire, and poet unite to become a life force in their flight away from their present locus.

The most jarring feature of the poem is the last line. Up to this point (lines 1–12) all the objects which play a role in the drama of desire are in commotion; but the confusion remains within the poet's (and the reader's) grasp. In contrast, the language of the final verse throws chaos into further chaos. "Sin embargo" posits a contradiction, a conflict with something that was already in conflict. The preterit "vine" jolts the temporal reference of the poem out of the present in which it comfortably resided, thereby questioning the very situation of the poem. In contrast to the wind, the appearance of "luz," with its godlike definite article, belies the fragmentation which set the tone for the body of the poem. Typically surrealistic, this last line is marginal; it seems unwilling to stay within the bounds of the poem as a whole. "Como el viento" is a discourse on the asymmetry of asymmetry and, in the last analysis, the exile of exile.

While the later poems of Cernuda are not as radically hostile to interpretation as some of the early ones, the opposing forces of desire are apparent throughout his writing. The tone of Cernuda's postexile poetry is, for the most part, reflective, as the subject, now an outsider, looks in on a lost desire. Yet the objectification of his life yearning results, ironically, in more ambivalence and division. In "Vereda del cuco" (*La realidad*, pp. 340–43; The Cuckoo's Path), one of Cernuda's most extensive reflections on desire, the poet compares himself to a bird moving along a path in search of water. The structure is uneven and unveils a series of synthetic contrasts whose paradoxical and illusory unity is another linguistic marker of the exilic condition. Past blends with present from beginning to end: "Cuántas veces has ido en otro tiempo / Camino de esta fuente" (lines 1–2; How many times have you followed / the path to this fountain at another time). The present of "this fountain" is also part of the poet's past. The subject's age is itself ambiguous, as in the previously cited verses, "niño ya no, ni hombre todavía" (line 18). The speaker is reticent as he travels along his path, but his pauses help him understand the thirst of his desire, which is at once sweet and bitter (line 29). The bittersweetness of past momentary satisfactions of desire marks the present experience of the poet's contemplation of the path. He watches himself battle with a shadow in order to reach a light, at which point (lines 34–35) he drinks the coveted water. But the water does not quench his thirst; on the contrary, it produces an even greater thirst (line 35). At the very center of the poem the lines treating the risk one must take to satisfy desire, "Para que sea perdido, Para que sea ganado" (p. 341; So that it may be lost, so that it may be won), pinpoint the paradox of the poem in its entirety: the loss and gain of following one's desire. The seemingly didactic tone of the poem, an affirmation of the need to realize one's desire, fades as it turns to the ambivalence of this very pursuit: "tormento divino" (line 68; divine torment), "silencio sonoro" (line 74; loud silence), "soledad poblada" (line 75; crowded solitude), "alba o noche" (line 77; dawn or night), "olvido o memoria" (line 78; oblivion or memory), "aceptando la muerte para crear la vida" (line 99; accepting death to create life), "muere y nace" (line 113; dies and is born). The presence of desire reveals itself through absence; similarly, to be in exile is to think oneself both present and absent. The concept of absence and the exile's futile search for presence is a trademark of Cernuda's language and, as some have suggested, an inherent paradox in language itself.

Oblivion

> Allá, allá lejos;
> Donde habite el olvido.
> (p. 150)

> (There, there far away,
> where oblivion dwells.)

Memory and its counterpart, oblivion, occupy important places in Cernuda's poetry. Not only do they provide Cernuda with essential components in the interplay between reality and desire, they embody the very act of writing. Just as the tenuousness of reality as illusory wish fulfillment frustrates the poet at every turn, so memory fills the vacuum of oblivion with imperfect copies in writing of what was once real. "¿Adónde va el amor cuando se olvida?" (Where does love go when it is forgotten?) Cernuda asks in a poem he titled "Old Question, Old Answer" (p. 485). To fill the abyss of oblivion with words is no consolation, for the poet is painfully aware that he has not re-created a reality, the ideal for which he thirsts, but has strayed further from it. For one such as Cernuda whose experience of exile is metaphysical, moral, and sexual as well as political, oblivion is a haunting and obsessive concept which engenders a fundamental question to which there is no response. Oblivion is one of the most distressing symptoms of those inflicted with the infirmity of exile, an existence rooted in an unverifiable past.[4]

The remembrance of a lost land, a home whose comforts and discomforts comprise much of the subject matter of Cernuda's later poetry, is evident even before his ultimate departure from Spain. In the early poetry oblivion takes a different form, but it is no less apparent than in the later volumes. In some poems, "¿Dónde huir?" (p. 44; "Where to Flee?"), "Destierro" (p. 88; "Exile"), "¿De qué país?" (p. 133; "From What Country?"), Cernuda seems to anticipate his own voice in exile, an expression which will crystallize into a tangible social experience with *Las nubes*. The geographic images of Cernuda's poems, however, are frequent throughout *La realidad y el deseo*. Cernuda speaks of oblivion in spatial terms; it is a cloudy locus conjured by the poet's incantations. Oblivion is a place, a dwelling for the nonexistent. The exotic place names of *Un río, un amor* such as Daytona, Durango, Nevada, Virginia, apparently inspired by jazz music (*Historial*, p. 909), are Cernuda's phonetic copies of the residence of things lost.

> Dentro de breves días será otoño en Virginia . . . .
> Ahora inútil pasar la mano sobre otoño.
> (p. 109)

(In a few days it will be autumn in Virginia . . . .
Now it is useless to pass your hand over autumn.)

In Virginia, as in Daytona, Durango, and Nevada, Cernuda evokes a geography of the mind as well as a yearning to realize it.

Sólo un lugar existe, cuyos días
Nada saben de aquello
Aunque todo allí sea mortal, el miedo, hasta las plumas;
Mas las olas abrazan a tanta luz aun viva. . . .
Olvidado fantasma con su collar de frío.
Mirad cómo sonríe hacia el amor Daytona.
(p. 51)

(Only one place exists, whose days
know nothing of all that,
though all there is mortal; fear, even feathers, yet the waves
embrace so much light still alive . . . .
Forgotten chimera with its collar of coldness.
Look at how Daytona smiles at love.)

In Cernuda's longest sustained discourse on oblivion, the volume of poems titled *Donde habite el olvido*, the word "donde" underscores the poet's conception of forgetfulness. The first poem (p. 150) in the collection sets the mood and defines the subject matter for the others. "Where" is an anaphoric conceit frequently followed by a plethora of verbs in the subjunctive (lines 3, 6, 8, 10, 17). The concept of a hypothetical dwelling place of oblivion structures this poem and engenders a variety of images, all of which evoke the nebulousness of oblivion itself: "gardens without dawn" (line 2), "a forgotten stone in the nettles" (line 4), "mist" (line 20). As the poet confirms through his repetition of the word "absence" (lines 20–21), what was at one time a land, a love, a memory, is no longer. Yet the absence is not absolute; it is a "leve ausencia" (light absence) whose trace is still felt "como carne de niño" (like the flesh of a child). The knowledge of the former existence of the forgotten—to know that at one time the forgotten took shape—intensifies the pains of oblivion. Absence characterizes the tone of this initial poem as well as the condition of exile, and there is a yearning for an elsewhere: "allá, allá lejos" (line 22).

Donde habite el olvido is filled with transparent images, typically surrealistic conceits which are statements on the formlessness of oblivion. Water, wind, clouds, and shadows occupy the space of forgetfulness in what the poet calls at one point "una verdad transparente" (p. 164; a transparent truth). Cernuda sees through the objects in the land of oblivion as he searches for a truth which is itself intangible: "un mar delirante" (p. 157; a delirious sea), "aire tranquilo en la nada" (p. 158; still air in nothingness), "el mar es un olvido" (p. 155; the sea is a thing forgotten). These images coalesce with the phonetic qualities of this collection, especially the echo, which appears as a mental construct — "Soy eco de algo" (p. 152; I am the echo of something), but also as repetitions of sounds, words and phrases, a device more noticeable in *Donde habite el olvido* than in other collections. The echo, like something forgotten, is a representation doomed to nothingness. In its chain of mimicry it yearns to duplicate its immediate predecessor, but it cannot. Like the transparent image, the echo must always defer to another entity. It cannot contain its own form. Such is the condition of exile: always other, never complete in and of itself.

Oblivion is also a relational concept, for there is a necessary interplay between the time and space of the present and that of the past. While these relations appear metaphorically in the early poems of *Un río, un amor* and *Donde habite el olvido*, Cernuda's physical departure from his homeland spawned a renewed contemplation of oblivion, this time within unfamiliar surroundings. In the poetry of *Las nubes*, *Vivir sin estar viviendo*, *Con las horas contadas*, and *La desolación de la quimera*, objects, situations, and occurrences are more easily identifiable than in the early poems. In this later poetry Cernuda refers to a real geography in relation to one literally left behind. In these collections the reader is as aware of exile as is the poet.

The poems of *Las nubes* were written during the first years of Cernuda's life outside of Spain (1937–40), a time marked by a civil war in the peninsula and the beginning of a world war in Europe. While this poetry reaffirms the existential and ontological dilemma of the early volumes, as well as Cernuda's eternal conflict between reality and desire, the deictics, or situational markers, of the poems acknowledge the existence of a real world filled with recognizable objects and human beings. Friends, poets, cathedrals, cemeteries, parks, monuments (specifically Philip II's palace at El Escorial) play significant roles within these "clouds" of memory and oblivion. Yet the very recognition of their existence is problematic, given the poetic context in which the people and objects appear. Cernuda seeks to resurrect the lost elements of his own past through his verse:

> También mi tierra la he perdido,
> Y si hoy hablo de ti es buscando recuerdos
> En el trágico ocio del poeta
> (p. 273)

> (I have also lost my land,
> and if today I speak of you, I do so searching for remembrances
> in the tragic idleness of the poet.)

The resurrection of life elsewhere, vividly narrated in one of the dramatic poems titled "Lazarus" (pp. 246–49), is central to the structure of *Las nubes*. Recollection is, for the poet, rebirth. Yet the revived entity, whether it be Lazarus, García Lorca (p. 208), Larra (p. 219), the Escorial (p. 272), Spain (p. 223), or the poet himself as a child (p. 225), does not remain in the condition in which it departed. Remembrance necessitates an awareness of having been nonexistent, an understanding which tempers the new life and renders it ambivalent. Cernuda conceives of oblivion in terms of an analogy: it is a form of death with an awareness of life, while memory, conversely, gives new life in the wake of unforgotten death.

The tangible social experiences, as well as the resuscitation of forgotten objects, people, and events, related in Cernuda's later poetry further reveal the relational dimension of exilic writing. Comparisons between a here and a there, a now and a then, these and others, are commonplace, especially in *Vivir sin estar viviendo* and *Como quien espera el alba*. Cernuda contemplates the surroundings of his new domicile and sees the traces of things from another time and place. In the new land all seems to point in the direction of an elsewhere; things have their imperfect correspondences in another place, and the mediation between the two loci is an arduous process which is never complete. Other flowers, other springs, other winds pervade this poetry so as to create a world in which nothing is whole without a reciprocal entity from another land. In "Otros tulipanes amarillos" (p. 328; "Other Yellow Tulips"), the recollection of the poet's former homeland and a former state of mind is touched off by a glimpse of "golden tulips" in a grey, wet ground (line 6). The flowers are "como son perdido en el aire sordo" (line 7; like a lost sound in the deaf air), for they remind the speaker of similar flowers from a land he once occupied. The first two stanzas are structured around a series of correspondences between the poet's present (lines 1–7) and his past (lines 8–14): "the springtime" becomes "another spring," the "land" is transformed into "another land," and the "light rain" reappears as the "light rain" of another moment. The image of the other tulips brings to mind the painful process of their remembrance and a longing not so much for Spanish soil (the specific locus is never mentioned) as for the youthful state of mind which contemplated the flowers years ago. The poet realizes that the moment is lost and that its seeming repetition (its remembrance) is illusory. The tulips of years gone by come to life by naming them, an act which leads only to further oblivion: "éstos con cuyos nombres se alimenta el olvido" (l. 40; these whose names nourish oblivion). The poem ends on a note of resignation as the poet admonishes himself to cope with his dilemma with silence: "aprende ese silencio antes que el tiempo llegue" (l. 44; learn that silence before the time comes). Silence is like a language from another land; the poet must learn it to assimilate a new environment. Ironically, however, silence can only lead the poet more deeply into exile.

In "Otros tulipanes amarillos," as in many poems written after his departure, Cernuda creates a geography of the forgotten through the anaphoric use of demonstratives as verbal pointers to another land.[5] The land of Cernuda's poems is filled with ambiguous directional signals whose information we can ascertain only through a polyreferential thought process. In the first line of "Otros aires" (p. 385; "Other Winds"), a poem written at the moment of Cernuda's arrival in the United States from England (the second departure), the poet asks, " "¿Cómo serán los árboles aquellos?' " ("What will those trees be like?"). The verse structures the rest of the poem as it does much of the poetry from 1930 to the final volume. It is itself a reference to a question asked at another time and thereby endows the demonstrative, "aquellos," with several referents. "Those trees" were hypothetical at the moment of the original question and remain so at the time of writing. But later the hypothesis differs: the poet gazes out his window and contemplates "those trees" from a distance through the hills and plains (line 4), yet they are less remote now than when the question was first asked. Maintaining their nebulous and evocative quality, the trees in this unfamiliar setting create a series of possibilities for the poet: new friends, love, new light, a promise, inspiration. Ironically, the very unfamiliarity of the new situation to which "those trees" allude creates a sense of wholeness: "extraño nada es, sino propicio / Y familiar" (lines 15–16; nothing here is strange, rather propitious / and familiar). The Cernuda of "Otros aires" is reborn, as was Lazarus, with the remembrance of a question. But this new wholeness remains an unrealizable desire, a hypothesis: "Una promesa, ¿oyes? / Acaso está sonando" (lines 25–26; a promise perhaps is ringing, do you hear?). The signposts to the realization of the promise—"here," "there," "others," "those," "this" —render the promise all too vague. Like the land of oblivion, the place to which "over there" refers is linguistically unreachable.

While oblivion is indeed the cause of stormy agony for this post-romantic writer, there are significant moments in which forgetfulness is a conscious choice by the poet as well as by the poet's enemies. In these instances oblivion becomes a weapon, at once the exile's defense against marginality and the homeland's arm against the outsider's denunciations. Cernuda is thus the victim and the perpetrator of oblivion's harms. Especially in *Desolación de la quimera*, but also in other volumes, the poet expresses his contempt for the Spaniards who stayed and vanquished and who used indifference and oblivion to perpetuate their own power. Cernuda's bitter voice, a familiar trademark, expresses itself most harshly in reference to the arrogance of those who choose not to remember. He submits in "A sus paisanos" (p. 526; "To his Countrymen"), whom he addresses in the second person plural, that upon his death oblivion will fall on him, making his departure from this world ("nothingness") complete:

> Y entonces la ignorancia,
> La indiferencia y el olvido, vuestras armas
> De siempre, sobre mí caerán, como la piedra,
> Cubriéndome por fin, lo mismo que cubristeis
> A otros que superiores a mí, esa ignorancia vuestra
> Precipitó en la nada.
> (lines 22–27)

> (Then ignorance,
> indifference and oblivion, your weapons
> will fall on me like a rock,
> covering me at last, in the same way as you covered
> others who, superior to me, were turned to nothingness
> by your ignorance.)

Desolación de la quimera may be read as a series of painful memories (the Civil War, the reading of Galdós, the "misunderstanding" of a friend, p. 501) against which oblivion is at times a palliative, at others, a death wish. Cernuda frequently invokes his own land and upbringing as a negative force with which he has to contend from birth. "Es lástima que fuera mi tierra" (p. 476; "It's a shame that it is my land"), the first part of "Spanish Diptych," is the title of a poem in which the poet chastises his Spanish heritage as if to cast his own cultural legacy into nothingness. In "Impresión de destierro" (p. 250; "Impression of exile"), a poem from a different collection but reminiscent of *Desolación*, Spain is merely a name that Cernuda chooses not to recall. This ironic gesture, like that of Cervantes in regard to Don Quijote's home town, is political; for in reality oblivion is never willful unless there are ulterior motives. Cernuda commits an aggressive act of denial of his birthplace. Admittedly, there are poems in which Cernuda describes his land in a more positive light, such as the second part of the "Diptych," "Bien está que fuera tu tierra" (p. 480; "It Is Good That It Was Your Land"). In these verses the poet recalls another Spain, a "noble" land, in juxtaposition to the one which the immediately preceding text so viciously defames: "La real para ti no es esa España obscena y deprimente, . . . Sino esta España viva y siempre noble / Que Galdós ha creado" (lines 167–70; The real Spain for you is not that one, obscene and depressing, . . . but this Spain, alive and always noble, / the one Galdós has created). But the second part of this dual-edged poem is equally ironic in that the Spain of nobility is fictional, an invention of Galdós and Cervantes. It is the "other" Spain: "your" land, not "my" land. It is Cernuda's projection, the force he will use to cast stupidity and cruelty (line 35) into the fires of oblivion.

Cernuda's politics of forgetfulness is yet another manifestation of exile's ambivalence. Spain is a problem whose solution will never be discovered precisely because of the poet's self-contradictions. For Cernuda the land is "good," yet it is "shameful;" it is real, yet a novelist's creation. By the same token oblivion is a solution, an act strategically taken against the arrogance of power though, in the long run, it is worse than death. "¿España?" asks a voice akin to that of the poet. "Un nombre. / España ha muerto" (p. 251; Spain? A name. / Spain has died).

Land

Mucho enseña el destierro de nuestra propia tierra.
(p. 272)

(Exile teaches much of our own land.)

Tierra nativa, más mía cuanto más lejana.
(p. 289)

(Native land, all the more mine farther away.)

The realization of desire, along with the losses and gains of oblivion, have political dimensions; yet the tension between social reality and poetic language manifests itself most clearly in one of Cernuda's favorite figures: *tierra*. In the midst of a body of poetry which seems at first glance indifferent to political forces, the resonances of a specific historical problem within a designated locus echo throughout *La realidad y el deseo*. While Cernuda's land is at some points a formless space, the persistent use of the word *tierra* in a variety of contexts (country, climate, earth, homeland, family, exile) underscores a social dilemma which initiated the obsession. His poetry is indeed narcissistic, but self-contemplation divides as well as isolates and thereby creates a dialogue of voices within one. The land is the ideology and the geography in which a heated dialogue takes place.[6]

Because of Cernuda's intensely metaphysical concerns, the specific reference place for his land is at times hidden within metaphorical gardens, winds, and oceans. Particularly in the early poems, the word land has no real geographic reference; it is a land of language: "Tierra indolente . . . Junto a las aguas quietas / Sueño y pienso que vivo" (p. 61; Indolent land . . . On the edge of still waters / I dream and think that I am alive).[7] But the insistence on a locus, no matter how amorphous or fictional, orients the poems and suggests possibilities of life outside this world, much in the same way as the exotic place names of Durango and Nevada evoke the existence of an elsewhere. But as Cernuda becomes older, his elsewhere moves closer. In *Invocaciones*, *Las nubes*, and *Como quien espera el alba* the yearning for the native land is no less evident than in the nostalgic autobiography of Rafael Alberti, *Arboleda perdida*. The gardens and oceans of Cernuda's later collections are of a specific time and place. Beaches, castles, and convents take form within an identifiable geography through titles such as "un español habla de su tierra" (p. 269; "A Spaniard Speaks of his Land"), and natural features act as emblems for a specific region: "bosque de plátanos" (p. 287; a forest of plane trees), "aquella tierra llana . . . adonde el limonero suspendía su fruto entre el ramaje" (p. 289; that flat land . . . where the lemon tree suspended its fruit among the branches). The Andalusian boy of the first poem of *Invocaciones* (p. 173) is at once the object of the desire and the geography of that desire. Hills, pines of perennial happiness, a nearby ocean, a dark river, all point to a lost place, concretely the shore of "el violento Atlántico" (line 43; the violent Atlantic). In several poems Cernuda re-creates the land of childhood, the memory of which has become bitterly painful. The brooding tone of "Niño muerto" (p. 225; "Dead Child"), for example, reflects a melancholy state of mind in the face of the loss of the old home, the fields of the village, and the old gray tower.

The nostalgic desire for the setting of earlier years becomes problematic as the social reality of that time invades the privacy of those memories. A case in point is "La familia" (p. 295), a social institution as well as a force in the poet's personal history. Cernuda's memory again comes into play as he re-creates the situation in which he grew up. The yearning for the home of happier days does not set the tone of this poem; it is rather a melancholic reflection on the austerity, inhibition, and personal guilt engendered by a hierarchical Andalusian family. The poet does not accuse; instead he accepts what he has become through familial influences even though there has been a spiritual, social, and geographical falling out, a separation between himself and his kin. Now, as a man with his own code of ethics, he seeks to understand and accept.

> No prevalezcan las puertas del infierno
> Sobre vosotros ni vuestras obras de la carne,
> Oh padre taciturno que no le conociste,
> Oh madre melancólica que no le comprehendiste.
> (lines 83–86)

> (May the doors of hell not prevail on you
> nor on your deeds of the flesh,
> Oh taciturn father whom you did not know,
> oh melancholy mother whom you did not understand.)

The ethical reversal of these lines ("obras de la carne"), typical of Cernuda's moral discourse, intensifies the separation and initiates a struggle between the two mutually exclusive forces, the poet and the family.[8] The family is another manifestation of the land: "el hogar . . . el nido de todos los hombres" (lines 14–15; the home . . . the nest of all men). Like the land, the family embodies a paradoxical force which both attracts and repels the subject.

Cernuda's critique of the family implies a larger issue, a historical dilemma encompassing the complete spectrum of the politics of Spanish exile. The rigidity of the patriarchal family leads to the intolerance, tyranny, and repression of a nation. Spain as a problem pervades *La realidad y el deseo* from beginning to end in much the same way as the theme of cultural identity and national character obsesses so many Spanish liberals, some of whom, such as Larra and Galdós, appear in some poems as characters. While the poet's dialogue with his own cultural tradition at first glance binds him to it, his dissonant and dissenting voice will never allow him to join the group. Cernuda's discourse is different and brands itself as such. The writers who deal with Spain as a problem (Larra, Galdós, Machado, Unamuno) do so as representatives of a movement or an ideology. They see Spain as a paradox. They participate in the consciousness and turmoil of a nation at war with itself. But Cernuda identifies with no one, except perhaps himself. The poems about his contemporaries, such as Juan Ramón Jiménez (p. 484), stress differences, not alliances. Even his objects of literary admiration (Góngora, Larra, Galdós, Lorca) do not take the form of allies in an ideological battle. They lose their identity; they are devices in service of the subject's poetic manipulation, for in the long run Cernuda's dialogue with his own tradition has been cut off. Exile, well before his departure from Spain, has rendered him eternally other.

The poetry dealing with Spain unveils opposing voices and social postures; it is difficult, if not impossible, to identify a consistent political stand on anything. Cernuda glorifies the history of his land with the remembrance of the Escorial ("El ruiseñor sobre la piedra"; "Nightingale on the Stone") and in another poem he extols the timelessness imposed by Philip II in the monarch's effort to create eternal harmony (p. 388). But in both texts the poet speaks as an outsider who can admire the virtues of his land only because of his position from outside: "mucho enseña el destierro de nuestra propia tierra." The poet feigns the voice of a foreigner who is able to look beyond the shortcomings of another culture (in reality his own) in order to find universal value.

Strangely coupled with these admiring odes is a selection of poems in diametric opposition, texts which characterize another Cernuda. The poet lashes out with a series of invectives, accusations, and curses all directed at the homeland. In these texts, "A un poeta muerto" (p. 208; "For a Dead Poet"), "Ser de Sansueña" (p. 386; "Being from Sansueña"), "Limbo" (p. 432), and "Díptico español," Cernuda assaults his own nation with a vengeance not found in other Spanish intellectuals who deal with similar issues. For Cernuda, being as concerned as he always is with origins and identity, the problem is not so much the social errors and injustices of his country but that he, a Spaniard by birth, must endure the shame of being Spanish. The attachment to a land is, in this case, not as much a condition but a being, as the title, "Ser de Sansueña," illustrates. Cernuda's native being will always provide a link to the Spanish soil, however tenuous, however abhorrent.

> Si soy español, lo soy
> A la manera de aquéllos que no pueden
> Ser otra cosa: y entre todas las cargas
> Que al nacer yo, el destino pusiera
> Sobre mí, ha sido ésa la más dura.
> No he cambiado de tierra
> Porque no es posible a quien su lengua une,
> Hasta la muerte, al menester de poesía.
> (p. 477)

> (If I am Spanish, I am so
> in the way of those who can
> be nothing else: and among all the burdens
> which destiny has given me upon birth,
> that one has been the most difficult.
> I have not changed my land [identity]
> because it is not possible for one who is bound
> by one's language
> until death to the craft of poetry.)

The Spaniard who wishes he were not, as Cernuda calls himself (p. 478), responds to the oblivion in which his land cast him with the vicarious pleasure of deeming that land unreal: through poetry he writes the land out of existence. While the land of Galdós is real, the nation that murdered Lorca, the land of the censors and the terrible Spaniards (p. 208), is a "limbo." Cernuda wishes destruction and fire on his land at one point (p. 433), and toward the end of his life, he seems to write as if the act of annihilation has been carried out: "Soy, sin tierra" (p. 527; I am without land).

The paradoxical and self-contradictory Spain over which Unamuno, Machado, and others of that generation brooded is not part of Cernuda's scenario, for his land is neither paradoxical nor self-contradictory. The paradox, self-contradiction, and ambivalence are not of the land but of the language. Home is no longer subject to change, no longer a region of social conflict and struggle. In the language of the exile, time within the land has ceased; everything is as it was. Home is now a metaphor, an eternal force pushing and pulling but never changing.

Cernuda's account of his own land's history does not claim accuracy, nor does it even pretend to offer a penetrating discourse on the ambiguities and tensions of his own culture, as many of his peers have done. Rather, it is a self-critique, a rendition of his own life on, through, and away from the land. It is also another manifestation of the lover's discourse, this time between the subject and the land, the elusive object of love. Like the dialogue with himself, Cernuda's appraisal of his land is a discourse which constantly turns on itself and questions its own motivations, as politics and social history become faint traces of a past, influences almost lost. Cernuda's introspection seems so pervasive that at times one wonders where the social issues of exile, the concrete conditions which set the process into motion, have gone. But for Cernuda the language of social history is the language of poetry; and by the same token the language of verse is the idiom of a fleeting personal history, the "dossier of a book."

V

Self-Exile: Juan Goytisolo

"When a person leaves,

it is because he has already gone." —Luis Cernuda

13   Exilic Signs of Identity

Nietzsche said in *The Use and Abuse of History* that when we read our own past, we become "gravediggers of the present" (p. 7). We deceive ourselves by thinking of the past as a tangible and immutable entity when in reality, history can only be understood in terms of fiction and imagination. To counter these abuses of history, he posits the concept of "the unhistorical man": one who is aware of historical processes yet has "the power, the art, of forgetting" them. In some ways the exile is caught in a Nietzschean bind, for by definition he or she is a slave of history, a history which, because of exilic distance, seems to lose its shape, its tangibility. The designation, "gravedigger of the present," serves as an apt description of many exiles, especially those who depart for political reasons. Yet by the same token, exile is a perfect place to engage in the self-conscious act, "the art, of forgetting," or ridding oneself of historical baggage. Brecht seemed aware of the problem when he advised his exilic subject (himself) "don't nail anything on the wall." Brecht was in a state of suspended animation in Denmark, and although he may have been at political odds with Nietzsche, he seemed to intuit the German philosopher's critique of history as he went into exile.

Similarly, the novels of James Joyce (an exile in his own right) may be read as historical negations, attempts to do away with a constraining, sterile, and dogmatic personal and social history. In *Portrait of the Artist*, Joyce writes the story of one who actively seeks the death of his own past through an exploration of that very past (the autobiographical trappings of the novel notwithstanding). Joyce's represents a uniquely modern form of exile: self-exile—a willful search, not unlike that of Cernuda, for the freedom from national origins, and as a consequence, from the linguistic and literary modes of a specific place or time. Oblivion is not always passive, and as an art (in Nietzsche's sense) the will to forget leads to a linguistic process of creation in which the very notion of creative representation is questioned. Many self-exiles force themselves to stand alone, as Cortázar called for, without their former tools and to perceive the new environment as a self-contained world where the relation between the sign and its referent becomes the relation between the sign and other signs.[1]

Among writers of contemporary Spanish fiction it is indisputably Juan Goytisolo whose work and life most clearly display the patterns of self-exile. For him exile has been a liberating experience; it has led him not only to places far from the Iberian Peninsula, including the Arab world, but to a new way of writing and seeing. Yet Goytisolo's act of self-exile, an attempt to rid himself of a former life through active forgetfulness, has been a difficult one. His case shows that just as it is impossible for the exile to return intact, to the place of origin, it is equally difficult for the self-exile to strip him or herself completely of a former existence—the signs of identity. The attempt, however, is worthy of consideration, for the tension between success and failure leads back to one of the most crucial issues in exile literature: the obliteration of a former identity.

It is no wonder that one of Goytisolo's favorite Spanish writers and source of his inspiration is Luis Cernuda. Goytisolo has said, publicly and in writing, that Cernuda is one of the few Spanish exiles who was able to benefit from the experience. In his essay on José María Blanco White he states that most Spanish romantics in exile from the tyranny of Ferdinand VII were unable to convert the exilic experience into a nourishing one ("Presentación crítica," pp. 84–86). Goytisolo sees both Blanco and Cernuda as exceptions. He goes so far as to use

Cernuda's life poetry as an implement of both destruction and a search: "Mejor la destrucción, el fuego" (better destruction, fire), a verse from Cernuda's poem "Limbo," is an epigraph to Goytisolo's novel, *Señas de identidad* (*Signs of Identity*). It is also emblematic of his will to rid himself of his own culture. The parallel between Goytisolo and Cernuda is an apt one, for the catalyzing force in both writers is animosity and conflict, a struggle which has political roots but turns into an existential, moral, even sexual separation from the mainstream, any mainstream: Franco's Spain, democratic Spain, or even that of the Spanish exile's archetypal refuge, Paris. As Goytisolo reads Cernuda, he writes his own disaffection and creates for himself a niche on the margins of both society and literature: "estoy definitivamente al otro lado con los parias de siempre" (*Juan sin tierra*, p. 320; I am definitively on the other side with the pariahs of always).

Paul Ilie has rightly observed, in his analysis of Goytisolo as both an inner exile and a self-exile, that there are generational issues to consider in understanding the intellectual exodus from Spain after the Civil War (*Literature and Inner Exile*, pp. 115–16). Goytisolo's career began relatively early and his direct experience of the war itself was almost nil, since he was only four years old when the fighting began. Given that Goytisolo belongs to the so-called mid-century generation of Spanish writers,[2] his exile encompasses a variety of historical stages and he stands behind and in direct relation to the original group of banished Spaniards who left during or immediately after the conflict. At one time he lived as a dissident within the dictatorship (whose censorship laws were among his most pressing reasons for leaving). He eventually became one of many Spanish expatriates living in Paris, and finally turned into an estranged member of that very group for temperamental, political, and literary reasons.

Goytisolo provides another example of multidimensional exile; and yet the dominant issue surrounding his life and work, especially the later work, is that of the self. As Ilie points out, Goytisolo's ultimate wish, as a remedy for the social and cultural ills from which exile arises, is for the annihilation of the self, or at least the conventional self determined by class, family, and national origin (p. 132). In this scheme self-exile involves the will to strip himself of his former vestments, to lay himself bare and to create a new self in and through his only remaining asset: language. The *señas* (signs) of Goytisolo's identity, as the title of his deepest exploration of exile (*Signs of Identity*) attests, refer not only to social phenomena, such as parents, ancestors, schools, possessions, places, and addresses, but to the linguistic representations of those phenomena: graphic and oral marks, texts, codes. In *Señas de identidad* the description of exile is itself part of a process of self-exile, as an uneasy relationship between life and language unfolds.

What sets Goytisolo's exilic search apart from that of most Spanish writers who left during or immediately after the war (with the possible exception of Cernuda) is not only the self-conscious nature of his search but its attention to language, both as a universal system of signs and as a specific structure defined according to cultural and geographical limits. Thus language in general and Spanish in particular are Goytisolo's main concenrs in his later writing, a body of texts which, as he himself states, commenced with *Señas de identidad*.[3]

Prior to *Señas* Goytisolo had been looking for the proper weapons to struggle against a society born of war, intolerance, and social injustice. Yet in a collection of essays titled *El furgón de cola* (*The Caboose*) he declared that the language of social criticism has become not only ineffective, but part of the problem (pp. 53–61). Furthermore, the conventions of the social novel, particularly the omniscient narrator who tells the stories of a variety of human beings from many strata of society, were to him as intellectually dishonest as they were hackneyed. To narrate in the words of a "diosecillo clásico" (classical little god), he stated, is to limit the pluralism of language, its ability to mask, to suggest, to signify several things at once. In self-imposed exile in Paris and after several attempts to forge a new language of social criticism, Goytisolo embarked on a literary journey of self-exploration. Social criticism thus becomes self-criticism, since, as a product of the very regime he criticized, he could no longer leave his own desires and influences out of the critique.

In *Señas* it is the self and its relation to language which stands as the text's point of departure. The autobiographical underpinnings of the novel have been pointed out by critics as well as by the author himself, and thus, autobiography appears again as one of the most important expressions of the condition of exile.[4] In this light *Señas* is a self-production in which exile is both the process and the product. The quasi-autobiographical protagonist, Alvaro Mendiola, returns to Spain from Paris to make a documentary film on the social ills causing emigration of workers and intellectuals. Already severely critical of his own culture and a resident of another country, Mendiola sees this return visit as an attempt to recapture his own past and thereby rise above it. His reading of Spain in the documentary is a self-reading, for as a second person narrator he tells how and why the film was made and that the end result has created further political, moral, and intellectual distance from his homeland. The process then is as exilic as the end result.

The writing of *Señas* is, on one level, a reconstruction of the protagonist's memory of the documentary and of the difficulties he had in realizing the project—censorship, interrogation, inaccessibility of vital information. All of these hardships are not unlike those encountered by the author himself at a previous time in his life. On another level *Señas* is a rewriting of Goytisolo's own previous work. The documentary serves as a metaphor for works such as *Campos de Nijar* and *La Chanca*, both of which are accounts of trips to southern Spain after the author had taken up residence in Paris. As Linda Levine has clearly shown in her study of Goytisolo (p. 15), *Señas* is filled with implicit and explicit references to Goytisolo's travelogues as well as to previous novels such as *Juegos de manos*. As Mendiola travels through Murcia and Alicante in search of people and landscapes for his film (as well as for his cultural roots) Goytisolo accounts for his own depiction of Spain at another time in his career. The first person description of La Chanca, a section of the city of Almería known for its Andalusian hospitality and for its Andalusian poverty, is recast in *Señas*. The effect is a change in focus from an objective depiction of inequality and social deprivation to the aesthetic and existential process of the portrayal. Thus Goytisolo re-creates himself at the moment of a former creation.

From Goytisolo's attempt at self-production in *Señas* one might conclude that the self in exile is an extremely fragmented one, and that the attempt to reconstruct it through memory only leads to further fragmentation. Again we witness the exilic process of recollecting (as in the works of Nabokov and Semprún); but this time, the textual and intertextual nature of the recollection stands out. Every aspect of the self—childhood, birthplace, social experience, schooling, movement from one culture to another, interaction with parents and family—has a linguistic manifestation, some sort of sign or signs representing each. Alvaro Mendiola, a deeply troubled human being, does not seem to know who he is, and his yearning for self-knowledge manifests itself in a close inspection of a series of texts. At his family's home in Barcelona he comes across photographs, documents, newspaper clippings, school records, lists, letters—signs of his cultural and individual identity. Each text sparks a series of images within the protagonist's memory.

A case in point is an atlas which Alvaro and his lover, Dolores, stumble on as they stroll through the park of Montjuich. The collection of maps is Goytisolo's gateway to Alvaro's memory, for it opens the story of the protagonist's travels with Dolores through various stages of their relationship. Through this book of places a second person narrator relates Alvaro's experiences in a boarding house in Paris, trips to Monaco, Venice, Geneva, and a political excursion to Cuba. In many ways the maps signify not only real places but real events. The reading of the atlas is Alvaro's reading of his life.

> El contenido del atlas geográfico es parte integrante de vuestra vida, e inclinándose sobre él, revivís el tiempo pasado.
> Elíptico, embrollado, su curso reproduce cabalmente los mean-

dros sinuosos de la memoria.
Hablan las voces del recuerdo.
Escuchad. (p. 318)

(The content of the geographical atlas is an integral part of your
lives, and as you look over it together, you relive the past.
Elliptical, embroiling, its course faithfully reproduces the sinu-
ous meanderings of memory.
The voices of remembrance speak.
Listen.)

The maps, then, have a dual function: they represent and they evoke.
Like photographs and all the other textual doors to memory, the atlas
signifies on several levels. It contains meandering and seemingly haphazard lines that represent not only a place but that place's geographical and natural characteristics. By the same token the map paves the
way to history, culture, and politics. The atlas also sparks the re-creation
of the events in a personal history, a history which becomes a narrative
as the protagonist recalls it. Ironically, the ultimate effect of the inspection of the atlas is not the resuscitation of history and personal experience, but their annihilation. The lines of the maps become more abstract
as the story continues, and the narrative reveals itself for what it really
is, a fiction. The atlas, thus, contributes to the fragmentation of a self
by dividing it into two: the real one, a tangible human being who
actually went to these places, and the representation of that human
being in language.

The attention to maps is emblematic of Alvaro and Goytisolo's exilic
search as well as of the geographical imbalance which leads to existential, psychological, and moral ambivalence. Goytisolo takes his exile
to an ontological limit as he questions the very reality of his new
condition, a dual condition: an exile and an entity of fiction. For the
self-banished Spaniard the separation between these two conditions
intensifies with the writing of an autobiographical novel. The emergence of a self-contained world of language unrelated to the politics

and history of the writer's country seems to be the work's culminating objective as well as a possible solution to the problem of exile. At several junctures in the novel, including the chapter devoted to the atlas, the protagonist finds himself far from the immediate circumstances which not only cast him into exile but brought him back momentarily. In these instances he appears lost in an artificial world in which memory is a game and oblivion, liberation. The vehicles to memory (the atlas, Mozart's *Requiem*, the glass of Fefiñanes) highlight the process of remembering, a process which ironically brings on the disappearance of the world outside the text.

However, for all the work's attention to artifice, to process, and to language, a real geography and a real political order linger hauntingly in the background, and, in spite of the attempt, they are never entirely obliterated. It is the very acknowledgment of a political reality which adds to the work's tension: the seemingly irreconcilable split between fiction and real life. Clearly, political life is one of the novel's primary concerns. Characters such as Professor Ayuso, one of the many Machado figures in Goytisolo's works and a staunch critic of the dictatorship, are vehicles to Alvaro's memory. Antonio's trials and difficulties after having served a prison sentence for a political crime and his alienation from the mainstream of Spanish society are another example.

Along with Ayuso, Antonio, and other characters who embody political struggles within the dictatorship stands another series of individuals whose stories are intricately linked to the politics of exile. They are the seemingly insignificant human beings, the multitude of exiles and immigrants who endured great economic and physical hardship after the war, some of whom had the audacity to write about it (as did those discussed in chapter 5). Goytisolo records some of these stories in a collection of italicized texts not directly connected to the plot line but whose first person accounts add to the intensity of Alvaro's dilemma. Insignificant individuals (in the framework of collective importance) appear once again in the exilic testimony. Goytisolo seems aware of the issue as he shifts focus from the disaffected intellectual, such as Ayuso or Antonio (the honorable young student), to living, breathing human beings—from symbols of dissidence to dissidence itself.

Even though malcontents of all persuasions populate Goytisolo's novelistic production before his exile, in Paris the author shows a growing concern for the authenticity of portrayal, especially of those who do not belong to his own class of intellectuals, such as workers, peasants, and marginal members of society. In his important interview with Rodriguez Monegal, Goytisolo suggested that he had grown dissatisfied with realistic attempts to imitate the lives of outcasts and that he was looking for more genuine representations of those human beings, people whom he considered his allies in spite of the social and intellectual distance (*"Destrucción,"* p. 50). A close look at Goytisolo's writing after the interview, especially *Señas*, reveals that in fact the author had changed his conception of character and character development. Psychology, political ideologies and struggles, identification, sympathy on the part of the reader with a personage, all seem to fade, and what emerges is life itself: testimony, at times fragmented and incoherent, that is, individual accounts of personal experience.

Testimony again appears as a manifestation of the exilic voice, and in *Señas* the narration of personal experience is one of the crucial themes of the novel. In the italicized sections of the novel Goytisolo plays the role of a transcriber who records the speech of others as he hears it. In so doing, he explores the relationship between language and experience. In these personal renditions of the flight from Spain after the war, plots emerge and fade, literary devices stand out, characters appear and disappear. The texts are ultimately transformed in the hands of the transcriber from testimony to literature.

> Esta silla y el cesto de mimbre que hay encima de ella valen para mí más que todos los amigos del mundo y han sido más fieles que ellos pues cuando este cesto pasaba las rejas de la carcel siempre llevaba dentro algo de comida y esta silla es la misma en la que me hicieron sentar los falangistas antes de meterme en la cárcel

y cuando yo estaba dentro de la cárcel el cesto de mimbre que está sobre la silla me llevaba la miseria que podía y cada día me alegraba cuando me venía a ver

esta silla y este cesto no tienen que agradecer nada a nadie pues muchos republicanos de antes andaban por la calle y el cesto no recibía de ellos ni un miserable céntimo

este cesto que iba a pedir limosna de puerta en puerta para llevarme de comer y esta silla a la que me ataron delante de mi mujer dicen que todo esto es verdad la silla en la que me pegaron con una fusta y el cesto con el que mi mujer pidió limosna . . . .

y esta silla y este cesto saben que cuanto digo es verdad verdadera . . . . (pp. 375–76)

(This chair and this wicker basket on top of it are worth more to me than all the friends in the world and they have been more loyal

when this basket passed by the bars of my jail cell it always brought some food and this chair is the same one that the falangists made me sit on before they put me in jail

and when I was in jail the wicker basket that was on the chair brought me whatever it could and every day I was happy when it came to see me

and this chair and this basket don't have to thank anyone for anything and many republicans from before walked up the street and the basket didn't get a penny from them

this basket that went begging from door to door to bring me something to eat and this chair that they tied me to in front of my wife say that all this is true, the chair I sat on while they whipped me and the basket my wife begged with . . . .

and this basket and this chair know that what I say is the truest of truths . . . .)

Goytisolo's motivation behind these first person renditions seems to be to nourish the protagonist's memory, as did the atlas. But these accounts also contribute to the analysis of the language of social reality.

In many ways more gripping and more convincing than the story of Antonio's difficulties with the police, these texts are also more complex. At first glance they stand in opposition to the plot line (the literary text): they are in italics and they are transcriptions of supposedly real events. Yet they are just as literary, or more so. In the previously quoted passage the personification of the chair and the wicker basket serves as the speaker's main rhetorical device. The two objects have proven their generosity and loyalty, in contrast to the comportment of human beings (the speaker's former friends refused to help). Even more important, the personification reveals an epistemological statement: the objects know—they witnessed the brutality and misery which the speaker had to endure. A flogging, the speaker's wife begging to keep her husband alive, friends turning their backs on the speaker in a moment of need—these stand as facts, undeniable truths, regardless of a perceiving subject, regardless of an impartial witness, with the exception, of course, of the chair and the basket: "and this basket and this chair know that what I say is the truest of truths." The speaker's redundancy comes, perhaps, from his lack of schooling, yet the rhetorical devices in his words suggest possibilities for the literariness of any text, even when the apparent intention is to expose the truth of what happened (a motivation clearly opposed to that of literature).

The rendition of the prison incidents, and other accounts of exilic experience transcribed in *Señas*, affirm the capacity of language to go beyond its easily accepted function of mirroring reality. Language has the power to create a reality all its own. Specifically, these texts are explorations of a testimonial reality as a defense against exile. Yet testimony is a vulnerable defense, for the reality of any event is subject to the scrutiny of language. The testimony of an individual's life, autobiography, is no exception, especially within the context of Goytisolo's novelistic manipulation, whereby he deals not only with the autobiographies of others but his own. Although the reality of these lives and experiences is questionable, there seems to be an acknowledgement that something has taken place. To manipulate that something, to turn it into a fiction, to exercise the "art of forgetting," is Goytisolo's objective. Furthermore, one cannot lose sight of the fact that the author's objective is a political one, for the manipulation is a countermanipulation. The stories of his autobiographical speakers are counterstories: they represent another truth, one opposed not only to the official rendition of what happened but to the very notion of an "official story."

> Transcritas durante los preparativos del rodaje del fallido documental, las biografías de los emigrados—primera ola de un mar en movimiento perpetuo—se erguían en medio del panorama campestre tranquilo y placentero como una grave y imperecedora acusación, todo el lento aprendizaje en el dolor, la vergüenza y la astucia, la injusticia y humillaciones de estos años cifrados en páginas escuetas y breves, rigurosas y estrictas, que ningún proceso, ningún bienestar, ninguna modernización—y era una certeza consoladora para ti—consiguirían nunca borrar. (p. 375)

> (Transcribed during the filming of the aborted documentary, the biographies of the immigrants [the first wave of an ocean in perpetual movement] stood out in the midst of a rural, calm, and pleasant panorama like a severe and undying accusation, all the slow and painful apprenticeship in the shame and cunning, in the injustice and humiliation of these years recounted in unpretentious and brief pages, rigorous and rigid, which no court, no well being, no modernization [and it was a consoling certainty for you] could possibly erase.)

The experience of exile and the attempt to record it do not allow the subject to forget politics easily, for in many cases (Goytisolo's included), politics are the root of the problem.[5] In exile, however, politics become diffuse, complex, and not as clearly delineated or explained. And in self-exile the situation is even more precarious, for behind the conscious act of rejection of an order or a regime lies a wish to forget, to pretend that politics do not exist. In *Señas* forgetting is in fact the protagonist's remedy for exile: "no te empecines más márchate fuera mira hacia otros horizontes danos a todos la espalda olvídate de nosotros y te olvidaremos tu pasión fue un error repáralo SALIDA SORTIE EXIT AUSGANG" (p. 421; do not insist any more, leave, look toward other horizons, turn your back on us, forget us and we will forget you, your passion was a mistake, fix it, . . .). Oblivion, in this context, is part of a creative process of forgetting. Yet one wonders how authentic such a process can be; how can we willfully forget something without deceiving ourselves? The political discourse of the novel, coupled with the protagonist's moral quandaries, renders the act of forgetting a tenuous one. The dictatorial regime is uneasily forgotten because it is part of the process of forgetting. It engages in a dialogue, albeit a hostile one, with the protagonist; it addresses itself in the first person plural as it utters its final words of feigned indifference to Alvaro's protests. A vestige of the "nosotros" will always remain within Alvaro, even the Alvaro who believes he has ridden himself of a former identity. By the same token the new identity of Goytisolo, the one who writes in a different language, free from the conventions of social realism and psychological development, cannot possibly forget those very conventions since they also are part of the process. In order to forget and thereby obliterate the signs of a former identity their existence must first be acknowledged. And in the aftermath of the obliteration, something will always remain: an article of clothing, a memory, a word, only to be destroyed again.

14 Exile as Nomad

Like James Joyce's novels, the writing of Juan Goytisolo becomes less representational after he moves away from his homeland. In Joyce's case, from *Portrait of the Artist* through *Ulysses* to the ultimate work of linguistic experimentation and play, *Finnegan's Wake*, the trajectory away from the proscriptive and constraining elements of Irish Catholicism is both literary and geographical. The chronology of Goytisolo's self-imposed exile has the same double-edged quality, as he continues where he left off in *Señas de identidad* with a work that has no pretense of realism or historical objectivity—*Reivindicación del Conde don Julián* (Count Julian). As we have seen in the previous chapter, *Señas* retains certain conventions of the historical novel even though its very conception represents an attempt to do away with those rules of writing. Beginning with *Don Julián*, up to his latest creative work, *Paisajes después de la batalla* (*Scenes After the Battle*), Goytisolo no longer writes in standard sentences, nor does he invent characters that are remotely similar to real human beings.

His ideology, both political and literary, has also changed. In the light of the political questioning that characterized *El furgón de cola*, Goytisolo collected a new series of his reflections on literature and culture, which had appeared in various European and American journals from about 1970 to 1976 (*Disidencias*). In these essays he was at times harshly critical of any writing in service of a specific political or social cause. The self-censorship called for by the Franco regime, he reiterated, was as stifling and bankrupt as that of politically committed writers who ignore the possibility of a reality that questions their own discourse. He stressed the need to go beyond the reflection of a hackneyed social and political reality (pp. 153–79).

Yet, also like Joyce, the distance from his homeland did not cure his obsession with it. In fact, it has been difficult for Goytisolo to find new material. Admittedly, his scenes have changed, as the very word, "scene," takes on new meaning in *Scenes After the Battle*. Today, his writing takes him to various parts of the globe, as the self-banished Spaniard becomes an exilic nomad, again both in a literary sense and a geographical one. Characters change names and identities freely, narrators tell several stories at once, including the story of the text's very genesis. Rules of reading are also questioned. Especially in *Don Julián* but also in subsequent novels, the author challenges the reader to interpret the text with and against other texts, suggesting that reading may be another form of writing. Yet for all these nuances and postmodern forms of expression and experimentation, Goytisolo's homeland looms over his writing even after its patriarch (Francisco Franco) dies and a democracy is shaped into existence by the author's former compatriots.

A ruthless attack on the reading of Spanish history and national character, *Reivindicación del Conde don Julián*, published in Mexico in 1970, is written by a man who has an exilic ax to grind.[1] Goytisolo's attack is not so much on Spain itself, its history, or even its people, but on its language, its beliefs, the oral and written codes of a nation that equates myth and legend to absolute truth. At the same time, *Don Julián* is the resumption of Alvaro's story in the light of all he has had to deal with in response to an authoritarian society. The novel (or text) is Alvaro's act of vengeance, the repossession of what he now sees as an occupied land. Goytisolo's inversion is an exilic (or self-exilic) one, for, like Cernuda, he posits a situation in which the exile expels: all that is undesirable within the old culture (tyranny, repression, religious and sexual intolerance) is trampled on and cast into oblivion. With the aid of a new conception of character, Goytisolo reenacts a crucial moment in Spanish history: the invasion of the peninsula by the Moslem hordes in 711 with Tarik at their helm. The narrator plays the role of Count Julian, the Christian lord of Ceuta who, also in an act of revenge, opened the gates of the city to the Moors thereby giving them free access to the peninsula. In many ways this novel represents the ultimate act of exilic return—the invasion of the old home.

Goytisolo brings a new dimension to the themes and language of exile, not only with the ironic inversions of *Don Julián*, but in his transformation of marginality from something pathetic and undesirable to something positive and universal. From exile, self-exile, revenge, and a gratifying act of repossession, Goytisolo takes his marginal figures beyond exile and celebrates those who are at home nowhere. He actually becomes one of these figures in his writing, a nomad who wanders not only from place to place but from the signs of those places to other signs. Especially in the works written after *Don Julián*, texts such as *Juan sin tierra* (whose publication date coincides with the year Franco died) and *Makbara*, Goytisolo seems to have found the voice and condition he was searching for in *Señas de identidad*.

Both in *Juan sin tierra* and in *Makbara*, the nomad, both as subject and object, takes on a significance not present in the texts written prior to 1975. Before that date, however, Goytisolo did show a growing interest in non-Western cultures, especially those immediately to the south of Spain. Islamic civilization and the figure of the warring nomad both serve as antagonizing elements in *Don Julián*, in opposition to the official history of Spain. Yet in the later novels the fascination with the Arab world as it relates to Spanish history becomes so intense that it stands alone without the initial link to anything Spanish. Many of the figures that populate *Juan sin tierra* are desert dwellers and travelers, some of whom have connections to the west but have been swallowed up by the desert. Two of the most representative are Père Foucauld and T. E. Lawrence, or Lawrence of Arabia. The real existence of both can be verified by autobiographical writings on their wandering through Northern Africa and the Middle East. In the case of Foucauld, a nineteenth-century French priest who wished to convert the Islamic infidels to Christianity, Goytisolo transcribes certain passages of his letters describing both his mystical zeal for martyrdom and his fascination with the desert.

> cette Afrique, ces missions d'infidèles appellent tellement la sainteté que seule obtiendra leur conversion: . . . il faut passer pour le désert, et y séjourner pour recevoir le grace de Dieu. (*Juan sin tierra*, p. 150)

> (this Africa, these missions ministering to infidels call forth so irresistibly the saintliness that will be the means of converting them: . . . one must pass through the desert, and linger there to receive the grace of God.)

In the case of T. E. Lawrence, Goytisolo does nearly the same. He paraphrases sections and reenacts scenes from the Britisher's celebrated autobiography, *Seven Pillars of Wisdom*, a text which stands alongside that of Goytisolo, as both writers consider themselves allies in the cause of a positive and liberating view of Arab culture: "alcanzarás el oasis más próximo gracias al fino instinto de los meharís: . . . Père Foucauld, Lawrence de Arabia?: entre los tuyos al fin, inmerso en su densísimo caldo humano" (p. 87) (will you reach the nearest oasis thanks to the refined instincts of the Meharis: . . . Père Foucauld, Lawrence of Arabia?: at last you are among them immersed in the utmost density of human warmth).[2]

The appropriation of both Foucauld and Lawrence, along with their texts, for ulterior motives is Goytisolo's act of nomadic pillaging. The nomad, unwilling to settle in one place or to become a productive member of any society, must borrow, beg, or steal in order to survive. Goytisolo's love of the desert draws him into the same activity. He subverts other texts, converts them into the allies of his own writing even though their intentions may be different. A desert dweller (or writer) must compensate for scarcity, and in Goytisolo's case it is not so much that there is no material to write about, but that, as an outsider, he must learn from other texts, assimilate them and convert them into new ones, which is, in the final analysis, the essence of any literary creation. Again, compensation and overcompensation appear as crucial aspects of exile literature, or perhaps any type of literature.

The protagonist of *Juan sin tierra* is, as the title suggests, a landless being, in this case a writer whose wanderings from place to place and from text to text are emblematic of Goytisolo's own conception of writing. Autobiography also continues to be Goytisolo's trademark in his later works, including those written after *Señas*: the entities which occupy the most significant positions of the texts tend to be subversive writers or outcasts who stand in symbolic relationship to the author. The narrators' ability to change identities at will, in both *Juan sin tierra* and *Makbara*, testifies to the literary possibilities and disguises of Goytisolo. It also points to a conception of writing as movement, or literary nomadism—a dynamic process in which nothing stays the same for long. Parody, travesty, changes in perspective and in pronouns, sometimes within one sentence (as in "descargó su conciencia, expusiste las razones de tu desvío, evoqué los incidentes [p. 38; he discharged his conscience, you argued the reasons for your deviation, I evoked the incidents]), all indicate a nomadic process of writing and a critique of the very notion of stability and continuity.

Makbara is perhaps the best example of nomadic writing not only because of the variety of locales in which the action supposedly takes place, but because of the narration itself. The text draws as much attention to the story-telling as it does to the story. The setting is the *makbara*, a transcription of Arabic referring to a public square or market place in which stories are told to passersby. The *makbara* frames the novel in such a way as to blur the barriers between fiction and reality, for the text enters the cultural and social reality of storytelling. The *makbara* also allows Goytisolo to play the role of the storyteller, the wandering troubadour of Arabian lore who entertains listeners by telling tales and by acting them out as he becomes the very characters he has created. He tells of the exploits of yet another exile, an "angel" descended to earth after having fallen from the grace of paradise, a Christian paradise which stands in opposition to Goytisolo's positive notion of movement and change. The former habitat of this outcast represents the dullness and boredom of perfection as well as the sterility, authority, and absolute power of the ideal.

> todo le aburría allá arriba: la empalagosa atmósfera del paternalismo, el celo servil de los colegas, la inaguantable esclavitud del horario: plentiud transmutada en vacío, perfección en estado opresivo, asfixiante . . . vuestro acervo sagrado, intangible, legado imperecedero del Padre. (pp. 37–38)

> (everything bored him up there: the sickening atmosphere of paternalism, the servile zeal of colleagues, the insufferable slavery of the clock: plenitude converted to emptiness, nauseating and oppressive perfection . . . your common property in the sacred, intangible, and imperishable legacy of the Father.)

The figure of the angel, as the above passage attests, is another in the long line of pariahs in Goytisolo's work. He, she, or it (and at times the plural forms of those pronouns) possesses the inherent ability to scandalize, shock, and repel all those who do not share its subversive and contaminating spirit. The novel begins with a cry of disgust, of "alarm" and "anguish" (p. 13), and from that point, the descriptions of the angel figure indicate the characteristics which separate it from the mainstream. The narrator (at times the angel itself) speaks of the figure as "a contaminating virus" with "dark bare feet" (p. 13), a "pariah, the infected one" (p. 16), a "fierce, wild, nomadic" entity who finds great satisfaction in "marauding, making dogs bark, [in] being the object of scorn" (p. 180). With the figure of the angel, Goytisolo combines the grotesque with a critique of established values. His principal figure is abhorrent, yet it is also a scapegoat. As people "beat it with a stick" (p. 180), they reveal their own inability to love, to move freely and without limits, to create. In this context the angel is not the least bit uncomfortable with its own alienation.

For one such as the angel, the only recourse is movement. Goytisolo celebrates his figure's determination to retain the qualities that society rejects, as the figure immerses itself in its own otherness and exile. Its exile is by no means passive, for not only does it counter a series of accepted norms, it threatens their authority. Neither the angel nor Goytisolo is content to allow the coexistence of an authoritarian structure with a free and dynamic one, since the objective is to destroy the very idea of authority. Merely stating the case against a political system does not go far enough in achieving the goal. The language of leftist politics, for example, comes under as severe attack in both *Juan sin tierra* (pp. 287–90) and *Makbara* (pp. 38–39) as does the society of mass consumption. Indeed, the angel figure is a contaminating force in leftist political circles much in the same way as the central figure of *Federico Sánchez* by Jorge Semprún. Unlike Semprún, however, Goytisolo opts for a seizure of signifying power, the power derived from writing an imaginative work, the power of language: "lenguaje corporal cuyo músculo es léxico: nervio, morfología: articulación, sintaxis" (pp. 212–13; corporal language whose muscular system is a lexicon, nervous system, a morphology, articulation, a syntax).

From Goytisolo's subversive writing, one may derive a political ideology not unlike anarchism, in this case both nomadic and linguistic. In one of the many ideologically engaging passages, Goytisolo puts forth a political credo which is at once a reference to the very text he is writing and to his own previous works, from *Señas* to *Makbara*:

> supervivencia del ideal nómada en términos de utopía: verso sin estado ni jefe, libre circulación de personas y bienes, territorio común, pastoreo, pura impulsión centrífuga: abolición de propiedad y jerarquía, rígida acotación espacial, dominio fundado en razones de sexo y edad, torpe acumulación de riqueza: asumir la fecunda libertad del gitano transgresor de fronteras: acampar en un vasto

presente de búsqueda y aventura: confundir mar con tierra y navegar por ésta con grácil tesitura de pescador: auspiciar estructuras de hospitalidad vagabunda, puertos francos de trueque y discusión, zocos, mercadillos de ideas. (*Makbara*, p. 205)

(survival of the nomadic ideal in utopian terms: a universe without a state or ruler, free movement of people and goods, common territory, pure centrifugal force, abolition of property and hierarchy, of a rigid division of space, of domination based on sex and age, of conspicuous consumption of wealth: to assume the role of the gypsy transgressor of borders: to camp in a vast present of searching and adventure: to confuse sea with land and navigate on the latter with the graceful art of the fisherman, to support structures of vagabond hospitality, free ports of trade and discussion, little marketplaces of ideas.)

With his synthesis of politics and writing, the self-exiled Goytisolo creates a set of precepts for a counterattack, another repossession of land in the same vein as *Count Julian*. The search for utopia, total freedom, a place where hierarchies no longer exist, is in effect a writerly search in which the land may become a sea and vice versa.

Beyond the critique of power and authority from the position of exile and self-exile, there is a fundamental problem which Goytisolo's later novels pose: the place of writing. In these texts the very notion of setting is problematic, since there are several ways the reader may position him or herself within them, especially in *Juan sin tierra* and *Makbara*. The assumption behind the notion of setting is that a literary text has the power to take both writer and reader to a locale other than the actual locale of the writing—a place where one is not. The literary text is, in many ways, a dialogue between places, for the very act of reading necessitates a willingness to tread on a different earth. Self-exile from the actual place of the text, then, is an important step in any signifying process. The text may be viewed as a space that beckons its readers into it. For the Goytisolo of *Makbara* and *Juan sin tierra* setting is relegated to a limitless blank page in which all other places are possible. The motif of the desert, so common in Goytisolo's work since *Don Julián*, is another manifestation of his exilic writing, for the text itself is the desert. Writing for Goytisolo is aimless wandering through an unfamiliar territory, an exotic land in which all stands at a distance.

Again, we recall Jacques Derrida's essay on Edmond Jabès's *Book of Questions*. Derrida reads Jabès as a writer whose exile occurs at the level of signification. Writing is, in this view, a nomadic process which involves a dispersal of meanings. In the terms of an exile, words leave home the moment they are written or uttered. They travel to other homes or significations in search of the one illusive and nonexistent single meaning, and in frustration set out for even further places. The place of the sign itself is where the speaker is not—"absence of locality" in Derrida's words ("The Question of the Book," p. 69). This universal absence is, in the poststructuralist scheme, why we are all in a state of exile, perpetually searching for signification: "If writing is not a tearing of the self toward the other within a confession of infinite separation, . . . then it destroys itself. It syncopates itself in the roundness of the egg and the plenitude of the identical. It is true that to go toward the other is also to negate oneself, and meaning is alienated from itself in the transition of writing." (pp. 75–76).

The relationship between Goytisolo's celebration of the writer or storyteller as nomad in *Makbara* and Derrida's conception (through Jabès) of "exile as writing" (p. 74) poses an important question for exile literature. In both there is a subversive intention. Derrida's debunking of logocentrism, or what he has characterized as the "metaphysics of presence," is behind his notion of exile in that exile is an apt condition to show the relationship between the center and the off-center of a structure. In another essay from the same collection, he attacks the notion of structure in the following terms: "Classical thought concerning structure could say that the center is, paradoxically, *within* the structure and *outside it*. The center is at the center of the totality, and yet, since the center does not belong to the totality (is not part of the totality), the totality *has its center elsewhere*" (p. 279, emphasis the author's). Goytisolo's wish to destabilize Spanish society, and as a consequence, Western society, is similar. His project is, in effect, to de-center Spanish history with factors and considerations that are outside its scope: Arab and Jewish culture, the other, the outcast, the transgressor. His approach to the problem via language and a transformation of perception is likewise similar to the Derridian attention to language and signification as a play of differences. The final paragraph of *Makbara* could have been the work of a Parisian poststructuralist.

> lectura en palimpsesto: caligrafía que diariamente se borra y retraza en el decurso de los años: precaria combinación de signos de mensaje incierto: infinitas posibilidades de juego a partir del espacio vacío: negrura, oquedad, silencio nocturno de la página todavía en blanco. (p. 222)

> (reading on a palimpsest: a calligraphy that erases itself each day and retraces its lines through the course of the years: a precarious combination of signs with an uncertain message: infinite possibilities of play in a vacant space that now appears: blackness, emptiness, the nighttime silence of the page still blank.)

Yet at the same time there are significant discrepancies between Derrida's and Goytisolo's conceptions of exile. At the risk of falling into the trap of logocentrism, I maintain that Goytisolo's exile is real, excessively real. The problems he faces are cultural ones, and just as significant is that he reads them as such. In spite of his attempts to transcend culture, he remains frustrated at those very attempts. He is still in exile even after Franco's death, because it is that specific exile which has given him a reason for being (as well as a career). In Derrida's reading of Jabès cultural factors also play an important role, especially the fact that Jabès writes both as a member of the Jewish community and as a dissident within that community. Yet for Derrida Jewishness is merely another elusive word, a structure that disintegrates as it falls prey to the scrutinies of language. By contrast, Spanishness, for Goytisolo, is an integral structure and the fact that he wishes its collapse does not dismiss his reading of nationality as a structure. Even as he attacks societies of mass consumption that have few links to Spain, there is an implicit reading of the histories of those societies as organic wholes, a reading that seems to replace one structure for another—Arabia for Spain, East for West, primitive societies for advanced ones. The notion of historical structure itself goes unquestioned. As an exile, history and politics are too crucial, too immediate, too tangible to forget with a stroke of the pen. For Derrida, on the other hand, "there can be no history without the gravity and labor of literality" ("Edmond Jabès," p. 64). Perhaps even more important, the immediate problems of nationality and the political developments within the homeland serve to offer Goytisolo an identity, those slippery signs, addresses, and codes that tell us who we are. To be in a state of total exile, a state of no return, as it were, is to lose all connections to a structure. And even though Goytisolo's identity, along with those of Alvaro, Don Julián, Juan Sin Tierra, and that elusive angel are counteridentities, there seems to be a certain comfort in them. Goytisolo and his self-characters appear to have found themselves in their homes away from home.

Nomadic Utopia

Related to a Derridian notion of exile, yet at the same time distinct from it, is Goytisolo's recurring image of utopia. Weary of playing the role of a critic of the status quo, whether it be in political or aesthetic terms, Goytisolo posits writing as paradise. The "ideal nómada" (nomadic ideal) already appears in *Makbara* (p. 205), and implicitly in *Juan sin tierra*, yet nowhere is Goytisolo's picture of utopia more crucial than in his most recent texts, *Paisajes después de la batalla*

(*Scenes After the Battle*) and *Coto vedado* (*Forbidden Garden*). It is significant that both works deal with autobiography in some way, the former as a discourse on the nature of autobiographical writing and the latter as an undisguised rendition of the real life of Juan Goytisolo. That both works focus on utopia in addition to autobiography might, at first glance, imply that Goytisolo's search for his own marks of identity has ended; yet this is not the case. It cannot be, given the concept of exile as movement and constant change, which the author never abandons. It seems that through his own writing Goytisolo has come to the realization that the very search initiated in *Señas de identidad* is not only endless but pleasurable. The process of writing is gratifying because there is no finality, no product that gives it a reason for being. It is also liberating, especially when released from the tyranny of clarity and certitude, two qualities which writing itself disavows due to the very nature of language. In this regard Goytisolo again takes on the characteristics of a Parisian poststructuralist, much like Roland Barthes, whose "pleasure of the text" is not unlike the concept of writing as play which Goytisolo affirms in his later novels.

Yet for all the similarities between these nomadic utopias on the one hand and the literary ideologies of Derrida and Barthes on the other, there are also strong ties between Goytisolo's utopia and the political aesthetic of exile. *Paisajes después de la batalla* focuses on a literary problem concerning the relationships among the author, the narrator, and the central figure of the text, who usually appears in the third person. This entity, not unlike the angel of *Makbara* (or for that matter other pariah figures in Goytisolo's later novels), seems to have conjured up a subversion in the order and stability of his surroundings. The surroundings themselves are clearly identifiable as Paris, and the subversion, unlike many other of Goytisolo's treasonous acts (such as the one committed by Don Julián), is a plausible one. The so-called "hecatomb" which comprises the beginning chapter refers to the results of a battle in which the "author of the outrageous deed" (p. 15) has changed the language of the street signs in Paris from French to Arabic. The subversive is a believable character: he lives in an apartment with a studio, he writes, he takes walks through identifiable streets whose names correspond to real streets in the French capital, and he has (of all things for a pariah to have) a wife. The types of subversions he engages in also have their parallels in reality: he writes obscene letters, he exposes himself, he writes graffiti, he incites the downtrodden to riot, at the same time contributing to propaganda for the other side, all in an effort to nourish himself with social conflict. Goytisolo's utopia, then, contains and deforms a variety of structures drawn from social reality, even though his vision of utopia is precisely the opposite: freedom from social reality.

In a telling passage of *Paisajes* (in a section titled "En el Paris de los trayectos que se bifurcan"; "In Paris's Bifurcating Passages") the narrator alludes to a story by Borges. Goytisolo parodies Borges by placing the Argentine's story within a context of urban reality—the metro system of Paris. The subterranean paths provide what the narrator sees as an infinite series of possibilities for travel and, by extension, for transcendence of the world's banalities.

> El metro de Paris, como el espacio en el que se inscribe su ajetreo diario, es vasto y rico en posibilidades: ramificaciones, encrucijadas, pasajes, trayectos de una sola dirección, desvíos, parábolas, media vueltas, elipses, cuppos di sacco. Examinar el plano del metro es ceder al recuerdo, evasión, desvarío, abrirse a la utopía, la ficción y la fábula: recorrer los monumentos, abominaciones y horrores de la ciudad, los monumentos, abominaciones y horrores propios, sin necesidad de moverse de casa. (p. 110).

> (The Paris metro, like the space in which it inscribes its daily bustle, is vast and rich in possibilities: ramifications, intersections, passages, one-way trips, detours, parabolas, half-turns, ellipses, cuppos di sacco. To inspect the subway map is to yield to memory, evasion, whim; to open oneself to utopia, to fiction, and to fable: to look over the monuments, abominations, and horrors

of the city, the monuments, abominations, and horrors of oneself, without the need to leave the house.)

Utopia, then, is writing itself. It is not only the text the reader has in his hands, it is Goytisolo's previous writerly journeys such as the ones in *Señas* that were also sparked by gazing at maps. The utopian text is one of evasion and oblivion. However, there is always something behind the escape such as "monuments, abominations, and horrors," for the exile, including the outcast of *Paisajes*, is constantly in flight from something. While Goytisolo's ideal is the eternal and blissful escape from the world, it is that very world which keeps him in motion and provides his own exile with a purpose.

Goytisolo's choice of something as real as a metro system, as well as his other choices in subject matter (urban terrorism, exhibitionism, sexual deviance, marital tension), is a commentary not only on Borgesian fantasy but on the liminal relationship between fiction and reality: that fiction draws on a certain closeness to reality as well as on a distance from it. The relationship between the author and the pariah of his text is another manifestation of this closeness, and, in the final analysis the tension between both is the central issue of this novel. The similarities between Goytisolo and the main character are apparent in the outward descriptions of the protagonist (his apartment in Paris, his writing, his knowledge of and fascination with Arab culture) and in the framework of the narration. The author strategically draws attention to himself not only as a real person, Juan Goytisolo, whose ideas shape the writing of the text, but as another fictional entity, a writer-character whose previous texts have played a role in the construction of the novel. In a parody of writerly acknowledgements, the author expresses his gratitude to those who have played some role in the writing of the work, including "el remoto e invisible escritor, Juan Goytisolo" (the remote and invisible writer, Juan Goytisolo) whose "dubious scientific fantasies" were a source of inspiration (p. 7). Thus by doubling himself, Goytisolo asks the fundamental question which any autobiography poses, "Who writes?" It is the same question Borges asks in his story, "Borges and I": what is the relationship between the living breathing human being and his or her own replication in the text?[3] Toward the end of the novel Goytisolo writes what I feel is the most revealing comment on his own enterprise, a statement that might well apply to all his writing since *Señas de identidad*, for the words point directly to both the aesthetics and the politics of exile.

escribir escribirme: tú yo mi texto el libro
yo: el escritor
yo: lo escrito
    lección sobre cosas territorios e Historia
    fábula sin ninguna moralidad
    simple geografía del exilio (p. 193)

(to write to write me: you I my text the book
I: the writer
I: the written
    a lesson on things territories and History
    a fable without a moral
    simple geography of exile)

Is the "simple geography of exile" a Derridian concept? Insofar as the phrase stands as a commentary on the text's own coming into being, one cannot deny that Goytisolo continues in the wake of postmodernist writers such as Severo Sarduy and Cabrera Infante who are also in exile and who constantly subvert the process of signification. Yet Goytisolo's linguistic subversion has deeply rooted political overtones in his clear opposition to tyranny of any sort, his lambasting of the language of leftist politics, and his mockery of the followers of political principles—the New Left, Marcuse, independence movements. Admittedly, Goytisolo feels at home nowhere (except perhaps in the blank page), yet his proximity to political reality does not allow him to read that reality as anything but an integral structure. Goytisolo expresses the self-exile's dilemma: how to rid oneself of the sounds and codes of a previous social reality.

A Forbidden Garden

Goytisolo's obsession with autobiography attests to his own self-exilic dilemma. Ironically, after *Paisajes*, which is in many ways a parody of confessional autobiographies, Goytisolo writes just that: a confessional autobiography laden with social commentary and self-explanation, a text he calls *Coto vedado* (*Forbidden Garden*). In his life story the author tells us that he has been a restless nomad throughout his life and that the comforts of a home, whether it takes the form of family, a country, a place, a love relationship, have never been a part of that life. He describes his childhood in Spain before the Civil War and his family members, especially those who made themselves a fortune in Cuba. He goes into detail about his sexual awakening and his ambivalent sexual preferences, about the atmosphere in the university during the dictatorship, his political vacillations, and his emergence into the world of the Parisian literati. With these renditions it becomes clear that for Goytisolo, exile is a career, literally and metaphorically. *Forbidden Garden* is an exposition of that exilic career, and as such, it begins to question certain decisions and consequences. Not only in this work but in other expository pieces, Goytisolo has been honest enough to admit that were it not for exile, his notoriety in Spain and in Europe would not have been what it is. His situation contrasts with the many exiles who fall into oblivion and, at times, into extreme physical and material hardship the moment they leave. The consequence for Goytisolo, who is painfully aware of the situation of some of his exilic colleagues, is the predictable one: guilt. Yet the author at no time falls into the trap of beating his breast. Like *Señas*, *Forbidden Garden* is Goytisolo's exploration of his own guilt and an attempt to rid himself of it, to find that sweet garden where the forbidden fruit is no longer forbidden.

Although the utopian and nomadic qualities of his previous works continue in *Forbidden Garden*, the narrative framework of his new text is different. It is typical of an exilic autobiography in its retrospective look at the author's own career and upbringing and in the way the author defends his life in an authoritarian society. In addition, there is no doubt that Goytisolo is the speaker, and his antagonists are identified by their real names—no disguises, no literary traps or ambiguity. The author's life is exposed lucidly and chronologically within the context of recent Spanish history and politics.

Yet the lucidity of *Forbidden Garden* is deceptive, and the autobiographical issues revealed in *Paisajes* are also the subject of *Coto vedado*. The work begins with an epigraph by René Char—"la lucidité est la blessure la plus raproché du soleil" (p. 5; lucidity is the sun's most reproachable insult)—which seems to disclaim the order and precision which characterize the body of the text. The disclaimer reappears in the form of italicized sections interspersed throughout the chronological development, sections reminiscent of the style of Goytisolo's later novels. In one of these subchapters the author interjects a series of vacillations about the motives behind his own work, suggesting that his enterprise is "inane," that it is the secular substitution for the sacrament of confession, and that his writing reveals an unconscious need for self-justification (pp. 40–41). While in the other sections the author in fact defends the choices he has made throughout his life, the italicized pages question those very choices. Goytisolo thus carries on a dialogue between two texts and two voices, and the ambivalence between them is the ambivalence of the work as a whole.

Goytisolo also brings into play the inner process of his own moral discourse, well in keeping with the patterns of other exilic autobiographies. The ethical language has the ultimate effect of splitting the self; it is another manifestation of Goytisolo's characteristic doubling and interplay between a *yo* and a *tú* (in this case, the I and the other or the "yo-otro"; p. 40). According to the speaker, the other has usurped the voice of the subject, as does a ventriloquist by speaking in the body and tone of something or someone else. In so doing, the speaker poses ethical problems to himself in a search for his own moral code. What emerges is a discourse of guilt. The specific moral issues are never cast aside by the other in favor of the ambivalences of ethical pondering. On the contrary, Goytisolo in the body of the other seems to take his own ethical code just as seriously as does the society which forced him into exile, as he paves the way for a bitter conflict between the two.

> solo conciencia hiriente de haber infringido las reglas del juego personal, de no estar a la altura del esfuerzo exigido, haber arrojado la toalla a mitad del camino, lamentablemente infiel a ti mismo y a los demás. (p. 41)

> (only the painful awareness of having broken the rules of the personal game, for not rising above the occasion demanded, for having thrown in the towel at midpoint, lamentably disloyal to yourself and to others.)

Goytisolo seeks to resolve the inanity of his own confession by inverting the principles on which a confession is based: he wants forgiveness for not sinning, that is, for not always answering to the call of subversion. The tension between sin and not-sin, between the self and the other, between the I and the you, and between the lucidly developed sections of the text and the italicized ones is never overcome; it is a conflict that the exile must live with.

In spite of the text's ambivalences, both moral and narrational, the garden of Goytisolo's title remains a forbidden one, and it is this very proscription which is the text's most outstanding object of attack. The ultimate question is the following: can the garden exist without its own antithesis? Regrettably, for the self-exile the answer is no, for the very concept of utopia emerges from the imperfection of the present. And by extension it is the present situation which compels the nomad to leave in search of new horizons.

The utopia Goytisolo seeks in his autobiography is not unlike other utopias conjured up by Western intellectuals. The garden of *Coto vedado* is another form of the mythical South and the disenchanted writer's attempt to find it. Like Rimbaud, Gauguin, Artaud, and the positive figures of *Juan sin tierra*, such as T. E. Lawrence, Goytisolo acts as if there were real directional signals to his utopia, all pointing southward. He follows his predecessors on their respective itineraries, including that of his favorite poet, Luis Cernuda, who said in an early poem, "Quisiera estar solo en el sur" (I would like to be alone in the south). More important for Goytisolo, like some of his rebellious fellow travelers, the South is not a myth, it exists; and his real life search for it, his travels to Andalusia, Cuba, the Islamic world, and most recently to Turkey, represent a form of writing, an autobiographical quest for a new geography. The South has been a theme in Goytisolo's writing throughout his career. In his *Forbidden Garden*, the book he calls "his only book" (p. 29) (as Cernuda referred to his autobiography), these southern lands take many forms. Goytisolo's recreation of his own life is structured around his trips to the South, both life trips and writerly ones. The ultimate consequence is that writing itself is a life voyage into a different and unfamiliar setting, as all the works from *Señas* to the present illustrate.

Goytisolo's South is indeed a real one, a geographical area filled with social controversy and conflict. It emerges from the colonizing power of its geographical opposite—the North, or in another sense, the West. The South's characteristic poverty and underdevelopment, its lack of importance in the eyes of the North (or West), its marginality, are what initially draws Goytisolo in a southward direction, an attraction based on a fundamental belief in social justice. From *Señas* to the *Garden*, Goytisolo tells us of his own repugnance at his family's activities in Cuba, of an ancestor's dealings with his slave mistress and the letter she wrote to the family asking for material protection. He decries the treatment of Arabs in Paris and in former French colonies, of blacks in New York, of homosexuals. But, as he seems aware, his solution is an impossible one: he wishes to join them, to become one of them, to adopt a different thought process, a new form of writing, in effect, an altered identity. In one of the italicized sections of *Forbidden Garden* he speaks of his attraction to the South in the following way.

> Acento ronco, gutural o cantarino del Sur, a través del cual se filtra quizá misteriosamente el amor a tu lengua: territorio conquistado palmo a palmo, a la escucha de voces transidas de resignación y pobreza: doble aprehensión gradual de una posible pertenencia y la índole aleatoria e incierta de tu otorgada, dudosa identidad. (p. 276)

> (Raw, guttural, or melodic dialect of the South, through which you filter the love for your language: a territory conquered inch by inch listening to voices overcome by resignation and poverty: a double and gradual apprehension of a possibility of belonging and the uncertain aleatory trait of your given and dubious identity.)

What makes *Forbidden Garden* a unique text in Goytisolo's corpus is his admission that Spain itself is another part of the South, an affirmation he previously denied. Curiously, Spain appears in the final section of *Coto vedado* as a land of reconciliation, a land that has become, after a long and rigorous process, part of what he has been seeking all along. In the culminating paragraph the second person narrator takes a final look at the author's break ("desamor," p. 276) with Spain. He points to Almería, Spain's south, as the locale which sets off the "impact" of the break. He then suggests that there remains a Spain which may serve as a substitute for the one left behind. He calls the alternative an "image of a captive and radiant scenery." In the final words of Goytisolo's autobiography, strangely enough, there are traces of that typically exilic phenomenon: nostalgia.

> El desamor a España . . . sujeto y motivo de nostalgia, proyección compensatoria de una patria frustrada, atisbo, vislumbre, presen-

timiento de un mundo todavía quimérico pero presente ya en tu espíritu en su muda, acechante proximidad. (p. 277)

(The break with Spain . . . subject and motive for nostalgia, a compensating projection of a frustrated nation, a look, a glimpse, a presentiment of a world still a chimera yet now present in your spirit in its silent and vigilant proximity.)

It seems that Spain, in its "vigilant proximity," is no longer as awesome as it was when Count Julian gazed at it in the initial pages of *Reivindicación*. Yet more important, Spain is now not only close but present, sculpted down to size so that it will fit into Goytisolo's nomadic utopia. Again the theme of proximity and presence in exilic writing emerges as an alternative to distance and pure artifice. Indeed, Derrida's "metaphysics of presence" is not easily overcome, and it is precisely that tension between presence and absence which remains in Goytisolo's work, in spite of the conciliatory tone of the last words of his autobiography. This text is as ambivalent in the final section as it is throughout, for here the two principal concepts, proximity and presence, are mutually exclusive.

The conciliatory nature of the end of Goytisolo's autobiography is deceptive, not so much in the spirit and tone of reconciliation as in the narrational "sense of an ending." Goytisolo had already played this trick on his readers with a grandiose culmination of *Juan sin tierra* in which he declared the end of writing itself, and "si en lo futuro escribes, será en otra lengua" (p. 319; if you write again, it will be in another tongue). He was referring, of course, to Arabic; but he was also referring to a metaphorical language of the outcast. Goytisolo's next novel was, not surprisingly, written in Spanish; what was curious about it was that *Makbara* was similar, if not identical, in scope and style to his supposed end-text. As an autobiography, *Coto vedado* presents similar problems, with its writerly contradiction between the end of the text and the continuation of the life. That contradiction is heightened by the deathlike quality of exilic experience—a death which seems to repeat itself. Predictably, Goytisolo has published a continuation of his autobiography, *En los reinos de taifa*; and it is likely that the self-text will not end there, just as Alberti will continue his *Arboleda perdida* until the final day of his exile, which will be the final day of his life.

Crossings

More than anything else exile literature has to do with crossings—not only physical or geographical, but conceptual. As I have protested throughout these pages, to deal with exile is to deal with many places (as well as disciplines) at once. As an exile writer crosses the border of the homeland into another surrounding he or she must begin to confront another reality, at times totally divorced from the former one. For the critic who deals with that writer's work, the task is equally unsettling. In both cases (the writer's and the critic's) the trajectory involves the shifting of ground from one nation to another, or at times from one language to another. Things no longer have a familiar name; one must rename them and subject them to different scrutinies.

In many ways exile literature as a topic presents a challenge to the very study of literature, especially to the more narrow approaches such as literary history, formalism, or even generic studies; for exile writing seems to cross all the limitations devised by these subdisciplines. And as I suggested in an early chapter, these crossings present yet another challenge to the broader discipline of literary theory. Rather than solve these problems, I have chosen to reflect on them and to live with the tensions they produce. Exile is indeed unsettling and one wonders if it is not contradictory to arrive at a settlement, for the most interesting literary theories, like the most interesting works of literature, are those that deal with difficult questions by raising yet more questions.

In one of the more defiant works of literary theory and criticism to have come out of Hispanic studies in many years, Gustavo Pérez Firmat discusses a concept which has great bearing on exile literature: liminality (*Literature and Liminality*). Through an elaboration of spatially and temporally unconnected texts (Zorrilla's *Don Juan Tenorio*, Valle-Inclán's *Las galas del difunto*, *Tiempo de silencio* by Luis Martín Santos, and the routines of Cuban stand-up comedians), he contributes to an understanding of one of literature's most salient qualities: the liminal. The term comes from anthropology, but Pérez Firmat suggests that it is essential to literature. Liminality refers to the moments in which lives are in a state of transition, precisely on the threshold between one stage and another. This is seen in individual lives in a rite of passage; it occurs collectively in carnival when debauchery and irreverence signal a period of religious austerity. Similarly, literature often finds itself on the threshold of something, in the middle ground between two mutually exclusive entities (literature and life, for example), or on the margins of both. Liminality serves as Pérez Firmat's connecting tissue within his motley group of texts, and it could very well serve as the essential link among the divergent pieces of exile writing.

As these chapters have attempted to show, an exile text always seems to be on the threshold of something. Like that dubious figure in Velázquez's *Las Meninas* who stands in the doorway behind the princess, one never knows whether the exilic text is on its way out or in — whether it forms part of the literary history of the new land or the old one, or whether its frame of references involves a new existence or a past one. An exiled author is one who must try to justify his or her existence in writing, and in so doing, that author creates a liminal space between the self and the text; hence the inclination in exile writers for autobiographical conveyance. Autobiographies are themselves liminal, and the ones written from exile are even more so.

The place of writing is another important and difficult aspect of exile literature, and, as I have pointed out, the spatial and temporal murkiness of exile leads to literary ambivalence. Whatever the designation, ambivalence or liminality, the subject of exile is always on shaky ground. He/she is neither here nor there, not in Madrid or in Paris, in Buchel (the Leverkuhn's farm in Saxony) or Thomas Mann's exilic refuge in Los Angeles, not on the shores of the Danish Sound (where Brecht went into one of his exiles) or in war-torn Germany, in the province of St. Petersburg where Nabokov was born or in Ithaca, New York, in Semprún's summer villa near Santander or in the concentration camp at Buchenwald, in Goytisolo's Barcelona or in Tangiers. The exile text itself shares this ambivalence when it resists definition or categorization: novelistic autobiographies and autobiographical novels, narratives that turn into political diatribes, expository works and exercises in erudition or truth-seeking which swell with anecdotes that are as fictional as they are truthful. Exile literature is also filled with real-life situations and historical realities that become stories, and vice versa (like Max Aub's diary of his return to Spain). Exile is precisely that shaky middle or liminal ground which tempts us to forsake the comforts and routine of the home in search of an elsewhere. Exile, in all its political ramifications and stimuli, begins with indignation and ends (if it ends) with questions.

Another version of these spatial and temporal crossings is transgression. Exile always involves a clash of some sort. Banished writers are at odds with an existing order, be that order political, literary, or both. The clash between the Spanish intellectuals who were forced to leave Spain (or others like Thomas Mann or Brecht) and the political reality of Europe in the thirties and forties was the subject of their writing. And the fact that these authors in exile were considered criminals by the political order of the homeland led to further acts of writerly criminality. For some, like Cernuda and Goytisolo, transgression became the impetus behind many of their literary creations as they celebrated their condition of exile. Thus the crossing of political barriers leads to the crossing of other barriers—literary norms, conventional morality.

For the critic David Williams, the exile is an "anti-poet . . . an undoer, an uncreator." His negative appraisal comes from his definition of literature as the binding and weaving of words. Williams argues that because of the loss of community and language, the exile must speak in a monological voice of self-absorption, unconnected to the raw material of literature itself ("The Exile as Uncreator," pp. 8–9). While very much opposed to Williams's narrow and normative scheme, the understanding of exile literature presented in these pages is not far from Williams's. In fact, most writers discussed here might even welcome the designation of anti-poet, especially the more brazen ones, such as Cernuda and Goytisolo, who consider it their mission to undo and unbind the language of their community. However, the language of the self (as seen in all the autobiographies and autobiographical conveyances of exile literature) is by no means monological. On the contrary, the notions of dialogue and dialogical writing seem to go hand in hand with exile literature, as we have witnessed in the many and multifaceted exchanges emerging from exilic situations: between the homeland and the new land, between the banishers and the banished, between memory and oblivion, between reality and desire, between fiction and reality, between a place and its elsewhere, between the self and the other, between an I and a you, between the poet and the text. One might go further, as does Derrida, to conceive the poet as the wandering Jew who writes in the absence of a locality, in a desert in which appearance and disappearance merge as in a mirage. For some postmodern critics the place of writing is precisely in exile, away from one's social group, away from the community of language embodied in a grammar. In being other, the exile ponders otherness and at times dares to assume that position in writing. The way home is the way of writing, which ironically leads us farther away: an eternal journey in which finality and origin are one and the same. The exile speaks this journey and in so doing speaks to the exile in us all.

Notes

Introduction

1   Sanz Villanueva's essay, "La narrativa en el exilio," is part of a six-volume collection of studies on Spanish Civil War exile culture compiled and directed by José Luis Abellán, *El exilio español de 1939*. Henceforth, parenthetical references to this important series of essays will be labeled "Abellán" along with volume and page numbers.

2   Paul Ilie's *Literature and Inner Exile* is one of the most penetrating treatments of post-Civil War exile and its counterpart, inner exile, to date. His work is filled with "cases," one in particular, "A Case History of Self-Exile; Juan Goytisolo" (pp. 114–34). Although my interests and objectives are different, I owe a great deal to Ilie's cultural history of exile after the Civil War.

3   As I have and will continue to protest, the study of exile literature is like the study of literature itself. Not surprisingly, many of the attempts to come to a general understanding of the issue often end up focusing on specific authors. From a political-sociological angle, both Terry Eagleton and Andrew Gurr come to interesting conclusions about cultural homelessness. See especially Eagleton's fascinating reading of Conrad's *Under Western Eyes* (*Exiles*, pp. 21–32). For an overview (a bit superficial) of the many European exile writers, particularly the modern ones, see Harry Levin's essay in *Refractions*, "Literature and Exile" (pp. 62–81). Asher Milbauer in *Transcending Exile* deals with exile as a dominant theme in Conrad, Nabokov, and I. B. Singer. The book suffers from an overly simple apprehension of the subject, in the light of what the author considers his noble rejection of the temptations of formalism and structuralism. Michael Seidel, on the other hand, fell into the trap (for better or for worse, probably the former) in his *Exile and the Narrative Imagination* when he conceived of the issue in purely

literary, specifically narrational, terms. He reaches conclusions about literary representations of exile that are similar to mine, yet his focus is different since he does not deal head-on with exile as a universal condition. Neither does he consider the concrete political entanglements of exile as a crucial aspect of his work. All in all, Seidel's is the most original treatment of exile literature I have read. The issue of *Books Abroad* (Spring 1976) on "The Writer in Exile" has a number of articles on the subject by Claudio Guillén, Czeslaw Milosz, Richard Exner, and the Hispanist, Biruté Ciplijauskaité (see especially Guillén's "On the Literature of Exile and Counter-Exile"). There is a similar issue of *Mosaic* (no. 8, 1975). The Germans have also shown intense interest in the phenomenon of exile as a determining factor in their literary history, as it is in the history of Spanish literature in this century. See John Spalek and Robert F. Bell's edition of essays on German exile literature, *Exile: The Writer's Experience*. See also Bruce Cook's *Brecht in Exile*. From a philosophical position of radical skepticism, Jacques Derrida treats exile in the writing of Edmond Jabès as a concept which shapes the act of writing and puts into question the very possibility of meaning. Echoing this view are two penetrating articles by Margaret Ferguson, "Saint Augustine's Region of Unlikeness" and "The Exile's Defense," in which the author deals with a Platonic notion of the fall as an anticipation of Derrida's ideas about exile as a condition for writing. The classical figure of exile leads inevitably to one of the most influential exilic writers: Dante. For a fascinating treatment of exile in *The Divine Comedy*, see Guiseppe Mazzotta's *Dante: Poet of the Desert*, a work as modern as it is painstakingly mindful of the cultural milieux surrounding the text. For Mazzotta, to read is to be cast into exile; the search for meaning is the pilgrim's search for the sublime.

I should note also that recent Latin American literature and criticism is filled with treatments of exile for obvious political reasons. Toward the end of his life the seemingly apolitical Julio Cortázar devoted many pages to the subject (see his *Argentina*), as have many Chilean writers—Ariel Dorfmann and Antonio Skarmeta among others. The Uruguayan, Mario Benedetti, has a great deal to say about exile as it pertains to the present political situation of Latin America in his *El desexilio*.

4 Another work which I find very appropriate to the study of exile literature is Gustavo Pérez Firmat's *Literature and Liminality*.

Chapter 1

1 Garcilaso wrote his first and second elegies while he was in Sicily. See Elias Rivers's edition of his *Poesías castellanas completas* (pp. 99–115).

2   This slogan was used by the Ministry of Information and Tourism under Franco to attract vacationers to Spain. It also characterizes the way many Spaniards, including some intellectuals, view their own culture.

3   For an interesting discussion of the literary canon and its formation, see the issue of *Comparative Criticism* (I, 1979) that deals exclusively with the subject.

4   Nabokov's assessment of Russian émigré intellectuals, a group to which he grudgingly belonged, was not positive. He saw them as powerless and politically inconsequential individuals whose passionate proclamations and declamations were of little interest in their respective new homes to anyone but themselves. His picture, however, by no means lacks sympathy. See *Speak, Memory* (pp. 280–88).

5   See *De una España peregrina*, as well as Ilie's lucid treatment of Bergamín (*Literature and Inner Exile*, pp. 11–12).

6   An exception is a paper delivered by Germán Gullón at the 1982 MLA Convention, "Dos modalidades discursivas: Camilo José Cela y Paulino Masip," which compares *Pascual Duarte* to a neglected novel by Masip, *El diario de Hamlet García*. Gullón's analysis shows that the importance attached to *Pascual Duarte* as the beginning of a new style in the Spanish novel is questionable considering the many narratives written in exile after the war.

Chapter 2

1   See the essays in Lemon and Reis, especially Boris Eichenbaum's "Theory of the Formal Method," pp. 99–139. See also Fredric Jameson's critique of formalism in *The Prison House of Language*.

2   Llorens's conception of exile literature in an essay from this collection, "El retorno de desterrado" (pp. 9–30), is surprisingly close to Ferguson's and even Derrida's. In the other essays of this volume Llorens continues to stress temporal and spatial instability and ambivalence. The Spanish intellectual's work on exile is, in my view, the most eloquent and gripping among that of the Hispanists, from his *Liberales y románticos*, through his treatment of José María Blanco White, to his own book of memoirs, *Memorias de una emigración*, which I shall discuss later. All translations are mine unless otherwise stated.

3   Ilie also discusses the fact that for writers, exile almost inevitably leads to some sort of moral discourse (*Literature and Inner Exile*, pp. 86–92).

4   The moral discourse of exile literature brings to mind Mikhail Bakhtin's concept of dialogue in his *Dialogical Imagination*. With a passage, a character, or even something as minute as one word, he argues, there may be a variety of historical

and ideological factors working with and against each other. In the case of writers whose very name represents the issues of his or her exile, the dialogical imagination is at work even before the reading of the text.

Chapter 3

1 See Spalek and Bell, *Exile: The Writer's Experience*, p. 92. Also Klaus Mann's autobiography, *The Turning Point*, is a revealing document, not only of a life in exile, but of the culture of exile from fascist Germany.

2 Spalek and Bell, p. 194. Strangely enough, this evocative phrase describing German exile is by Adolf Berle, the U.S. secretary of state in the early forties, in an attempt to persuade Thomas Mann into a more active role in the aid of his fellow exiles. "Sterile complexity" is indeed an apt description of how the author of *Doctor Faustus* perceived the political entanglements and polemics in which Brecht participated. For a comprehensive biography of Brecht, see Ronald Hayman's *Brecht*. It is beyond me how anyone could possibly make Bertolt Brecht's life seem dull, but Hayman has succeeded in doing so, perhaps because he is a nonexile writing an exilic biography.

3 Critics tend to view Brecht's radical politics as a detriment to his creative endeavors, as in Herbert Lenhart's argument in Spalek and Bell that both Brecht and Mann were "victimized by their ideologies" (p. 200). Yet in Brecht's case political issues are not only the catalysts for many of his most important works, they make for unresolved tensions between the reality of a world threatened by fascist terror and the world he creates in his literary texts.

4 For the development of Brecht's dramatic theory, especially his understanding of "epic theater," see John Willett's edition, *Brecht on Theater*. The chronological organization of Brecht's essays shows that the seeds of his theory of theatrical alienation are present before his exile, but the full development of the idea, evidenced in "A Short Organum for the Theater," does not occur until 1947, the year of his departure to the United States (pp. 179–205).

5 Jesús López Pacheco's edition of Brecht's exile poetry (*Poemas y canciones*, trans. Vicente Romano) contains translations that are more coherent and less pretentious than those by various American translators in Willett's edition of Brecht's poetry. All subsequent references to Brecht's poems are from López Pacheco.

6 To my knowledge, the posthumously published dialogue has not been translated into English. I am using a French edition, *Dialogues d'exilés* (Paris: L'Arche, 1961).

7 In addition to the autobiography, *Speak, Memory* (pp. 280–88), see Simon Karlinsky's edition of *The Nabokov-Wilson Letters, 1940–1971*.

Chapter 4

1 See O'Gorman, *The Invention of America*.

2 See Abellán's own contribution to his collection of essays in *El exilio español de 1939*, "Filosofía y pensamiento: su función en el exilio de 1939" (pp. 151–208). See also his *Filosofía española en América (1936–1966)* as well as Marielena Zelaya's *Testimonios Americanos*.

3 Ayala's essay raises interesting questions in the light of recent critical attention to reader-response in the literary text. See especially Hans Robert Jauss's *Toward an Aesthetic of Reception* for the social and historical issues involved in this aspect of literary theory.

Chapter 5

1 The figure of the prison guard as victim is one of the most pervasive images in the prison camp memoirs of the Spanish Civil War. Raposo devotes much of his book to the description of the Senegalese, as does Bravo Tellado. His embittered irony manifests itself throughout his memoirs, as in his reference to "la dulce y hermosa Francia" (*Memorias de un Español*, p. 18). Andreu speaks of himself and his fellow exiles as "the players in a comedy" (*Los brazos*, p. 14). In an ironically lighthearted rendering of his prison experience, Fillol tells of his escape to yet another prison, that of the French Resistance, whose members used Spanish exiles and concentration camp survivors as "volunteers" in suicide missions (*Los perdedores*, pp. 80–84). Castillo, an intellectual, writes a scathing account of the French who complied with the occupying Germans and who refused to offer any assistance to the Spanish exiles (*El incendio*).

Chapter 6

1 For a theory of autobiography, see James Olney's *Metaphors of Self* and his edition of essays on the subject, *Autobiography*. For a view of autobiography from a modern critical perspective, see Paul Jay, *Being in the Text*.

2 *Greguería* literally means street noise or hubbub. Gómez de la Serna used this word to designate his self-styled humor and wordplay.

3 Both Santos Sanz Villanueva (Abellán, IV, 142) and Vicente Llorens (Abellán, I, 97, 98) do not consider Gómez de la Serna an exile. His exclusion is based on the facts that the bulk of his work was written prior to his exile, that his exile was voluntary, and that he did not disassociate himself from the Franco regime. Yet is it

not possible to find examples of Spaniards who meet at least one of these criteria and who are more commonly considered exiles? Juan Ramón Jiménez, Luis Cernuda, and Alejandro Casona are examples, not to mention the many self-exiles such as Juan Goytisolo and Fernando Arrabal. Many of those who crossed the Spanish border into France in 1939 did so voluntarily. Some of the written accounts show that many wished they had taken their chances in Spain rather than suffer the torments and imprisonment of Vichy France. See Antonio Ferres and José Ortega (*Literatura española del último exilio*) for a new categorization of exiled Spanish writers.

4 For a collection of essays on Spanish autobiographies see Philippe Lejeune et al., *L'Autobiographie en Espagne*. It is interesting that of all the autobiographies considered in this French collection, over half are by exiles. Autobiographies by well-known exiled writers of the Spanish Civil War which are not included in this book are María Teresa León's *Memorias de la melancolía* and Emilio Prados's autobiography *Recuerdos de mi vida*, published posthumously by Carlos Blanco Aguinaga in *Emilio Prados, vida y obra*. See also Francisco Ayala's recently published autobiography, *Recuerdos y olvidos*.

5 See Aurora Albornoz's discussion of these poets in the context of their exiles (Abellán, IV, 11–108).

Chapter 7

1 Sanz Villanueva devotes relatively little space to Barea (Abellán, IV, 152–4). Barea's name does not even appear in most of the general studies on the contemporary Spanish novel. An exception is Gonzalo Sobejano's *Novela española de nuestro tiempo* (pp. 60–65). Barea's Civil War saga first appeared in an English edition and became known in the English-speaking world as one of the most representative depictions of the war by a Republican Spaniard. The vagaries of literary history notwithstanding, Barea's importance as a writer has diminished drastically since the fifties. His novel was censored in Spain and his fellow writers in exile could not understand why the non-Spanish world chose his work as the most authentic picture of the conflict from the Loyalist side (personal conversation with Manuel Andújar, February 1986).

2 Salabert's novel first appeared in French as *L'Exile intérieur* and will appear in Carlos Gurméndez's series published by Anthropos, Memoria Rota: Exilios y Heterodoxias (Barcelona). Both this series and a similar one in Plaza y Janés (Barcelona) are making efforts to give these novels some new life by reissuing them in Spanish editions. Were it not for Gurméndez and a few other Spaniards (usually

the ones old enough to remember), the Spanish reading public would still be suffering from cultural blindness regarding their writers in exile. It is my impression that some, including young intellectuals, still do.

3 It is perhaps an uncanny coincidence that Mora and Semprún are cousins, both the grandchildren of the famous conservative statesman and aristocrat, Antonio Maura. It is not so uncanny, however, that at least two of Antonio Maura's younger progeny would turn out to be raving radicals.

4 Jack Sinnigen in *Narrativa e ideología* begins a discussion of the use of parentheses in the *Autobiografía*, yet he does not delve into the aesthetic consequences of such a device. Indeed the preponderance of parentheses tells us a great deal about exilic life and literature. Even López Barrantes speaks of his own life as a continuing parenthesis (*Mi exilio*, p. 379).

5 See Tzevatan Todorov's words on the subject in a celebrated issue of *Communications* in which the critic attacks realism almost as if he were writing a manifesto.

Chapter 8

1 An exhaustive biography of Aub has not yet appeared, but there is an interesting and informative (albeit incomplete) one by Rafael Prats Rivelles, titled *Max Aub*. For the most complete work on Aub's narratives, see Ignacio Soldevila Durante, *La obra narrativa de Max Aub*. See also Francisco Longoria, *El arte narrativo de Max Aub* and Luis López Molina, *Notas sobre Max Aub*. Marra-López also deals with Max Aub in his *Narrativa española fuera de España* (pp. 177–215).

2 See Marra-López on the political and social conversion in Aub as a result of the Second Republic and the Civil War (*Narrativa española*, pp. 181–82).

3 The five novels in the series are *Campo cerrado*, *Campo abierto*, *Campo de sangre*, *Campo del Moro*, *Campo de los almendros*.

4 See Aub's speech on *Guernica* delivered in Paris in 1937 at the inauguration of the new Spanish pavilion in the French capital. The oration is included in *Hablo como hombre* (pp. 13–16).

5 In an excellent article which appeared in the *Nation* (August 31, 1985, pp. 152–56), Arthur Danto discusses the political and aesthetic differences between the concepts of memorial and monument, specifically in regard to the Vietnam Memorial and the Washington Monument. A memorial to exiles, such as Aub's, adds another dimension to Danto's distinction, since it must clash with the surroundings in which it is produced. The very absence of the former surrounding seems to add a touch of the ridiculous to an otherwise earnest attempt to remember. It is also interesting to read *Guernica* as a memorial.

6 Marra-López says that the abundant rhetorical adornments in the *Laberinto* "burn out" the dramatic situations (*Narrativa española*, p. 189). In like manner Emir Rodríguez Monegal (*Tres testigos*, p. 81) submits that Aub's verbal "jugueteo" (play) destroys the tragic nature of a particular episode.

7 Margaret Sayers Peden helped with this translation.

Chapter 9

1 Although the first version of *Luis Alvarez Petraña* was published in 1934, Aub continued the fictional biography in exile by adding further information. Two more editions were published in 1965 and in 1971. I am using the 1971 edition, which contains the previous two.

It is interesting that the novelized biography ("biografía novelada") was in vogue among Spanish intellectuals in the twenties. See Luis Fernández Cifuentes discussion in his *Teoría y mercado de la novela*, pp. 342–51, as well as Gustavo Pérez Firmat's essay, "La biografía vanguardista." It is no less interesting that many vanguardist writers of that period who later went into exile (Ayala, Chacel, Alberti, Moreno Villa) continued their interest in biography by writing autobiographies. As we shall see, Aub's novelized biographies may be read as autobiographies.

2 Aub was a friend and admirer of Dos Passos. See Prats Rivelles (*Max Aub*, p. 51).

3 Soldevila Durante takes exception (*La obra narrativa*, pp. 148–56) and attaches great importance to Aub's interest in the new aesthetic movements of the early part of this century. Soldevila's book on Aub is remarkably insightful and cognizant of the theoretical implications of Aub's works.

4 Leonor is curiously reminiscent of the main character(s) in Buñuel's film, *The Obscure Object of Desire*.

Chapter 10

1 Aub himself wrote three plays dealing with this issue, each titled *La vuelta* (1947, 1960, 1964). See *Las vueltas*. In *La gallina ciega* Aub seems to be playing the main role of these plays.

Chapter 11

1 Latin American intellectuals have recently shown much interest in exile literature. See Grinor Rojo's *Muerte y resurrección*. Also of note are the novels of Antonio Skarmeta, a Chilean, such as *Soñé que la nieve ardía* and a beautiful narrative about Neruda, *Ardiente paciencia*.

2 Douglas Barnette has collected a group of Cernuda's poems that deal specifically with exile in *El exilio en la poesía de Luis Cernuda*. See also his informative introduction on Cernuda and the poetry of exile in that volume (pp. 9–30).

3 All citations from *La realidad* are found in the Harris and Martisany edition (*Poesía completa*).

4 The specific titles and dates of the collections of *La realidad* are as follows: *Perfil del aire* (*Profile of the Air*, 1927), now known as *Primeras poesías*, *Egloga, elegía, oda* (*Ecloque, Elegy, Ode*, 1928), *Un río, un amor* (*One River, One Love*, 1929), *Los placeres prohibidos* (*Forbidden Pleasures*, 1931), *Donde habite el olvido* (*Where Oblivion Dwells*, 1933), *Invocaciones* (*Invocations*, 1935), *La nubes* (*Clouds*, 1940), *Como quien espera el alba* (*As One Waiting for the Dawn*, 1944), *Vivir sin estar viviendo* (*Living Without Being Alive*, 1949), *Con las horas contadas* (*With Time Running Out*, 1956), *Desolación de la quimera* (*The Chimera's Desolation*, 1962).

Chapter 12

1 Examples are Harris's *Luis Cernuda: A Study of the Poetry* and Philip Silver's *"Et in Arcadia Ego."* Both are valuable thematic studies that attempt to integrate the poet's life with his poetry. Silver examines "literary themes as configurations of a vital, pre-literary theme" (p. xiv). Alexander Coleman in *Other Voices* treads beyond the life and works approach by incorporating psychological categories as well as an assessment of Cernuda's dramatic technique (pp. 112–38). The final chapter on "The Other" (pp. 139–81) is an interesting discussion of Cernuda's doubling through the use of the *yo* and *tú*. See also C. B. Morris's discussion of Cernuda in *Surrealism and Spain* (pp. 78–101). For an accurate synthesis of the philosophical underpinnings of the relationship between reality and desire, see Salvador Jiménez Fajardo's book on Cernuda published in the Twayne series, a remarkably insightful analysis given the limitations of the series.

2 In Octavio Paz's "La palabra edificante," one of the most provocative readings of Cernuda to date, the issue of homosexuality in the poetry is treated as an ethical category (pp. 143, 149–52), an affirmation of a "different truth" (p. 150). Paz proclaims that unlike Genet, who rarely offered a reversal of conventional morality (black becomes white, sin is virtue), Cernuda celebrates difference and questions the very reality of the conventional world: "To recognize oneself as a homosexual is to accept the difference between oneself and others. But who are the others? . . . They are everyone and no one. Public health is collective infirmity sanctified by power. . . . My body is real; is sin real?" (pp. 150–51)

3 For biographical and textual data concerning Cernuda's participation in the surrealist movement, see Capote Benot, *El surrealismo en la poesía de Luis Cernuda*, and Morris (*Surrealism in Spain*, pp. 76–101). For a formal assessment of Cernuda's surrealist poetry, especially in *Un río, un amor*, see Summerhill ("Cernuda's Flirtation with Surrealism"). Cernuda himself discusses his own surrealist influences in the autobiography (*Historial*, pp. 905–906).

4 The noted Cuban writer José Lezama Lima sees in an early edition of *La realidad* (1936) verbal diffusion and voluptuousness, which the vacuum of oblivion ironically engenders. He compares Cernuda's "olvido" to Proust's "vertiginous parade of impressions" ("*Soledades habitadas*," p. 52).

5 Demonstratives permeate *La realidad*, especially in the postexile volumes. At some points Cernuda becomes particularly engaged in this type of verbal pointing: the interplay among the words "este," "aquel," and "aquella" (p. 420; this and that), "la tierra tuya aquella antes" (p. 438; your land that land before). Also, the culminating lines of "Spanish Diptych" rely on demonstratives for their emotive resonance: "¿Qué herencia sino ésa recibimos? / ¿Qué herencia sino ésa dejaremos?" (p. 479; What legacy but that one do we receive? / What legacy but that one will we leave behind?). This is reminiscent of "Vivir para ver esto / Vivir para ser esto" (p. 387; To live to see this / To live to be this).

6 Critics tend to shy away from the ideological content of Cernuda's poetry. Silver, however, does deal with political and historical themes in the poetry (*A Study of the Poetry of Luis Cernuda*, pp. 163–204).

7 In addition to the poems with exotic place names (Daytona, etc.) for titles, further examples are Poem V of *Primeras poesías*, "Elegía," "Quisiera estar solo en el sur" ("I Would Like to be Alone in the South"), "De qué país" ("From What Country"), Poem XV of *Donde habite el olvido*, "Los fantasmas del deseo" ("The Ghosts of Desire"). In the *Historial*, Cernuda says that he borrowed these names from Hollywood movies (p. 911).

8 In his essay on Cernuda, Paz argues that in *La realidad* one hears a didactic voice addressed to the subject who speaks it as well as to those who understand its language. Cernuda writes not only to tell his own truth, for his truth is also that of his language and his people. The poet speaks the voice of liberation, says Paz, by uttering the mute words of his compatriots. As one who raises an architecture, Cernuda edifies us with the rocks of his scandalous words ("La palabra edificante," pp. 159–60).

Chapter 13

1   Paul Jay discusses the Nietzschean concept of history in relation to autobiography and to Joyce's *Portrait of the Artist* (*Being in the Text*, pp. 115–40). See also Helen Cixious, *The Exile of James Joyce*.

2   José María Castellet was the first to distinguish between older contemporary Spanish novelists who experienced the war firsthand and those younger writers such as Goytisolo who were too young to have those direct experiences ("Veinte años," pp. 290–95).

3   See Emir Rodríguez Monegal's interview of Goytisolo in *Mundo Nuevo* 11 (1967), pp. 46–60.

4   Linda Levine discusses the autobiographical aspect of *Señas* in her thorough analyses of Goytisolo's novels up to *Don Julián* (*Juan Goytisolo*, pp. 13–67). See also Maryellen Bieder's "A Case of Altered Identity: Two Editions of Juan Goytisolo's *Señas de identidad*."

5   Most North American Hispanists dismiss the political nature of Goytisolo's novelistic discourse. Robert Spires's chapter on Goytisolo in his *Beyond the Metafictional Mode* is an example (pp. 72–88), even though the literary discussion of *Juan sin tierra* is a penetrating one. In the Afterword, however, Spires seems to question his own choice (a deeply ideological one) to ignore any political or social dimension to the works he has analyzed (pp. 125–28).

Chapter 14

1   In an interesting discussion of Goytisolo's later work Gonzalo Sobejano ("Valores figurativos y compositivos de la soledad en la novela de Juan Goytisolo") states that Goytisolo's exilic dilemma comes from the necessity of reviewing his own land from the perspective of a tourist. The exile is a "transcendental tourist" who perceives the lost home as " 'other' " (p. 25), an exotic and unfamiliar land. Sobejano's treatment of Goytisolo is based on the figure of solitude both in Spanish and non-Spanish literature.

2   See my study of Goytisolo's later writing: *Trilogy of Treason* (pp. 120–27).

3   For a discussion of *Paisajes* as a parody of autobiography, see Claudia Schaefer-Rodríguez, "Goytisolo Through the Looking Glass."

Bibliography

Abellán, José Luis, ed. *El exilio español de 1939.* 6 vols. I, *La emigración republicana de 1939.* II, *Guerra y política.* III, *Revistas, pensamiento educación.* IV, *Cultura y literatura.* V, *Arte y ciencia.* VI, *Cataluña, Euskadi, Galicia.* Madrid: Taurus, 1976.

———. *Filosofía española en América.* Madrid: Guadarrama, 1967.

Alberti, Rafael. *La arboleda perdida: memorias.* Barcelona: Seix Barral, 1981.

———. *Marinero en tierra.* In *Poesía 1924–1944.* Buenos Aires: Losada, 1946.

———. *Poemas del destierro y la espera.* Madrid: Austral, 1976.

Albornoz, Aurora. "Poesía de la España peregrina." In *El exilio español de 1939,* edited by José Luis Abellán, vol. 4, pp. 13–108. Madrid: Taurus, 1976.

Alfaya, Javier. "Españoles en los campos de concentración nazis." In *El exilio español de 1939,* edited by José Luis Abellán, vol. 2, pp. 91–120. Madrid: Taurus, 1976.

Amieva, Celso. *Almohada de arena.* Mexico: Suplemento de Ecuador, 1960.

Andreu, Lorenzo. *Los brazos del pulpo.* Madrid: Sala editorial, 1972.

Andújar, Manuel. "Crisis de la nostalgia." In *Andalucía e Hispanoamérica: crisol de mestizajes,* pp. 105–19. Sevilla: Edisur, 1982.

———. *Cristal herido.* Barcelona: Anthropos, 1985.

———. *Historias de una historia.* Barcelona: Anthropos, 1986.

———. "Las revistas culturales y literarias del exilio en Hispanoamérica." In *El exilio español de 1939,* edited by José Luis Abellán, vol. 3, pp. 23–92. Madrid: Taurus, 1976.

———. *Saint-Cyprien, plage: campo de concentración.* Mexico: Moncayo, 1942.

Arana, José Ramón. *El cura de Almuniaced.* Mexico: Aquellare, 1950.

Aranguren, José Luis. "La evolución espiritual de los españoles en la emigración." In *Crítica y meditación,* pp. 131–66. Madrid: Taurus, 1955.

Aub, Max. *Campo abierto*. Mexico: Tezontle, 1951.

———. *Campo cerrado*. Madrid: Alfaguara, 1978. Mexico: Tezontle, 1943.

———. *Campo de sangre*. Mexico: Tezontle, 1944.

———. *Campo del Moro*. Mexico: Mortiz, 1963.

———. *Campo de los almendros*. Mexico: Mortiz, 1968.

———. *Conversaciones con Luis Buñuel*. Madrid: Aguilar, 1985.

———. *Diario de Djelfa*. Mexico: Fondo de Cultura, 1944.

———. *Hablo como hombre*. Mexico: Mortiz, 1967.

———. *Jusep Torres Campalans*. Barcelona: Plaza y Janés, 1984.

———. *La gallina ciega: diario español*. Mexico: Mortiz, 1970.

———. *Las vueltas*. Mexico: Mortiz, 1965.

———. *Vida y obra de Luis Alvarez Petraña*. Barcelona: Seix Barral, 1971.

Ayala, Francisco. *La cabeza del cordero*. Buenos Aires: Francisco Ayala, 1944.

———. "Para quién escribimos nosotros." In *El escritor y la sociedad de masas*. Buenos Aires: Sur, 1958.

———. *Recuerdos y olvidos: del paraíso al destierro*. Madrid: Alianza, 1984.

Bakhtin, Mikhail. *The Dialogical Imagination*. Edited by Michael Holquist. Translated by Carl Emerson and Michael Holquist. Austin: University of Texas Press, 1983.

Barea, Arturo. *La forja de un rebelde*. 3 vols. 1, *La forja*. 2, *La ruta*. 3, *La llama*. Buenos Aires: Losada, 1958. (*The Forging of a Rebel*. Translated by Ilsa Barea. New York: Reynal and Hitchcock, 1946.)

Barnette, Douglas. *El exilio en la poesía de Luis Cernuda*. El Ferrol, La Coruña: Esquio, 1984.

Bartra, Agustí. *Cristo de 200000 brazos*. Barcelona: Plaza y Janés, 1970.

Benedetti, Mario. *El desexilio y otras conjeturas*. Madrid: Ediciones El País, 1984.

Bergamín, José. *De una España peregrina*. Madrid: Ali-Borak, 1972.

———. *El pasajero peregrino español en América*. Mexico: Seneca, 1943.

———. *En el pozo de la angustia*. Barcelona: Anthropos, 1985.

Bieder, Maryellen. "A Case of Altered Identity: Two Editions of Juan Goytisolo's *Señas de identidad*." *Modern Language Notes* 89 (1974):298–310.

Blanco Aguinaga, Carlos. *Emilio Prados: Vida y obra. Bibliografía y antología*. New York: Las Américas, 1960.

Blanco White, José María. *The Life of the Reverend Joseph Blanco White: Written by Himself*. Edited by John Hamilton Thom. London: John Chapman, 1845.

Borges, Jorge Luis. *Ficciones*. Buenos Aires: Emecé, 1956.

Botella, Virgilio. *Así cayeron los dados*. Paris: Imprimerie des Gondoles, 1959.

Bravo Tellado, A. A. *El peso de la derrota*. Madrid: Edifrans, 1974.

Brecht, Bertolt. *Dialogues d'exilés*. Translated by Gilbert Badia and Jean Baudrillard. Paris: L'Arche, 1961.

———. *The Life of Galileo*. Translated by Howard Benton. London: Methuen, 1980.

———. *Mother Courage*. Translated by Eric Bentley. New York: Grove Press, 1980.

———. *Poemas y canciones*. Edited by Jesús López Pacheco. Translated by Vicente Romano. Madrid: Alianza, 1980.

———. *Poems*. Edited by John Willett and Ralph Manheim. 3 vols. London: Methuen, 1976.

———. "A Short Organum for the Theater." In *Brecht on Theater*, edited and translated by John Willett, pp. 179–205. London: Methuen, 1964.

Brook, Paulita. *Isabel la Católica*. Mexico: Colecciones Nuevas, 1944.

Capote Benot, José María. *El surrealismo en la poesía de Luis Cernuda*. Seville: Publicaciones de la Universidad, 1976.

Castellet, José María. "Veinte años de novela española." *Cuadernos Americanos* 126 (1963):282–95.

Castillo, Isabel del. *El incendio: ideas y recuerdos*. Buenos Aires: Editorial Américalee, 1954.

Cernuda, Luis. *Historial de un libro (La realidad y el deseo)*. In *Prosa completa*, edited by Derek Harris and Luis Martisany. Barcelona: Barral Editores, 1975.

———. *La realidad y el deseo*. In *Poesía completa*, edited by Derek Harris and Luis Martisany. Barcelona: Barral Editores, 1977.

Chacel, Rosa. *Desde el amanecer: autobiografía de mis primeros años*. Madrid: Revista de Occidente, 1972.

Ciplijauskaité, Biruté. "Nationalization of Arcadia in Exile Poetry." *Books Abroad* 50 (1976):295–302.

Cixious, Helen. *The Exile of James Joyce*. Translated by Sally Purcell. New York: David Lewis, 1972.

Coleman, Alexander. *Other Voices: A Study of the Late Poetry of Luis Cernuda*. University of North Carolina Studies in Romance Languages and Literatures, no. 81. Chapel Hill: University of North Carolina Press, 1969.

Cook, Bruce. *Brecht in Exile*. New York: Holt, Rinehart and Winston, 1982.

Cortázar, Julio. "Exilio y literatura." In *Argentina: años de alambradas culturales*, pp. 16–25. Barcelona: Muchnik Editores, 1984.

Dante Alighieri. *La divina comedia*. Translated by Bartolomé Mitre. Buenos Aires: Editorial Sopena, 1944.

Danto, Arthur. "The Vietnam Veteran's Memorial." *The Nation* (August 31, 1985):152–55.

Derrida, Jacques. "Edmond Jabès and the Question of the Book." In *Writing and*

Difference, translated by Alan Bass. Chicago: University of Chicago Press, 1978.

———. *Writing and Difference*. Translated by Alan Bass. Chicago: University of Chicago Press, 1978.

Dieste, Rafael. *Rojo farol amante*. Madrid: Hiperión, 1983.

Dorfman, Ariel. *Ultima canción de Manuel Sendero*. Mexico: Siglo Veintiuno, 1982.

Dos Passos, John. *Manhattan Transfer*. Boston: Houghton, Mifflin, 1953.

Durán, Manuel. "La generación del 36 vista desde el exilio." In *De Valle-Inclán a León Felipe*, pp. 191–209. Mexico: Finisterre, 1974.

Eagleton, Terry. *Exiles and Emigrés*. New York: Schocken Books, 1970.

Esteves, Arturo. *Búsqueda en la noche*. Buenos Aires: Buena Era, 1957.

Exner, Richard. "Exul Poeta: Theme and Variation." *Books Abroad* 50 (1976):285–95.

Felipe, León. *Español del éxodo y del llanto*. Mexico: Colección Málaga, 1973.

Ferguson, Margaret. "Saint Augustine's Region of Unlikeness: The Crossing of Exile and Language." *Georgia Review* 29 (1975):842–64.

———. "The Exile's Defense: *La Deffence et illustration de la langue francoyse*." *PMLA* 93 (1977):275–89.

Fernández Cifuentes, Luis. *Teoría y mercado de la novela en España: Del 98 a la República*. Madrid: Gredos, 1982.

Ferres, Antonio and José Ortega. *Literatura española del último exilio*. New York: Guardian Press, 1975.

Fillol, Vicente. *Los perdedores: Memorias de un exiliado español*. Madrid: Gaceta Ilustrada, 1973.

Gaos, José. "La adaptación de un español a la sociedad hispanoamericana." *Revista de Occidente* (May 4, 1966):177.

García Bacca, David. *Introducción literaria a la filosofía*. Caracas: Ediciones de la Universidad Central, 1945.

Garcilaso de la Vega. *Poesías castellanas completas*. Edited by Elias Rivers. Madrid: Castalia, 1969.

Garfias, Pedro. *Antología Poética*. Mexico: Finisterre, 1970.

Gómez de la Serna, Ramón. *Automoribundia*. 2 vols. Madrid: Guadarrama, 1974.

González, Valentín (El Campesino). *Jusqu'à la mort*. Translated by and in collaboration with Maurice Padiou. Paris: Albin Michel, 1978.

———. *Yo escogí la esclavitud*. In collaboration with Julián Gorkin. Barcelona: Plaza y Janés, 1977.

Goytisolo, Juan. *La Chanca*. Paris: Librería española, 1962.

———. *Coto vedado*. Barcelona: Seix Barral, 1985.

———. *Disidencias*. Barcelona: Seix Barral, 1977.

———. *El furgón de cola*. Barcelona: Seix Barral, 1976.

————. *Juan sin tierra*. Barcelona: Seix Barral, 1975.

————. *En los reinos de taifa*. Barcelona: Seix Barral, 1986.

————. *Makbara*. Barcelona: Seix Barral, 1980.

————. *Paisajes después de la batalla*. Barcelona: Montesinos, 1982.

————. "Presentación crítica." In *Obra Inglesa de José María Blanco White*, pp. 1–98. Barcelona: Seix Barral, 1972.

————. *Reivindicación del Conde don Julián*. Mexico: Mortiz, 1970.

————. *Señas de identidad*. Mexico: Mortiz, 1969.

Grimm, Reinhold. "Identity and Difference: On Comparative Studies Within a Single Language." *Profession 86* (1986):28–29.

Guilarte, Cecilia de. *Nació en España: novela o lo que el lector prefiera*. Mexico: S. E., 1944.

Guillén, Claudio. "On the Literature of Exile and Counter-Exile." *Books Abroad* 50 (1976):271–80.

Guillén, Jorge. *Cántico*. Barcelona: Editorial Labor, 1963.

Gullón, Germán. "Dos modalidades discursivas: Camilo José Cela y Paulino Masip." Paper delivered at annual meeting of MLA, 1982.

————. "El ensayo y la crítica." In *El exilio español de 1939*. Edited by José Luis Abellán, vol. 4, pp. 249–86. Madrid: Taurus, 1976.

Gurr, Andrew. *Writers in Exile: The Creative Use of Home in Modern Literature*. Harvester Studies in Contemporary Literature and Culture, no. 4. Brighton, England: Harvester Press, 1981.

Harris, Derek, ed. *Luis Cernuda*. Madrid: Taurus, 1977.

————. *Luis Cernuda: A Study of the Poetry*. London: Tamesis, 1973.

Hayman, Ronald. *Brecht: A Biography*. New York: Oxford University Press, 1983.

Ilie, Paul. *Literature and Inner Exile: Authoritarian Spain, 1939–1975*. Baltimore: Johns Hopkins University Press, 1980.

Jameson, Fredric. *The Prison House of Language: A Critical Account of Structuralism and Russian Formalism*. Princeton, N.J.: Princeton University Press, 1972.

Jauss, Hans Robert. *Toward an Aesthetic of Reception*. Translated by Timothy Bahti. Theory and History of Literature, no. 2. Minneapolis: University of Minnesota Press, 1982.

Jay, Paul. *Being in the Text*. Ithaca, N.Y.: Cornell University Press, 1984.

Jiménez Fajardo, Salvador. *Luis Cernuda*. Twayne World Author Series, no. 455. Boston: G. K. Hall, 1978.

Joyce, James. *Portrait of the Artist as a Young Man*. London: Cape, 1969.

Karlinsky, Simon. *The Nabokov-Wilson Letters, 1940–1971*. New York: Harper and Row, 1979.

Lejeune, Philippe, et al. *L'Autobiographie en Espagne*. Etudes Hispaniques, no. 5. Actes du IIe Colloque Internationale de la Baume-les Aix, May 1981. Aix-en-Provence: Université de Provence, 1982.

Lemon, Lee, and Marion Reis. *Russian Formalist Criticism: Four Essays*. Lincoln: University of Nebraska Press, 1965.

Lenhart, Herbert. "Thomas Mann, Bertolt Brecht, and the Free Germany Movement." In *Exile: The Writer's Experience*, edited by John Spalek and Robert Bell. University of North Carolina Series in Germanic Languages and Literatures, no. 99. Chapel Hill: University of North Carolina Press, 1982.

León, Fray Luis de. *Los nombres de Cristo*. Edited by Cristobal Cuevas García. Madrid: Cátedra, 1977.

León, María Teresa. *Memorias de la melancolía*. Buenos Aires: Losada, 1970.

Levin, Harry. *Refractions: Essays in Comparative Literature*. New York: Oxford University Press, 1966.

Levine, Linda Gould. *Juan Goytisolo: La destrucción creadora*. Mexico: Mortiz, 1976.

Lezama Lima, José. "Soledades habitadas por Cernuda." In *Luis Cernuda*, edited by Derek Harris. Madrid: Taurus, 1977.

Llorens, Vicente. *Aspectos de la literatura española*. Madrid: Castalia, 1974.

———. *La emigración republicana*. In *El exilio español de 1939*, edited by José Luis Abellán, vol. I. Madrid: Taurus, 1976.

———. *Liberales y románticos: una emigración española en inglaterra*. Madrid: Castalia, 1968.

———. *Literatura, historia, política*. Madrid: Revista de Occidente, 1967.

———. *Memorias de una emigración: Santo Domingo, 1939–1945*. Barcelona: Ariel, 1975.

Longoria, Francisco. *El arte narrativo de Max Aub*. Madrid: Playor, 1977.

López Barrantes, Ramón. *Mi exilio*. Madrid: G. del Toro, 1974.

López Molina, Luis. *Notas sobre Max Aub*. Castellón de la Plana: Armengot, 1970.

Mann, Klaus. *The Turning Point*. New York: L. B. Fischer, 1942.

Mann, Thomas. *Doctor Faustus*. Translated by H. T. Lowe-Porter. New York: Penguin, 1983.

———. *Doctor Faustus: The Genesis of a Novel*. Translated by Richard and Carla Winston. London: Secker, 1961.

Marichal, Juan. "De algunas consecuencias intelectuales de la Guerra Civil Española." In *El nuevo pensamiento político español*, pp. 65–77. Mexico: Finisterre, 1974.

Marra-López, José Ramón. *Narrativa española fuera de España*. Madrid: Guadarrama, 1966.

Martínez, Carlos. *Crónica de una emigración (la de los republicanos españoles en 1939)*. Mexico: Libro-Mex, 1959.

Masip, Paulino. *Diario de Hamlet García*. Mexico: León Sánchez, 1944. (2d ed. Barcelona: Anthropos, 1987.)

Mazzotta, Giuseppe. *Dante: Poet of the Desert*. Princeton, N.J.: Princeton University Press, 1979.

Méndez, Concha. *Vida a vida o vida o río*. Madrid: Caballo Griego para la Poesía, 1978.

Milbauer, Asher. *Transcending Exile: Conrad, Nabokov, I. B. Singer*. Gainesville: University Presses of Florida, 1985.

Milosz, Czeslaw. "Note on Exile." *Books Abroad* 50 (1976):281–84.

Mora, Constancia de la. *Doble esplendor*. Barcelona: Destino, 1971.

Moreno Villa, José. *Vida en claro*. Mexico: Fondo de Cultura Económica, 1944.

Morris, C. B. *Surrealism in Spain*. Cambridge: Cambridge University Press, 1972.

Nabokov, Vladimir. *Pnin*. New York: Penguin, 1983.

———. *Speak, Memory: An Autobiography Revisited*. New York: Putnam, 1979.

Nietzsche, Friedrich. *The Use and Abuse of History*. Translated by Adrian Collins. Indianapolis: Bobbs-Merrill, 1957.

O'Gorman, Edmundo. *The Invention of America: An Inquiry into the Historical Nature of the New World and the Meaning of Its History*. Bloomington: Indiana University Press, 1961.

Olney, James. *Autobiography: Essays Theoretical and Critical*. Princeton, N.J.: Princeton University Press, 1980.

———. *Metaphors of the Self: The Meaning of Autobiography*. Princeton, N.J.: Princeton University Press, 1972.

Otaola, Salvador. *El cortejo*. Mexico: Mortiz, 1963.

———. *La librería de Arana: historia y fantasía*. Mexico: Aquelarre, 1952.

———. *Los hombres*. Mexico: Aquelarre, 1950.

Ovid. *Tristia*. Translated by L. R. Lind. Athens: University of Georgia Press, 1975.

Pamies, Teresa. *Cuando éramos capitanes: memorias de aquella guerra*. Barcelona: Dopesa, 1974.

Pasternak, Boris. *Doctor Zhivago*. Translated by Max Hayward and Manya Harari. New York: Pantheon, 1958.

Paz, Octavio. "La palabra edificante." In *Luis Cernuda*, edited by Derek Harris, pp. 138–60. Madrid: Taurus, 1972.

Pérez Firmat, Gustavo. *Literature and Liminality: Festive Readings in the Hispanic Tradition*. Durham, N.C.: Duke University Press, 1986.

———. "La biografía vanguardista." In *Prosa Hispánica de vanguardia*, edited by

Fernando Burgos. Madrid: Orígenes, 1986.

Pina, Francisco. *Charles Chaplin: genio de la desventura y la ironía*. Mexico: Aquelarre, 1952.

Poema del Cid. Edited by Ramón Menendez Pidal and Alfonso Reyes. Madrid: Espasa Calpe, 1967.

Prados, Emilio. *Signos del ser*. Madrid: Papeles de Son Armadans, 1962.

Prats Rivelles, Rafael. *Max Aub*. Madrid: Espasa, 1978.

Raposo, Alemosio. *Memorias de un español en el exilio*. Valencia: Ediciones Aura, 1968.

Rejano, Juan. *La mirada del hombre*. Madrid: Casa de Campo, 1978.

————. *Pasos y sombras*. Mexico: Aquelarre, 1953.

Reyes Nevares, Salvador, et al. *El exilio español en Mexico*. Mexico: Fondo de Cultura Económica, 1982.

Rodríguez Monegal, Emir. "Destrucción de la España sagrada." *Mundo Nuevo* 11 (1967):46–60.

————. *Tres testigos de la guerra civil: Max Aub, Ramón Sender, Arturo Barea*. Caracas: Monte Avila, 1971.

Rojo, Grinor. *Muerte y resurrección del teatro chileno*. Madrid: Michay, 1985.

Ros, Antonio. *Horas de angustia y esperanza*. Mexico: Tezontle, 1944.

Sachs, Nelly. *The Seeker and Other Poems*. Translated by Ruth Mead, Matthew Mead, and Michael Hamburger. New York: Farrar, Straus and Giroux, 1970.

Said, Edward. *Palestinian Lives: After the Last Sky*. Photographs by Jean Mohr. New York: Pantheon, 1985, 1986.

————. *The World, the Text, and the Critic*. Cambridge, Mass.: Harvard University Press, 1983.

Salabert, Miguel. *El exilio interior*. Barcelona: Anthropos, 1987. (*L'Exil intérieur*. Translated by Claude Couffon. Paris: Julliard, 1961.)

Salazar Chapela, Esteban. *Perico en Londres*. Buenos Aires: Losada, 1947.

Sanz Villanueva, Santos. "La narrativa en el exilio." In *El exilio español de 1939*, edited by José Luis Abellán, vol. 4, pp. 109–82. Madrid: Taurus, 1976.

Schaefer-Rodríguez, Claudia. "Goytisolo Through the Looking Glass: *Paisajes después de la batalla*, Autobiography and Parody." *Journal of the Midwest Modern Language Association* 19 (1986):13–29.

Seidel, Michael. *Exile and the Narrative Imagination*. New Haven, Conn.: Yale University Press, 1986.

Semprún, Jorge. *Autobiografía de Federico Sánchez*. Barcelona: Planeta, 1977.

————. *El largo viaje*. Translated by Jacqueline and Rafael Conte. Barcelona: Seix Barral, 1976.

Sender, Ramón. *Crónica del alba*. Barcelona: Destino, 1977.

Serrano Poncela, Segundo. *Habitación para hombre solo*. Barcelona: Seix Barral, 1963.

———. *La viña de Nabot*. Madrid: Ediciones Albia, 1974.

Silver, Philip. *"Et in Arcadia Ego": A Study of the Poetry of Luis Cernuda*. London: Tamesis, 1965.

Sinnigen, Jack. *Narrativa e ideología*. Madrid: Nuestra Cultura, 1982.

Skarmeta, Antonio. *Ardiente paciencia*. Buenos Aires: Editorial Sudamericana, 1985.

———. *Soñé que la nieve ardía*. Barcelona: Plaza y Janés, 1984.

Sobejano, Gonzalo. *Novela española de nuestro tiempo (en busca del pueblo perdido)*. Madrid: Prensa Española, 1975.

———. "Valores figurativos y compositivos de la soledad en la novela de Juan Goytisolo." *Voces* 1 (1981):23–32.

Soldevila Durante, Ignacio. *La obra narrativa de Max Aub*. Madrid: Gredos, 1973.

Solzhenitsyn, Alexander. *The Gulag Archipelago*. Translated by Thomas P. Whitney. New York: Harper and Row, 1978.

Spalek, John, and Robert F. Bell, eds. *Exile: The Writer's Experience*. University of North Carolina Studies in Germanic Languages and Literatures, no. 99. Chapel Hill: University of North Carolina Press, 1982.

Spires, Robert. *Beyond the Metafictional Mode: Directions in the Modern Spanish Novel*. Romance Languages, no. 30. Lexington: University Press of Kentucky, 1984.

Steiner, George. *After Babel: Aspects of Language and Translation*. New York: Oxford University Press, 1977.

———. *Extraterritorial: Papers on Literature and the Language Revolution*. New York: Atheneum, 1977.

Summerhill, Stephen J. *"Un río, un amor*: Cernuda's Flirtation with Surrealism." *Journal of Spanish Studies: Twentieth Century* 6 (1978):151–57.

Tabori, Paul. *Anatomy of Exile*. London: Harrap, 1972.

Todorov, Tzevetan. "Introduction." *Communications* 11 (1968):1–4.

Ugarte, Michael. *Trilogy of Treason: An Intertextual Study of Juan Goytisolo*. Columbia: University of Missouri Press, 1982.

Unamuno, Miguel de. *Agonía del Cristianismo, Mi religión y otros ensayos*. New York: Las Américas, 1967.

Valdés, Juan. *Diálogo de la lengua*. Edited by Juan Lope Blanch. Madrid: Castalia, 1969.

Willett, John, trans. and ed. *Brecht on Theater*. London: Methuen, 1964.

Williams, David. "The Exile as Uncreator." *Mosaic* 8 (1975):1–14.

Zambrano, María. "Los intelectuales en el drama de España." In *Senderos*, pp. 27–70. Barcelona: Anthropos, 1986.

———. *Pensamiento y poesía en la vida española*. Mexico: Casa de España, 1939.

Zelaya Kolker, Marielena. *Testimonios americanos de los escritores transterrados de 1939*. Madrid: Instituto de Cooperación Iberoamericana, 1985.

Index

About the Author

Michael Ugarte is Associate Professor of Romance Languages, University of
Missouri, Columbia, and author of *Trilogy of Treason*, a book on Juan Goytisolo.
He also has written numerous articles on modern Spanish literature.

Library of Congress Cataloging-in-Publication Data
Ugarte, Michael, 1949–
Shifting ground : Spanish Civil War exile literature / by Michael
Ugarte.
p.   cm.   Bibliography: p.   Includes index.   ISBN 0-8223-0857-6
1. Spanish literature — Foreign countries — History and criticism.
2. Spanish literature — 20th century — History and criticism.
3. Exiles' writings, Spanish — History and criticism. 4. Politics
and literature — Spain. 5. Spain — History — Civil War, 1936-1939-
-Literature and the war. I. Title.
PQ7020.U36 1988
860'.9'920694 — dc19   88-16957 CIP